Day Care:
Curriculum
Considerations

Michael Langenbach

University of Oklahoma

Teanna West Neskora

CHARLES E. MERRILL PUBLISHING COMPANY
A Bell & Howell Company
Columbus   Toronto   London   Sydney

Published by
CHARLES E. MERRILL PUBLISHING COMPANY
A Bell & Howell Company
Columbus, Ohio 43216

We wish to acknowledge the children, staff, and parents of Middle Earth Day Care Center whose cooperation and encouragement enabled us to try out and report many of the ideas contained herein.

To Mary Ann and Danny

International Standard Book Number: 0-675-08544-6

Library of Congress Catalog Card Number: 76-47317

Printed in the United States of America

1   2   3   4   5   6   7   8—80   79   78   77   76   75

Preface

Day care for children has been the weak, if not unplanned for, sister of all institutions serving the public. Except for the recent attention some legislators, members of a few professional organizations, and members of some women's liberation groups have paid to day care facilities, the burden of improving the quality of day care in the United States has been shouldered by the overworked and underpaid day care staff members and the parents of children receiving the care. Our intention is to help spread responsibility for the quality of day care by treating it as a legitimate educational enterprise.

Day care institutions suffer the image of being exclusively concerned with physical care, and many times have been charged with delivering that poorly. Our belief is that few day care facilities willingly limit their offerings to physical care. Financial constraints and lack of professional training account for most of the shortcomings of these agencies. With the advent of professional training for day care personnel, an improvement in the quality of developmental and educational services offered to children should be realized.

The cycle of no training leading to dimunutive salaries needs to be broken. Offering professional training to in-service and prospective day care teachers ought to enhance programs and improve bargaining positions for teachers requesting higher salaries. City, state, and federal funds may be required to meet the economic challenges, but there is ample precedent and overwhelming justification for such support. Day care facilities may have to relinquish some of their autonomy in the processes of increasing their budgets, but increased funds and professional training promise more and better programs from which children could benefit.

We believe the quality of day care programs can be improved by meeting the following goals: first, day care teachers and directors must have knowledge and skills related to child care and curriculum development; second, more money must be channeled into day care operations to compensate for the quality of services delivered; and finally, there must be a national commitment to families and children, one result of which would be the greater availability of high-quality day care programs. It is not axiomatic that these goals be achieved in this order, or any linear form. Those interested in the fate of day care need to work on all of these goals as well as others, perhaps simultaneously, in order to break the cycle of incomplete skills, underfinanced programs, and indifferent attitudes.

It is our hope that this book serves the following purposes: first, that it adequately describes day care as a legitimate educational enterprise; second, that it provides useful suggestions for developing a day care curriculum; and third, that it presents views of development and research findings that should provide a perspective for thinking about and working with a day care curriculum. The book should be useful to day care teachers in service as well as preservice teachers enrolled in training programs at both the undergraduate and graduate levels.

Table of Contents

Introduction

Every day millions of young children are placed in some type of day care facility. The number of centers is increasing as family and employment patterns change. The quality of services any child receives in a day care setting is a function of many factors. Assuming safe and healthful facilities are available, the greatest impact on young children in these settings will come from the adults who provide the care and manage the activities. Teaching in a day care setting is a combination of art and science. It is the science side of it—the knowing and the skillful doing—with which we are concerned in this book. There are some concepts and generalizations as well as their applications that must be shared if the quality of day care is to continue to improve.

One of the most pressing problems now facing day care facilities is to lend some coherence to their overall programs. Goals, objectives, activities, and evaluation procedures need to be thought through, sorted out, and organized in a manner that improves the performance of day care personnel. A curriculum can be a useful tool for day care in that it can be the vehicle for achieving coherence and clarifying the direction of day care services.

Unfortunately, the word *curriculum* often conjures up strange images, one of which is a collection of rigid prescriptions imposed by higher authorities. Our use of the term is not intended to frighten or threaten the imaginative teachers in day care. We submit, simply, that a consistent delivery of high-quality services to children is tenuous at best when no coherent guide is available to help teachers plan programs and activities that will help children. Another image of curriculum in the literature of day care includes vast collections of creative recipes for play dough and other arts and crafts. Even though such collections can be useful to day care teachers, this conception of curriculum is too narrow. We use the term in a broader sense. In short, we conceive curriculum as a comprehensive document and an ongoing process that describes programs and provides opportunities for the systematic improvement of practices. A third image of the word curriculum is to associate it with particular goals and objectives or the kinds of activities and experiences the children will have. In years past people referred to

1

"separate subjects curriculum," "integrated curriculum," or "whole child curriculum." More recently labels such as "cognitive curriculum," "humanistic curriculum," and "relevance curriculum" have replaced the older labels.* None of the labels, either old or new, adequately represents the point of view we hold. Indeed, we wince at the prospect of "day care curriculum" coming to mean something we do not intend. What we hope it conveys is a device or vehicle that is useful for day care personnel in carrying out their responsibilities to children. A day care curriculum may be cognitively oriented, humanistically oriented, or some combination of a number of orientations. We believe its design or character is entirely at the discretion and best thinking of the people related directly and indirectly to the day care setting.

The position put forth in this book is in one sense value free; that is, we hold no breech for one orientation or emphasis over another. In another sense, however, we do embrace certain values related to our neutral position. We believe any person or group of people responsible for the care of children for large parts of the day has an obligation to provide the best care possible, and a description of the kinds of goals, objectives, activities, and experiences planned for the children. Some random and fortuitous experiences are inevitable whenever people interact and more so when young children interact, but the majority of experiences children have should be accounted for if some semblance of purposefulness as opposed to mindlessness is to prevail.

We believe the primary responsibilities of the people engaged in day care curriculum development include the following:

1. Realization of the value of a curriculum as a vehicle for improving the quality of care given children.
2. Familiarization with a conceptual model of a day care curriculum as a document and a system.
3. Knowledge of information related to children.

Quality care for children is directly related to how well the day care staff meets each of these three responsibilities. This book is an attempt to integrate pertinent information regarding these responsibilities.

The book is divided into five sections. Section One is a conceptual treatment of day care and curriculum. Chapter One discusses day care in terms of rationales and value-based suggestions about how day care might be considered. Chapter Two contains discussions of curriculum as a document and as a system. Section Two contains two chapters that treat curriculum development in more specific terms. Chapter Three has suggestions for selecting and organizing the resources for curriculum development as well as suggestions for actually developing the purpose/philosophy, goals, objectives, and activities. Chapter Four includes suggestions for implementing, evaluating, and revising the curriculum. The third section, entitled "Some Views of Children," is made up of four chapters. Chapter Five contains four views of intelligence and intellectual development. Chapter Six is a discussion of psychological and social development. Chapter Seven includes language, moral, physical, and motor development. The last

---

*See, for example, Elliot W. Eisner and Elizabeth Vallance, eds., *Conflicting Conceptions of Curriculum* (Berkeley, Calif.: McCutchen Publishing Corp., 1974).

chapter in Section Three contains two integrated theories of development. Section Four, "Sample Applications," includes four chapters wherein examples of goals, objectives, and activities are discussed. Each of the four chapters is devoted to children of a particular age range and represents an illustration of the possibilities of putting into practice the theoretical considerations made earlier. The final section is entitled "Overview." It contains a chapter on research with illustrative discussions of three research areas that pertain to day care curriculum. The last chapter is a view of day care needs and a look ahead to what the future holds for day care in this country.

Section One

Conceptual Considerations

Before one can attach much meaning to the words *day care* or *curriculum,* more precise definitions and descriptions must be offered. The first chapter in this section contains a conceptual framework for day care that includes rationales and suggestions. The second chapter discusses curriculum as a plan and a system.

Chapter One

Day Care

. . . it is not a question of whether or not there will be changes in the way in which we bring up our children, but rather what direction the changes will take.

Urie Bronfenbrenner, Two Worlds of Childhood
(New York: Russell Sage Foundation, 1970), p. 119.

Simply defined, *day care* is child care in the absence of parents. It may be all-day care, all-night care, or simply a two-hour drop-in arrangement. Our concern in this book is with child care given outside the child's home and in the company of other children. Day care outside the child's home can be provided either in a family day care home or in a day care center. Family day care is offered in a home with special provisions for a small group of children. Day care centers accommodate larger numbers of children.

Rationales for Day Care

Traditionally, the term *day care* brought to mind visions of unhappy, undernourished children with dirty clothes, runny noses, and apathetic faces huddled together in an ill-heated slum with no toys to play with and nothing to do. Women who left their children in day care facilities were frowned upon and considered negligent and irresponsible. The primary reason that day care had such a negative image was the then-current belief that young children separated from their mothers suffer detrimental effects. It was accepted almost unequivocally until the early 1960s that children belong in the home with their mothers. Another universally held "truth" that greatly affected the young child up until this time was the notion that the years from birth to six were primarily for playing and physical growth and very little else. The emotional and intellectual development of children were often left to chance until the beginning of formal schooling.

In recent decades, a new perspective has been brought to the concept of day care and the period of early childhood has gained an increased appreciation.[1] The current position held by many professionals concerned with young children is that the right kind of day care setting can foster children's emotional development and help sustain their attachment to their mothers and other family members. Day care can be seen as a supportive institution concerned with strengthening the relationship between the family and the child.

7

The years from birth to six have now been recognized universally by psychologists and educators as the period of life in which the most rapid intellectual development occurs.[2] For many areas of intellectual development, a firm foundation acquired at this age is critical. Language, concept formation, and problem-solving ability are but a few of the many skills that a young child needs to encounter and begin to master at this time. Quality day care programs aimed at the intellectual, social, and emotional needs of the individual child and the strengthening of the family unit can have an enormously positive influence on the child and the family.

Tradition is very strong, however, and there are many people in this country today who maintain that children should not be cared for in groups but should be cared for at home by their own mothers.[3] The arguments for and against day care continue and will probably continue for some time to come, but the issue soon becomes academic because many mothers are working, and their young children are in some type of day care setting. The relevant question is no longer whether or not there should be day care for America's children but what kind of day care should be provided for the millions who need it. Our task here then is not to debate the issue of whether or not children should be in day care but to examine why they are and to analyze what needs to be done to create the best possible day care situations for children, families, and society.

Changing Family and Employment Patterns

Fifty years ago most people in America lived their adult years in or near the same town in which they spent their childhood. This practice was a very practical one, and it attributed to an extended family arrangement in which three or more generations of one family all accepted a certain amount of responsibility for each other. If for any reason parents could not properly care for their children, there were grandparents, aunts, and cousins available to assume the task. Today our society is much more mobile, and it is not unusual for adults to live hundreds and thousands of miles away from any relative. The nuclear family that consists of one or two parents and their one or more children has become the norm. What happens if the parents in these nuclear families are unable to provide adequate care for their children and relatives are not available to provide assistance? In many cases young children simply do not receive adequate care. Quality day care could provide a safe, stimulating environment for these children and at the same time assist the parents in the care of their children.

Women in America are often caught in the middle of a conflict over which they have little control. They have accepted for decades that their role was in the home caring for their own children, yet more and more women are joining the labor force for economic or other reasons. In 1973, 35 million women were in the labor force (two-fifths of the total labor force), and the majority of them worked for economic reasons.[4] The standard of living continues to rise in the United States, and many women have gone to work to improve the living standards of their own families. At the same time that the standard of living has been increasing, America has been experiencing one of the greatest inflationary periods in its history. Prices on even basic necessities continue to rise. Many women who set out to improve the lot of their families have found their employment a necessity just to maintain their present living standard. Inflated costs of living and high economic aspirations have increased the number of cases in which a family needs the income of both parents to maintain the living standard it has set for itself.

It is predicted that there will be a tremendous increase in the number of working women in the near future.[5] Continued economic pressure from inflation is only one of several reasons for this expected influx of women workers.

There are also legislative as well as social conditions that indicate the inevitability of many more women in the work force.

Title VII of the Civil Rights Act prohibits discrimination in employment. For the first time in history women and other minorities are competing with white men as equals in the job market. Employers are required to hire specified numbers of people representing all minority groups. What is your sex? What is your race? should no longer be the first two questions asked by an employer. The only relevant question should be, What are your qualifications? Women are meeting the demands of employers by training to meet employment qualifications. There is no doubt that there will be increasing numbers of semiprofessional and professional women in the future.

Legislation has also been passed that affects the status of the woman who is a welfare recipient. Under the Work Incentive Program any woman who does not have children under six and who is capable of working is required to accept either training for a job or gainful employment if it is available. If this program is successful, not only will it reduce the number of families receiving welfare but it will increase the number of women working outside the home.

America also has a rapidly increasing number of families headed by females who are the sole or primary support of the family. In 1973, the Department of Labor statistics indicated that three-fifths of all women workers (21 million) were single, divorced, widowed, or separated, or had husbands whose earnings were less than $7,000 per year.[6] The divorce rate in America is climbing steadily and all indications are that it will continue to rise.[7] There has also been a more general acceptance of unmarried women who give birth to and raise their own children. Another social development that creates one-parent families is the practice of allowing single men or women to adopt children. Regardless of how the one-parent family occurs we are seeing more and more of them, and when there is only one adult in a family, there is seldom a choice of whether or not to work. Gainful employment is a necessity.

We indicated earlier that the living standard in America is steadily increasing. This means that the demands of consumers are rising. Americans want more goods and services. As the demands increase, industries need more people in the labor force to meet them. More and more women will be needed in the labor force as industry tries to keep up with growing demands. Working women in America have become a necessity to our national economy.

We have seen that millions of women in America are working today and much evidence points to the probability of more working women in the future. What impact does this have on young children? In 1973, 4.8 million working women had 6 million children under six years of age.[8] It is predicted that there will be 5.3 million working mothers with children under six by 1980 and that in the very near future the large majority of children under six will have working mothers.[9] Good care for their children is one of the first concerns of these mothers. In 1969 there were only 640,000 licensed day care slots to serve the 4.5 million children.[10] Quality care for the other 4 million children today and in the future is dependent on a national commitment to meeting the needs of young children and their families, for now it is accurate to say that there are millions of children in need of quality day care who are not receiving it.

Liberation as Justification

In the early years of this country men and women contributed equally to the support and functioning of their families. The roles and responsibilities that each assumed might have been rigorously divided according to sex, but, nevertheless, the full contribution of both was needed to sustain the family. Our society has become more technical and the men have moved into jobs away from the home and family. As this move occurred the woman has been forced from her role of being an economically contributing family member to one of being economically dependent on the man. The husband's role as the provider and the wife's as the tender of the hearth emerged early in this country's history and still exists in many homes today. Until recently this pattern changed very little.

During national crisis situations, such as war times and the depression, women's labor was needed and women were expected to work for the country's good. Other than during times of war, if women did work outside the home they were relegated to the lowest paying jobs or given lower pay for doing the same job as a man. The Day Care and Child Development Council indicated that women of our world today have become mere tools used to stabilize an economy.[11]

Many American women have taken a stand against this second-class role to which they have been assigned. These women are insisting on being productive, contributing members of society with all of the responsibilities that go with this role. There are many social changes occurring in our country now that are adding strength to the women's movement and to the liberation of men and women from traditional roles.

There are more educational advantages available for all people in America than ever before. The trend is toward more education for women. The more education a woman has, the greater the probability she will be employed.[12] Women who have trained for a career want to use their education and skills and often find both are in demand in the labor market.

Many of the social changes mentioned previously have been influenced by and are influencing the women's movement. Many women feel trapped by traditional roles and expectations and are choosing divorce as an avenue to personal independence. Involvement and employment outside the home for these women is a necessity. But even more American women are opting for liberation within marriage. Marriage is no longer seen as an obstacle to pursuing careers and interests outside the home. Many women, both married and single, have elected to work for a myriad of personal reasons: to achieve financial independence, to pursue interests outside the home, to make a contribution to society, to enjoy contact with many and varied people, and to be a part of the "real" world. Women's liberation does not imply that one must be employed outside the home to be a fulfilled, contributing member of society. It means simply that women and men have equal rights to activities within the home and outside the home, for employment or not for employment in whatever way is personally satisfying to each.

Quality child care facilities are seen by many as a necessity to free women to become productive members of society. The argument offered by most women's groups is that women with children will never have employment and educational opportunities equal with men until they are assured of high-quality child care for their children. Quality care provides for the physical safety, health, emotional, social, and intellectual development of young children. Good day care can benefit the child and in turn benefit the entire family. When children are receiving kind, loving care in a safe, stimulating environment, mothers are freed from constant concern for their children's safety and well-being. They are thus able to direct their energies toward seeking a happier, more productive life for themselves and their families. Quality day care serves a double purpose. It frees the woman to become a productive member of society while it provides children with a healthy environment in which to develop. However, the kind of day care to which we are referring is very expensive, and most working mothers cannot afford to pay even a fraction of what it costs. Governmental subsidy is seen as a necessity by most women's groups if quality day care is to become a reality for American children.

Disadvantaged Children

There are millions of American children today who are disadvantaged in some way. Many disadvantages are obvious while others are more subtle, but they can all be detrimental in handicapping a child for a lifetime. We have already stated, but it bears repeating again, that the first six·years of a child's life are critical. During these years children should acquire language, cognitive structures that are necessary to build on later, emotional stability, a healthy body, social skills, and a healthy attitude toward themselves and others. When children are deprived of opportunities to develop in these areas, the probability of their being emotionally, intellectually, physically, and socially sound as adults is not good. High-quality developmental day care for disadvantaged children is seen by many professionals as a mechanism to supplement the home environment so that these children will have a better chance for success in life.

Children of Low-Income Families.   Over 3 million children under six years of age in America live in families whose income is below the poverty level.[13] There are many low-income parents who provide good care for their children, but there are many who do not have the skills, knowledge, or finances to meet their children's pressing needs. If we examine briefly the environment in which most of these children live, the disadvantages with which they are expected to cope become apparent. Typical housing for these families are urban slums, rural shanties, or migrant shacks. These children are subjected to poor sanitary conditions, crowded living quarters, inadequate clothing and lack of heating in cold weather. Closely associated with the physical environment are the health conditions to which these children are exposed: inadequate and unbalanced meals, lack of dental care, no immunizations, few medical services, and no help for emotional disorders. If we continue to examine the emotional setting, we often find frustrated parents who see no way out of poverty and thus no way to improve their way of life. We also find hostility toward the rest of society for creating a state of poverty that seems inescapable in this country.

Many people argue that we as a society owe these children opportunities out of this stifling environment. Developmental day care is seen as a reasonable method to assist these children and their families out of the poverty trap. Developmental day care should provide health and dental services; nutritious meals; a clean, safe, warm building; a spacious grassy play area; and many daily experiences to promote language and cognitive growth. It should also provide parent education and assistance to the family. Day care should not be viewed as the answer to all of the ills of our complex society, but it can play an important role in a broad-based social reform to assist America's poor.

Children of Handicapped Parents.   Handicapped parents who cannot properly meet all of the needs of a growing, active child can be divided into two groups: the physically unable and the emotionally unable. The temporal variability within each of these groups is tremendous. A physical disability could be a temporary state created by an accident or by surgery in which the parent is hospitalized or bedridden. In this kind of situation day care would only be needed temporarily until the parent recovers. Some parents, however, are permanently disabled and either cannot care for the child or require less demanding activity for the sake of their own health. In these instances day care may need to be extended until the child is well into elementary school and mature enough to provide some self-care with the assistance of the parent.

Child abuse commonly occurs in homes where parents are not emotionally capable of caring for their children. If children are not abused physically in these instances, they may be abused mentally, thereby being deprived of the kind of emotional support that only a stable adult can provide. Statistics are readily available on the growing number of alcoholic housewives in America.[14] What the statistics fail to answer is what kind of care these women are capable of providing for their children. The obvious answer is these women are not at all equipped to deal with the complex needs of a young child. Nor are parents who are heavy drug users capable of caring for children without assistance. Day care for children from these homes can help prevent the parent's handicap from having a disastrous effect on the child. Day care for all or part of the day until the other parent or an older sibling returns to the home appears to be a reasonable intermediate step that must be taken until these parents can be assisted to overcome their problems.

Handicapped Children.   Adequate day care is becoming a real concern for parents of handicapped children. Presently, there are few facilities that accept handicapped children, usually because of the expense involved. But these children need the professional assistance that a well-staffed day care center could provide. The trend is away from isolating physically and mentally handicapped children from other children. The idea receiving much support today is that handicapped children should be mainstreamed as much as possible so that they and we begin to learn from one another. A day care setting that is geared to meet the needs of all children can provide for this integration to occur when children are young and open.

Many families with handicapped children are facing the same situation that is confronted by many other American families. Mothers must go to work for economic reasons. Other mothers choose to stay at home and care for their own child, but caring for children is a demanding, often exhausting job. Caring for a handicapped child can be even more demanding. Occasional day care for the children who otherwise stay at home is necessary to give the mothers some time for other activities. Quality day care for handicapped children is urgently needed, but it cannot be so expensive that it becomes prohibitive. We must find ways to assist these families and these children toward more comfortable and more normal lives.

Suggestions for Day Care

These suggestions are based on our values, views of children, and experiences of working in day care settings. The reader may hold different values, views, and experiences that would lead to other suggestions. Ours are offered for consideration.

We have just considered several reasons why the number of children receiving some kind of day care is growing and why it will probably continue to grow. The well-being of America's young children has certainly not been the force behind the movement. Economic, political, and social pressures have created the need for day care. Traditionally, the needs and the role of the children were given little significance in the day care programs found in America. There has been a shift in this attitude toward more concern for children, but greater effort will be necessary to increase the number of quality day care settings. The emphasis of day care programs must be to provide for optimum development through meeting the needs of each individual child.

Each child is a multifaceted organism, and day care programs should be designed to consider all aspects of the child. First, the child is a unique individual with abilities, ambitions, thoughts, and desires that belong to no one else. Programs should be developed that allow the differences in children to grow. Next, the role of the child as a family member should be considered. Families are the primary socializing agent of children, so programs should be offered that allow families to play an important role in deciding what kind of day care their child will receive. As we turn toward another facet of the child, we must realize that the values, attitudes, and habits acquired during childhood are often lasting ones. It is the responsibility of a good day care program to provide an environment that will prepare each child to live comfortably as an adult in our complex society. Let us examine some ways that day care programs should contribute to a child's total life.

Assist in Total Development

Throughout the years one area or another of the child's development has been singled out for special attention in day care programs. During the early part of the century, the physical well-being of the child was the primary objective. Then day care was influenced by the goals of many nursery schools during the forties and fifties, and the program objectives began to focus on the social development of the young child. The advent of Head Start in 1965 influenced early childhood programs, making the cognitive development of children the first priority of many day care programs.

Day care programs must move from the notion of caring primarily for any one area of development and accept the responsibility for providing an environment that fosters the child's total development. Developmental day care means care that provides opportunities for the social, intellectual, emotional, and physical development of the child. Children enrolled in day care should be given opportunities for optimum growth in all of these areas, and these areas must be viewed as being interrelated. Social development cannot be treated separately from the physical growth of the child, nor can intellectual development be considered without respect for emotional development. The total needs of the child must be examined and avenues found to meet these needs if the day care environment is to be helpful, stimulating, and supportive.

We cannot assume that the needs of each child will be met in the same ways. Children differ in many ways: physical growth, appearance, health, biological inheritance, interests, abilities, experiences, family life style, family social status, ethnic origin, and family size to name only a few. The goal of a good day care program should not be to minimize these differences and to create sameness among the children but to capitalize on the differences and to assist each child to become a totally unique person.

It is customary and completely acceptable that there be broad, common goals that are applicable to all children. These goals might relate to such areas as safety, nutrition, health care, and language development. Once these broad goals are set, however, individual differences among the children dictate that we allow each child to develop in his or her own style and in such a way as to maintain his or her heritage and individuality.

The idea of self-concept is very closely related to the idea of individual differences. It is the teachers' responsibility to assist children to accept their differences and to be satisfied with themselves as worthy people. Programs that stress one particular area of development can be damaging to the child who lacks skills in that area. The lack of achievement in any given area of development is often due to a maturational delay rather than inability. If young children do not succeed academically, it may well be because they are not socially and emotionally prepared to handle academic situations. Failure in the physical area can often be attributed to lack of body coordination that has not yet developed. Teachers have a responsibility to provide opportunities for all children to succeed in many ways every day. Children need success experiences upon which to build self-confidence and a willingness to try new and more difficult tasks. We will never have a society of well-adjusted adults until children are encouraged to think well of themselves and to be happy with who and what they are.

Strengthen the Family

The relationship between the teacher and the child in a day care setting is often a very important one for the child. The teacher assists the child in many necessary functions such as eating, sleeping, toileting, playing, and learning each day. It would be an unusual situation if there were not a special closeness between the teacher and the child, but people who care for children must guard against usurping the roles and responsibilities of the parents. It's crucial that parents remain the most important adult figures in a child's life. When the child is in day care, the teacher's role should be to supplement the family. In no way should the day care situation attempt to replace the necessary positive relationship between a parent and the child. If a healthy relationship does not exist between the parent and the child, the teacher should assist the family to develop this kind of relationship. Parents and teachers should share a sense of joint responsibility if the child is to receive optimum benefit from the day care experience.

Harmonious, cooperative relationships are more easily formed between teachers and parents if parents are welcome at all times in the day care setting. Parent involvement is vital for a successful day care program. Parents should be encouraged to participate in the activities anytime during the day. Parents can gain an understanding of their children when they share daily activities with them and observe them interacting with others.

Special efforts may be necessary to encourage parents to become involved in the day care setting. Some parents may be reluctant because their previous school and social agency experiences have been unpleasant. Other parents are often bogged down in work, and lack of time becomes the barrier. Day care personnel must recognize these problems and accept the challenge to involve the parents in the program.

There are many traditional avenues used in public school to encourage parents to become interested and active in the school. These include home visits, special invitations to visit the school, and all-school functions such as Halloween parties. These methods have worked equally well in day care programs. However, another successful approach is ensuring that parents have opportunities to make decisions that directly affect their children. If day care is to act as a strengthening service to families it must provide the kind of support that families need and want. The most effective way to ensure that the families' desires are known is to give parents responsibilities for making decisions about the program that affects their children.

School-age children require a day care program that considers their interests and levels of development.

Care for Older Children

Most day care literature deals with day care for children from birth to six years of age. This is not, however, the only kind of day care that is needed in this country. A strong belief held by many, including the authors, is that high-quality, developmental day care should be made available at all times in many places for all ages who need it at a price that families can afford to pay. When the last child in the family enters school, the family's need for out-of-home care has certainly not vanished. Many people, including parents, never think of day care for children once they enter school, but examine for a moment the number of reasons why children do not attend school each year: summer vacation, holidays, teacher meetings, teacher strikes, weekends, bad weather, and illness of the child. Children are in school less than one-half of the days in a year. Most states require schools to teach about 175 days. Children of working mothers require supervision on the remaining days as well as before and after school.

When children enter kindergarten or first grade, their needs are not very different from those of a preschool child. The social and emotional abilities of children this age are not developed sufficiently so that they can cope with their own problems and make intelligent decisions about their activities. These abilities develop slowly through guidance and support from caring adults. Children of this age need the security of a friendly adult each day to help them in their development and to give direction to their daily activities.

More than two-thirds of the children of working mothers are from six to fourteen years of age.[15] There must be an increase in the amount and availability of out-of-school care to accommodate these children. Programs must be developed that consider the self-respect of the child; provide opportunities for the child to develop and mature; and allow friends, activities, and interests to be selected rather than forced. The few facilities that exist for the school-age child are typically operated for the care of pre-schoolers, and accept but do not plan for school-age children. The school-age child feels out of place, cramped, oversupervised and insulted by many of the rules that are inappropriate for older children. If school-age care is to succeed in day care settings caring for younger children, there will have to be programs designed, rules formulated, equipment purchased, and staff hired with this age group in mind.

There are many alternatives available for providing good care for school-age children. Family day care homes and day care centers located near the school, out-of-school programs located in existing school facilities, and recreational programs such as the YMCA and YWCA are other possible ways to provide for the care of the school-age child. All of these and many other alternatives should be available so that children and parents can select the program that is most compatible with the needs of the child and the family.

Maintain Cultural Pluralism

We have recognized that young children have basic needs that are necessary for optimum development, and we have charged day care programs with the responsibility for meeting these needs. We must stop and remember, however, that even though many of the primary goals for all day care programs will be the same, the programs themselves should be diverse lest we fall into the trap of providing identical opportunities for all children.

It would be very presumptuous to focus all day care programs toward middle-class mores and values. Many institutions have wrongly insisted that all Americans disregard their own tradition, language, and religion and adopt traditional European customs, the standard English language and the Christian religion if they are to be at all successful in this country. Minority groups have taken a stand against this degradation and are demanding that their distinct cultures be retained and respected. Day care programs must follow this lead and provide diversity so that all parents can choose the program most appropriate for their children and families. Programs should vary in the languages that are spoken to the children, the kinds of food that are served, the ways the food is eaten, the types of music and musical instruments presented, the types of

Day care settings can assist children of all races to be accepting and appreciative of the culture of their friends and neighbors.

literature that are read, the social expectations held for the children, the religious holidays observed, the appropriate dress, and many other ways.

The healthy self-concept each child should achieve will only be possible if children are assisted to feel neither inferior nor superior because of their heritage but are encouraged to be proud of their culture and accepting and appreciative of their friends' and neighbors' cultures.

Closely tied to the maintaining of cultural pluralism is the belief that discrimination in any form is especially damaging to impressionable children who have no way of sorting discriminatory behavior from other behavior. While maintaining cultural differences and pride, we must provide opportunities for children to learn about and live with others who are different from themselves. Day care programs should provide the ideal setting for young children to learn to respect and enjoy people who are a different race, sex, or age. Day care personnel must be keenly aware of providing a nondiscriminatory environment to free children from sexual and racial prejudice about themselves and others.

Summary

Day care is child care in the absence of parents that takes place away from a child's home and in the company of other children. Except in times of national emergency, day care has not received special attention. The primary obstacle for those interested in improving day care services has been the traditional belief that young children should never be separated from their mothers. Recent recognition of the importance of the first few years of life and the realization that many children need day care have drawn attention to day care as an opportunity for making a positive impact on young children.

The reasons why day care is necessary include changing family and employment patterns, liberation of women and men from stereotyped roles, and special services needed by disadvantaged children. The children in this last group include those from low-income families, children whose parents are handicapped, and handicapped children themselves.

Our suggestions, based on our values and experiences, pertain to the potential of day care in this country. There should be efforts to assist each child in his or her total development and not emphasize one sphere of development at the expense of another. Day care should strengthen the family by offering supplemental help to children and their families. There should be accommodations for school-age children and children from different cultural backgrounds.

NOTES

1. In 1969 the Office of Child Development was established within Health, Education and Welfare, and since then many states have established similar offices.
2. Benjamin S. Bloom, *Stability and Change in Human Characteristics* (New York: John Wiley & Sons, 1964).
3. The Presidential veto of a comprehensive child care bill reflected a concern that the national government would be encroaching upon the "family-centered approach." Office of the President, Economic Opportunity amendment of 1971—Veto Message (H. Doc. No. 92-48) (1971).
4. Employment Standards Administration, Women's Bureau, "Women Workers Today" (Washington, D.C.: U.S. Department of Labor, 1974), p. 1.
5. Ibid., pp. 7-8.
6. Ibid., p. 2.
7. Margaret Mead, "Too Many Divorces, Too Soon," *Redbook Magazine* 142 (1974): 72-74.
8. Employment Standards Administration, Women's Bureau, "Women Workers Today," p. 3.
9. Annie L. Butler, "The Child's Right to Quality Day Care" (A position paper) (Washington, D.C.: Association for Childhood Education International, N November 1970).
10. Employment Standards Administration, Women's Bureau, "Day Care Services: Industry's Involvement" (Washington D.C.: U.S. Department of Labor, 1971), p. 6. See also "The Woman Question in Child Care" (A position paper) (Washington, D.C.: The Day Care and Child Development Council of America, n. d.), p. 16.
11. "The Woman Question in Child Care," pp. 11-13.
12. Employment Standards Administration, Women's Bureau, "Women Workers Today," p. 3.
13. U.S. Bureau of the Census, "Characteristics of the Low Income Population: 1972," *Current Population Reports* (Washington, D.C.: U.S. Government Printing Office, Series P-60 No. 91, 1973), p. 55.
14. "Alcoholism and Women," *Alcohol Health and Research World,* Summer 1974, p. 4.
15. Gertrude L. Hoffman, *School Age Child Care* (Washington D.C.: U.S. Department of Health, Education and Welfare, Publication No. (SRS) 73-23066, n.d.), p. 1.

Suggested Readings

Bloom, Benjamin S. *Stability and Change in Human Characteristics.* New York: John Wiley & Sons, 1964. An examination of child development studies, both longitudinal and cross sectional that amply indicates the potential for growth during a child's early years.

Hoffman, Gertrude L. *School Age Child Care.* Washington, D.C.: U.S. Department of Health, Education and Welfare No. (SRS) 73-23006, n.d. An excellent description of the state of the art regarding child care for school-age children.

Swenson, Janet P. *Alternatives in Quality Child Care.* Washington, D.C.: The Day Care and Child Development Council of America, 1972. An excellent treatment of children and child care with clear implications for planning a day care setting.

"The Woman Question in Child Care." (A position paper) Washington, D.C.: The Day Care and Child Development Council of America, n.d. A brief summary of the role of child care in women's liberation.

Suggested Activities

1. Conduct a survey of how many and what kinds of day care facilities are present in your community or a section thereof. How many are community sponsored? church affiliated? private? What are the differences, if any?

2. Inquire at several day care centers regarding their waiting lists. Try to assess the need for more day care slots in your area.

3. Summarize the state and local licensing requirements for different types of day care. Are state and local requirements the same? If not, how do they differ?

Chapter Two

Curriculum

Those who set out to do anything at all in the world must have as a rule some kind of plan of action. "As a rule," I say, because very great things have been done without a plan, by a simple advance on chaos and old night. As a rule, however, a plan is very useful and necessary, so long as it does not blind one to the aim of the work and so make the means appear to be a greater thing than the end for which they are designed.

Margaret McMillan, The Nursery School
(New York: E. P. Dutton Co., 1921), p. 317.

There are many definitions of *curriculum* that range from the very narrow and specific to broad, general statements. We see little value in rehashing the arguments that support or attack various positions. A workable solution to the definition dilemma is to be clear and consistent in how the word is used and get on with the business of making useful suggestions for developing and improving services offered to children. The conceptualization of curriculum and its attendant concerns ought to be broad enough to permit adaptation to specific settings, all of which have unique characteristics that may need to be maintained.

Definitions

Curriculum has been used to mean only the goals and objectives or intended outcomes for children.[1] Others use it to mean all the experiences children have for which the school assumes responsibility.[2] For our purposes we will define *curriculum* in two ways. First, *curriculum* will refer to a written plan for the experiences for children.[3] Many such documents have been written for school-age children, and we see no reason why they cannot be written for younger children. An analysis of curricula written for older children reveals that such documents contain certain characteristics that can apply to day care.[4] The second use of the word *curriculum* will be to describe the activities of the people involved in developing, using, and revising the document. A curriculum system is that part of a day care operation that involves developing, using, and revising the plan for children.

The definitions of *curriculum* we will use are straightforward but can become unclear when, for example, we consider a day care setting that has no document that is a written plan for the experiences of children. Does it follow then that such a setting has no curriculum? It depends. One could infer the curriculum to be whatever the teachers use as a point of departure for planning for children. The curriculum in this instance would probably be an assortment of early childhood education textbooks and manuals, government publications, past experience, other teachers' or parents' suggestions, or any number of miscellaneous sources. In a setting where there is little or no planning for children, we can infer that no curriculum exists. Our assumption is that the lack of a unified, carefully thought-out and considered source for planning children's experiences promotes slipshod teaching and virtually no accountability or responsibility.

Charles Silberman conducted an extensive study of public schools during the late sixties.[5] He concluded that a kind of mindlessness permeated most school settings. This definition of mindlessness was "the failure or refusal to think seriously about educational purpose, the reluctance to question established practice."[6] One of our major premises is that developing a curriculum—that is, a written plan for the experiences for children—will help reduce the likelihood of day care personnel being mindless about their responsibilities. Developing a curriculum forces the people involved to think seriously about their purposes and question established practice.

It is important to indicate some meanings associated with curriculum that we do *not* intend. We are not suggesting that a curriculum be a rigid, inflexible document that is imposed by higher authorities on unsuspecting teachers. A curriculum should be very much a working draft of the best thinking available, but one that is tentative and continually tested by teachers and children. Although there are commercial sources for such curricular items as goals and objectives, activities, and evaluative devices, we are not suggesting an uncritical adoption of such aids. The curriculum should be tailored to meet specific needs and interests of children, teachers, and parents. If the curriculum is perceived as an obstacle to teachers, something is wrong. It should be an aid to teachers and a clarifying explanation to parents.

Nor are we intending to convey something mysterious or magical about curriculum. There is a great deal that is unknown about teaching and learning, and the presence of a curriculum will not account for the unknown. A curriculum can only be a plan or record of what is known about teaching and learning. There is enough known now, we believe, to warrant making some systematic use of it.

Finally, we do not believe that having a curriculum will permit a director or a parent to say with confidence exactly what is happening in any one classroom with any group of children at any one time. That is not an ideal to which day care should aspire. Using a curriculum for planning specific activities should not preclude creativity on the part of teachers or children. Rather, the curriculum should be a reasonable account of the purposes and goals the activities are serving. A curriculum cannot take the place of teachers and should not unduly hamper them. However, teachers can be more effective individually and as a group over a period of time if they work together from common purposes and goals contained in the curriculum.

A simple illustration of the way we are using curriculum is the case of a teacher taking a group of five year olds on a train ride to a nearby town. Ideally this activity should have been selected on the basis of its appropriateness to the goals and objectives selected for the children in the group. What we are proposing is that such an activity reflect the needs of the children and be related to other activities in a reasonable way. For example, the train ride may be an experience designed to increase vocabulary development related to transportation. It may be related to learning more about the people in the neighboring town. Many goals and objectives might be served by a simple train ride, and we believe they can be served more effectively if planning precedes the activity. By planning, we mean an attempt at thinking through all possible benefits and tie-ins that might accrue to such an experience. Such thinking ought to lead to certain expectations that might otherwise be overlooked. Other kinds of activities can be indicated by such planning. The train ride is important, but the context out of which it grows and the subsequent activities it helps to create are just as important.

Characteristics of a Curriculum Document

When curriculum refers to a written plan for the experiences for children, it pertains to both day care centers and day care homes. An analysis of over a thousand curriculum documents indicated that they contain any or all of the following sections:

1. Directions for use.
2. A brief historical account of curriculum development.
3. A statement of purposes or philosophy.
4. A statement of goals and objectives toward which the staff is working.
5. Activities that ought to contribute to achieving the goals and objectives.
6. An evaluative scheme.
7. A plan for continual revision of the curriculum.

It is not our intention to make something complicated that appears to be simple on the surface. Our experience with day care centers, both public and private, as well as with elementary schools, convinces us of the importance of making as explicit as possible the topics included in the document called curriculum. But let us add this point. Developing such a document need not precede offering day care services, nor should it so engulf the staff that they have little time for planning and meeting their daily responsibilities.[7] What follows, then, is a topical discussion of each part of the curriculum in terms of a rationale for its inclusion and suggestions for its treatment.

Directions for Use.   This section includes suggestions on how the total document should be used by teachers and viewed by parents. Some organizations may want to be very specific regarding the use of suggested activities, while others may wish to delegate more responsibility to teachers for generating their own activities. Whatever the case, readers will know from reading this section the intended use of the document.

History.   Providing an historical perspective to the curriculum development efforts of a center will help answer the inevitable question, What did you use for guidance in the past? Without a curriculum document, day care centers functioned, sometimes well, on a basic set of assumptions held by the majority of staff members. With high rates of turnover in staff to which many centers are accustomed, one can see the precariousness of maintaining some continuity of effort toward certain goals and objectives. The historical section brings new parents and staff up to date in terms of knowing the kinds of planning efforts made in the past, whether or not parents were involved, what outcomes there were, and so forth.

Purpose or Philosophy.   This section is undoubtedly the most difficult to develop. It is the section wherein a center states its rationale for offering the kinds of services it provides. It should also contain the basic assumptions from which goals are produced and activities planned. A significant difference between goals, activities, and day-to-day routines could be explained by different assumptions about children as learners.

For example, if children are assumed to be essentially passive receivers as opposed to active inquirers, the kinds of activities presented to the children should reflect that assumption. The process of discussing and developing this section can have the beneficial effect of making everyone involved more aware of and sensitive to the fundamental concerns of the parents and staff. Two examples of statements of purpose/philosophy appear in Appendix A.

Goals and Objectives.   Whereas the section on purposes and philosophy deals with the reason for being, other than employment-related needs of parents, this section becomes more specific in regard to exactly what it is the day care setting endeavors to achieve through the experiences offered to children. A goal is a broad, global statement and an objective is a more precise and definite statement of an aspect of a goal. Goals and objectives can be found in the professional literature (see Appendices B and C), but the staff and parents should not be overlooked as primary sources. Sorting out the many goals and objectives can be laborious. Some guidelines for developing this section are:

1. Realize no perfect system of sorting exists.
2. Realize a great deal of overlap will result regardless of how goals and objectives are sorted.
3. Try categorizing goals and objectives according to physical, affective, and cognitive domains.
4. Try organizing goals and objectives by age levels.
5. Try rank ordering goals and objectives—some will be more important than others.

The collection of goals and objectives, however they are organized, will always be subject to review for additions, modifications, and deletions. It will not be possible to assemble an exhaustive list, but the major intentions of the day care setting should be represented in this section.

Activities.   This section, whatever form it may take, has been the conceptual model many people associate with curriculum. This is the section that serves as the resource for selecting the children's daily experiences. Just as there are many sources for obtaining objectives, there is a nearly limitless supply of general and specific suggestions for activities.

The activities, of course, should be reflective of and purposeful in regard to the goals and objectives. One method of organizing the activities is to establish an activity bank, categorized according to goals, objectives, or ages of children. There is no best way to organize the activities. The important thing is that there be a large enough collection of them so that all goals and objectives are represented, and that they be organized in a manner that makes them accessible to teachers. Even more than with objectives, the collection and organization of activities are continuous processes in which curriculum developers are engaged.

Evaluative scheme.   All activities and experiences can be examined for positive and negative effects. The examination can be formal, as in the case of using developmental inventories or tests of intellectual development, or informal, as in the case of teachers or parents collecting impressionistic data. There are four kinds of evaluation.[8] Placement evaluation occurs when decisions are made about placing children with teachers. Diagnostic evaluation is used when special problems emerge in a child. Visual and auditory screening of all children in a day care setting may reveal special cases requiring more intensive diagnosis. Formative evaluation is carried out during the year to provide feedback to teachers and parents about the appropriateness of methods, activities, objectives, goals, and purpose or philosophy. Formative evaluation is most helpful in revising the curriculum. Summative evaluation is focused on ascertaining the children's progress toward goals. The evaluative scheme indicates the kinds of evaluations recommended and how the information generated by the evaluations will be used.

Plan for Revision.   Everybody agrees any kind of educational plan should be subject to continual revisions, but one looks in vain for many examples of systematic work toward revising a curriculum. This section of the curriculum could outline not only the individuals or groups who would be responsible for revision, but suggestions for topics and reporting of such work. Making these plans explicit provides some assurance that the curriculum will continue to reflect current needs and interests of all parties involved.

Figure 1 is a representation of the essential characteristics of a curriculum document. It shows the relationships between the purpose/philosophy, goals, objectives, activities, and evaluation.

Usefulness of a Curriculum Document

Developing a curriculum as a written document that includes most, if not all, of the sections previously described is not an easy task. Some of the difficulty can be traced to personnel having little appreciation for the usefulness of such a document. There are at least three reasons to warrant spending the time and energy in developing and writing a curriculum. The reasons are interrelated but will be discussed separately.

Any intelligent undertaking, especially if it is to extend over time, requires planning. Plans dealing with humans as opposed to those for things are tentative and necessarily more general than specific. The important point, however, is that the responsibility of caring for children's needs is serious enough to warrant thoughtful planning. One caution related to planning should be remembered. An architect or engineer can be exact in his or her specifications and prescriptions for a building. Young children are much less predictable in terms of what is currently known about human behavior in groups. Specific expectations can be held for children, but provisions for a variety of methods of attaining them should be made. Selecting only specific objectives that are measurable can promote a kind of mechanistic approach to working with children. If many behaviors can be stated in irreducible degrees of specificity, it does not necessarily follow that these should be used exclusively for planning.

Another reason for developing and using a curriculum has to do with the responsibility of the helping professions. Many day care facilities function without a curriculum as a document, and many public and private schools have gotten along without a written curriculum. But nearly all schools, and some day care centers, are mandated into existence. They are domesticated organizations in that management control over admission and client control over participation are lacking.[9] Schools, especially public schools, will be open year after year and criticized as often, so long as they shirk the responsibility of being accountable to themselves and the people they serve. These

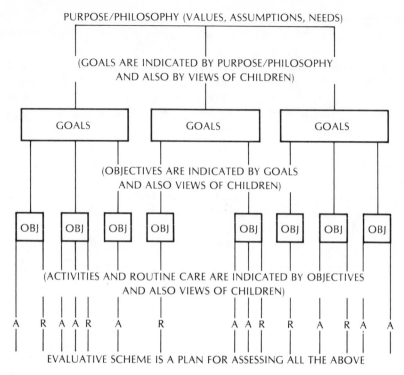

Figure 1 Relationship of Essential Curriculum Components

organizations have no vital need to demonstrate professional responsibility or intelligent planning. On the other hand, day care personnel must be responsible to themselves and the people they serve.

Finally, any group of individuals, brought together for common interests and goals will take on special characteristics that are unique to them individually as well as a group. Those characteristics and that uniqueness will have an impact on the total setting. The curriculum ought to reflect that uniqueness and through it communicate to anyone who is interested that this day care setting is not exactly like any other one.

It matters little whether or not a curriculum contains all the sections previously discussed. What does matter is that teachers and parents have a reliable source of information regarding what a particular day care setting considers important and the ways in which its personnel will work toward accomplishing its purposes and goals. The curriculum can be a useful vehicle for achieving this purpose.

Curriculum as a System

The curriculum system of a day care facility is an abstraction. It is easier to write and talk about than it is to see, but discussions of the curriculum system should reflect actual behaviors of the people involved. Essentially, the system refers to the following activities:

1. Selecting people to participate in developing the curriculum.
2. Organizing people into work groups.

3. Developing the curriculum.
4. Implementing the curriculum.
5. Evaluating the curriculum.
6. Revising the curriculum.

Selecting.   Selecting or determining who will be involved in curriculum development can be the responsibility of the governing body or the director. Whenever possible, the people who will be expected to carry out what the curriculum suggests should be active participants in its planning and development.[10]

Organizing.   Organizing the people into work groups can be determined best by the people involved. There are some general guidelines for organizing that will be discussed in Chapter Three.

Developing.   Exactly how the curriculum is developed depends upon the expertise available. Essentially the finished product should have some resemblance to the earlier description of the curriculum document. Techniques or strategies for developing and testing specific objectives and activities may range from adopting what has been tried before to more systematic synthesizing. There is no one best way to develop a curriculum. If parents and teachers believe a curriculum will help them clarify their goals and objectives, provide a base from which they can venture forth with new techniques, and make some assessment of all their efforts, a curriculum can be written with less difficulty than most would expect. Suggestions for curriculum development can be found in Chapters Three and Four.

Implementing.   Implementing the curriculum means to use or do what was said would be used or done. As simple as that sounds, most curriculum systems fail at that juncture; that is, in spite of the many hours and great amount of energy put into curriculum development, there is seldom any monitoring or follow-up to see if the curriculum is ever used. This seems to be especially true in large systems in which teachers may feel a kind of impersonal imposition regarding expectations of curriculum use. As was indicated earlier, the best safeguard against teachers not using the curriculum is to involve them in its planning.

Evaluating.   Evaluating whatever is done in day care should be a decision-bound process; that is, decisions need to be made regarding the appropriateness of goals and objectives, methods or activities used to achieve them, and materials or support services used by the teacher. The kinds of decisions made depend upon the kind of evaluation, for example, formative or summative. The initial concern of the curriculum worker in day care is that there be a systematic evaluation procedure that helps care givers improve their services to children.

Revising.   Revising the curriculum is a continual process. There will always be items in the curriculum that require modification or addition, just as new ideas will need to be tried and included. The revision can usually be carried out by the same individuals who developed the original document. It is perhaps most apparent when discussing the revising aspect of a curriculum system that many of these activities could be happening simultaneously. There need be nothing linear or lockstep about the process of curriculum development and revision. People are too spontaneous for that to ever result. As long as it is possible to see some semblance of interrelatedness in activities in which people are involved, one can have some confidence that the output of such a system will result in increased understanding of what the programs and practices represent. Suggestions for revising the curriculum can be found in Chapter Four.

Summary

Curriculum has been associated with many different meanings. Two definitions of curriculum will be used in this book:

1. A curriculum is a written plan for the experiences for children.
2. A curriculum system is that set of activities and decisions associated with developing, using, and revising the plan for children.

As a plan for the experiences for children, the curriculum should serve as a guide to teachers in their daily planning of specific activities. Investing time and energy in developing a curriculum, and using and revising it should mitigate against the mindlessness that permeates so many of our institutions.

A curriculum document can consist of the following components or sections:

1. Directions for use
2. History
3. Purpose or philosophy
4. Goals and objectives
5. Activities
6. Evaluative scheme
7. Plan for revision

The essential components are purpose/philosophy, goals, objectives, activities, and evaluative scheme. Three reasons for using a curriculum are:

1. Important activities require planning.
2. Helping professions are responsible to their clients.
3. Unique characteristics of a group should be maintained.

A curriculum system consists of six activities:

1. Selecting people to participate in curriculum development.
2. Organizing people into work groups.
3. Developing the curriculum.
4. Implementing the curriculum.
5. Evaluating the curriculum.
6. Revising the curriculum.

NOTES

1. Mauritz Johnson, Jr., "Definitions and Models in Curriculum Theory," *Educational Theory* 17 (1967): 127-40.

2. Ronald C. Doll, *Curriculum Improvement: Decision Making and Process* (Boston: Allyn & Bacon, 1977), p. 22.

3. This definition is a more general version of Beauchamp's "written plan depicting the scope and arrangement of the projected educational program for a school," in George A. Beauchamp, *Curriculum Theory,* 3d ed. (Wilmette, Ill.: The Kagg Press, 1975), p. 130.

4. Michael Langenbach, M. T. Hinkemeyer, and G. A. Beauchamp, "An Empirical Analysis of Curriculum Design" (Washington, D.C.: *Research in Education,* ED045 582,6, April 1971), p. 146.

5. Charles E. Silberman, *Crisis in the Classroom: The Remaking of American Education* (New York: Random House, 1970).

6. Ibid., p. 11.

7. For some practical suggestions on writing or taping parts of the curriculum, see Jonathon Kozol, *Free Schools* (Boston: Houghton Mifflin Co., 1972), pp. 63-65.

8. George F. Madaus and P. W. Airasion, "Placement, Formative, Diagnostic and Summative Evaluation of Classroom Learning." (Paper presented at the Annual Convention of the American Educational Research Association, Minneapolis, Minn., March 1970.) For a more comprehensive treatment of formative and summative evaluation, see Benjamin S. Bloom, J. Hastings, and George F. Madaus, *Handbook on Formative and Summative Evaluation of Student Learning* (New York: McGraw-Hill Book Co., 1971).

9. See Richard O. Carlson, "Environmental Constraints and Organizational Consequences: The Public School and Its Clients," in *Behavioral Science and Educational Administration,* ed. Daniel E. Griffiths (Chicago: University of Chicago Press, 1964), pp 262-76.

10. For empirical studies supporting this suggestion, see John J. Johansen, "The Relationships between Teachers' Perceptions of Influence in Local Curriculum Decision Making and Curriculum Implementation," *The Journal of Educational Research* 61 (1967): 81-83 and Michael Langenbach, "Development of an Instrument to Measure Teachers' Attitudes Toward Curriculum Use and Planning," *The Journal of Educational Research* 66 (1972): 35-38.

Suggested Readings

Beauchamp, George A. *Curriculum Theory.* 3d ed. Wilmette, Ill.: The Kagg Press, 1975. A conceptual model for considering curriculum as a written document and as a system through which such a document is developed, used, and evaluated.

Doll, Ronald C. *Curriculum Improvement: Decision Making and Process.* 3d ed. Boston: Allyn & Bacon, 1974. A comprehensive treatment of historical, phychological, and social forces affecting the process of curriculum development.

Manning, Duane. *Toward a Humanistic Curriculum.* New York: Harper & Row, Publishers, 1971. A humanistic treatment of curriculum topics emphasizing concern for all aspects of children's growth and development.

Taba, Hilda. *Curriculum Development: Theory and Practice.* New York: Harcourt, Brace Jovanovich, 1962. A thorough account of the foundations, process, and strategies of curriculum development.

Suggested Activities

1. Visit several day care settings. Ask what sources teachers use to plan activities for children. Discuss your findings and the implications.

2. Visit several day care settings. Try to determine the purpose or philosophy of each. Discuss the differences and similarities.

3. Observe some children in a day care setting. Are the activities in which they engage and/or their general behavior reflective of certain purposes or philosophies?

Section Two

Curriculum Development

Whenever people in school settings talk about and plan for the educational experiences of the children they serve, they are engaging in some form of curriculum development. A final product in the form of a plan or a list of goals may or may not be the result of such communications, but the process is one of curriculum development. It is also a curriculum development process when psychologists and sociologists formulate goals for a Head Start program. Curriculum development can involve teachers, parents, school administrators, child development specialists, curriculum specialists, and others who have an interest in providing quality care and education for children. Curriculum development can also be a one-person endeavor as will be shown in Chapter Three.

There is no "right" way to go about the process, but descriptions of some options can help in getting started. The same is true for implementing, evaluating, and revising a curriculum. No one way is foolproof. What will work in one setting may or may not work in another. What will apply to all day care settings and what is the thesis of this book is that children in day care are more likely to profit from the experience if routines and activities are planned according to goals and the purpose/philosophy of the staff and families being served. This thesis can be manifested most readily, we believe, by the development and use of a curriculum. Some suggestions for the development of a curriculum are contained in Chapter Three. Using, evaluating, and revising a curriculum are discussed in Chapter Four.

Chapter Three

Beginning the Process of Curriculum Development

The inescapable fact is that every day care center, whether it knows it or not, is a school. The choice is never between custodial care and education. The choice is between unplanned and planned education, conscious and unconscious education, between bad education and good education.

James L. Hymes, Jr., Teaching the Child Under Six, *2d ed.*
(Columbus, Oh.: Charles E. Merrill Publishing Co., 1974), p. 30.

One looks in vain for many practical suggestions for curriculum development. Chapter Two was conceptual and abstract about actual procedures of organizing and writing the various sections of a curriculum because it was an attempt to generalize about many different situations. Much of the professional literature is equally vague about curriculum development procedures. Worse yet, as was pointed out earlier, many sources define curriculum as such an all-encompassing phenomenon that the very definition defies specificity.

There are legitimate reasons for avoiding specific recommendations. One is that in spite of a lot of experience with the process of curriculum development, no one has empirically verified what procedures work best with certain people in specified conditions.[1] There may be a fear, also, that if concrete suggestions are tried and fail, one's credibility as a writer in the field is weakened. We believe there is a great deal of ambiguity surrounding curriculum development as it is treated in the professional literature. Until there are some systematic research studies documenting the activities, problems, and possible solutions to the problems encountered when developing a curriculum, in-service professionals will have to approach curriculum development with an open mind and expect to raise more questions than they can answer.

The curriculum system mentioned in Chapter Two referred to the following activities:

1. Selecting people to participate in developing the curriculum.
2. Organizing people into work groups.
3. Developing the curriculum.
4. Implementing the curriculum.
5. Evaluating the curriculum.
6. Revising the curriculum.

The first three of these activities will be discussed in terms of a hypothetical day care setting. The last three will be discussed in Chapter Four. The setting will be a center

33

serving about 100 children from infants to five year olds all day and elementary-age children before and after school. Readers interested in family day care homes can extrapolate from some of the suggestions related to centers, but will find more specific attention under the heading, "Individual Efforts."

Selecting People to Participate

The responsibility for selecting people to participate in developing the curriculum usually rests with the director. The director has the authority to make such decisions except in those cases where a governing board or some higher office management, as in the case of day care networks, retains the authority for such decisions. In our hypothetical center, we will àssume the director has the authority to select people who will be involved in the curriculum development for that center. The actual selection is based on two other assumptions. One is that the director wants a curriculum, and the other is that the director wants other people to be involved in its development.

If the director does not want a curriculum for the center, there is little likelihood one will ever be developed. In such a case, teachers may develop their own curriculum for their own classrooms, either individually or as a group effort.

The director may want a curriculum but not want other people involved in the decisions related to its development. If this is the case, then the director will have full responsibility for curriculum development, and it will probably take the form of adopting in whole or in part from the various curricula that are described in the professional literature or are commercially available. Adopting a curriculum from some external source has advantages and disadvantages, both of which will be discussed shortly, but let us proceed with the hypothetical case and assume that the director wants a curriculum and wants to have other people participate in its development.

The teachers should be involved in curriculum development because there is some evidence to suggest that a teacher will be more likely to use the curriculum if he or she has participated in developing it. Teachers' attitudes toward the curriculum are more likely to be positive if they have been involved in its development. Head teachers and assistants, full time and part time, aides and volunteers in the center should be encouraged to participate. We see little to be lost and much to be gained by involving as many of the staff as possible.

The children's parents should also be involved in curriculum development. Ideally, any day care setting should serve as a supplement to the parents and families it serves. To be supplemental means to help work toward similar goals and meet certain needs and purposes. There can be little confidence in the degree to which a day care setting is supplemental if the people responsible for the setting do not know the goals, needs, and purposes of the parents and families they serve. The parents will contribute a perspective somewhat different from that of the teachers and director, but all the groups should work together because of their common concern—providing the best possible care for the children. Parents can make important contributions to the statement of purpose/philosophy and goals. Teachers, too, should contribute to the development of these curriculum sections, but their indispensable expertise along with the director's would be in their contributions to the sections of objectives, activities, and evaluation.

Moving slightly from the ideal, however, we face what in many situations approaches the real conditions. The overwhelming majority of the parents are either working or going to school. Expecting them or at least very many of them to devote much time to curriculum development may be unrealistic. They should be encouraged to participate, however, and night care for their children could be offered if necessary. It is equally unrealistic to expect all teachers to be interested in curriculum development. They, too, work all day. Incentives such as additional pay or compensating time off can be considered. Alternative arrangements for meeting during the day might be arranged. Some teachers may resist participation on the grounds that they see little use for a curriculum. They may be converted, once immersed in the process, but probably the most that can be expected is some degree of participation and cooperation when needed. There is a fine line between a teacher's unwillingness to cooperate on the grounds that he or she has legitimate objections to certain procedures and one's unwillingness to cooperate based on less professional grounds. It is simply unrealistic to expect all teachers to be equally open and cooperative. The variation among teachers is natural. Ideally, the variations in points of view, philosophy, etc. should be capitalized on and not ignored or resisted in terms of some ideal that has everybody agreeing to everything. Assuming then that a group of parents, the staff, and the director are in general agreement that having a curriculum would be helpful to their common purpose—providing the best possible care for the children—what kinds of suggestions can be made about the best way to organize the groups for working?

Organizing People into Work Groups

Suggestions for organizing people into work groups have been made in the form of guidelines by Parker.[2] The guidelines that follow represent a distillation of generalizations that evolved from working with in-service teachers in a variety of settings. The guidelines are offered here as starting points for day care personnel to consider when organizing work groups.

Planning Procedures

Authoritarian statements regarding procedures to be used in the solution of problems are out of place. This guideline is extremely difficult to follow, but it is most important. The leader who says, "Now, let's all sit facing each other in a circle," or "First we must select a chairman," or, especially, "We will follow Robert's Rules of Order," soon finds himself or herself in trouble. There may be some synthetic progress at the first meeting, but the members present will carefully avoid saying what they mean unless they spend whatever time is needed to develop their own procedures.

Working on Significant Problems.

Problems are significant to an individual when she or he can become involved emotionally as well as intellectually, when the problem can be seen as a basis for action, and when solution of the problem seems to be demanded. Needless to say, a problem may have significance for an individual even if she or he does not suggest it. Otherwise, group discussion would be fruitless and impossible. All, including the leader, share in the responsibility for suggesting problems.

Developing Opportunities for Relating

We know that attitudes are modifiable, that they can be changed in group situations, and that such changes involve personal relationships between the individual concerned and the other members of the group. If the feelings are negative, the attitudes may change but not in the direction of the group. Such nonconformity, especially if it persists after full discussion of such facts as are known, must not only be accepted by the group, but treasured. Conflict such as that just described need not and should not produce personal animosities. However, the unruffled acceptance of difference is the mark of an adult, and like much of adult behavior, it must be learned.

Creating an Atmosphere of Mutual Respect and Support

People who know a situation thoroughly usually feel secure. There are even some fortunate people who feel secure in a situation that is essentially strange to them. Perhaps these are the ones best qualified to assume the role of leadership. Those who are insecure are best helped if given the time and opportunity to become thoroughly familiar with the new situation. Individuals in official positions who are unable to forget their status should be excluded from the group. Otherwise, the group will find it profitable to disband, for the decisions will be those of such individuals rather than those of the group. Basic to the democratic procedure is acceptance of the worth of each individual.[3]

In our hypothetical example, a group of parents, teachers, and the director are organized in a manner that satisfies them. They are ready then to get started with curriculum development.

Developing the Curriculum

Just as there is no right way to organize people for working, there is no single right way to develop a curriculum. Several options are available, and each will be discussed to illustrate some starting procedures.

Adopting or Adapting from External Sources

The wholesale adoption of a curriculum or significant parts thereof can be accomplished by writing to a publisher or sponsor and purchasing it. Sometimes the essential components of a curriculum (purpose/philosophy, goals, objectives, and activities) are described in the professional literature and can be put into useable form with a minimum of difficulty. Some of the available curricula are especially geared to children who are labelled as disadvantaged, but a few purport to be designed for any and all children. The advantage of using the adoption or adaptation option is that it saves a lot of time and energy. The disadvantage is the possibility of a lack of fit between the published curriculum and the children, parents, and teachers. Another disadvantage is that the adoption virtually precludes active teacher involvement in the actual development, thereby making it less likely for the teachers to be enthusiastic about using it.

The people responsible for curriculum development can pick and choose from several curricula those sections or components that are judged to be appropriate for their center. The advantage of this variation is that a better fit will obtain between the assembled curriculum and children, parents, and teachers. The disadvantage is that some curricula are based on different kinds of assumptions and selecting from several may yield a document that has little internal consistency.

Another external source is the curriculum consultant. Perhaps a college or university nearby can be prevailed upon for this resource. A consultant could be asked to come in and write the curriculum. This has the same advantage as the first option and helps ensure that the curriculum will reflect the uniqueness of the center. Such consultants rarely come free, however, and not all consultants value input from parents and teachers. It is possible, of course, that a consultant would direct the activities and involve both parents and staff, thereby providing the expertise but not at the expense of the unique needs of the setting or the involvement of interested parties.

For our purpose, we will assume our hypothetical group of parents, teachers, and director choose to develop their own curriculum and rule out the adoption of a commercial one. Furthermore, let us assume the use of a consultant is not feasible. What options remain?

Inventory of Actions

One possible beginning would be to make an inventory of all the general actions of the staff while working. For example, in this setting the children are greeted, made to feel welcome, and comfortable, and in some way accommodated at the start of the day. Breakfast is served at 8:15 and lasts until 9:00 A.M. when all the food services are removed from the room. After this there is time for some play or work activities. The elementary-age children leave for school. Preparation for lunch begins about 11:15 A.M. After lunch, from 12:15 to 1:00 P.M. the children may be out doors for some free or structured play. Inside at 1:15 it is story time, a quieting down activity preparatory to nap time. Naps last from one to two hours; early risers are able to engage in quiet indoor activity or outdoor play. Another play/work activity may begin about 3:00, lasting for a half to a full hour. Snacks are served during this time and cleanup and preparation for leaving begin about 4:00 P.M. most of the children play out doors, weather permitting, until their parents come to pick them up. The elementary children return to the center, have a snack, and then have about an hour before their parents come for them.

The inventory of a typical day's activities makes it clear very quickly that everyday is full of routine. Routine includes warm, friendly greetings, happy and secure handling, and otherwise structuring and maintaining a safe and healthy environment for children. At first glance some may erroneously think that routine care is not part of the curriculum, but it is and should be for two reasons.

First, routine care, or what some might call standard operating procedures, accounts for so much of the time in a day care setting that teachers miss many opportunities for helping children if it is not considered a part of the curriculum. A unique characteristic of day care is that the extended day presents numerous opportunities for learning experiences to occur. Teachers and children in a day care setting do not have the time constraints common to many other educational settings. Worthwhile experiences can take place throughout the day as the children receive routine care and encounter special activities.

The second reason routines are not be be overlooked is that they could take on the characteristics of the hidden curriculum.[4] The routines of an educational setting can be more overwhelming to the children than any other phenomenon if they are unplanned and taken for granted. Indeed, two characteristics of the hidden curriculum are:

1. It is often at odds with the purpose/philosophy and goals of the visible curriculum.
2. It has a more pervasive impact on the children than the visible curriculum.

It would be an error, in our judgment, if routine care were unplanned and unscrutinized. We believe the routines should receive the same kind of scrutiny and consideration as any activity or other part of the day.

The curriculum should speak to aspects of routine because opportunities will be present for learning experiences to occur during the process of routine care. There can be many times in the ministering of routine care that goals and objectives of the curriculum can be met. It seems useful to us, however, to separate time designated for routine care from undesignated time to see when and where other opportunities exist for meeting goals. It may become apparent, for instance, that a two-hour time period exists nearly every day between breakfast cleanup and preparation for lunch. The question is, What kinds of goals might be worked toward during those periods of time? Before answering that question, attention must be paid to the purpose/philosophy of the center that is agreed upon by those participating in curriculum development. It may be more logical or rational to begin with establishing a statement of purpose/philosophy first, but our experience has been that those discussions, unless anchored to some reality base, can become endless and not particularly helpful. Our generalization is made cautiously, however, because others may find more success in beginning the process of curriculum development by first considering a statement of purpose/philosophy. We believe the statement of purpose/philosophy should be developed by parents, teachers, and the director.

One of the primary reasons for having a curriculum is to capture the unique characteristics of a particular center. When parents, teachers, and the director engage in the process of hammering out those unique characteristics—purpose/philosophy, basic assumptions, priorities, whatever—it can be a revealing if not traumatic experience for everyone involved. Indeed, the uniqueness of purpose/philosophy may take a somewhat different form when several people begin to reduce it to words. One conviction we hold is that that experience is good for the organization. We cannot cite empirical evidence to support that claim, but we believe it nonetheless.

The one purpose common to all day care settings is to provide out-of-home care to children. Other purposes, what some would call philosophy and what we refer to as purpose/philosophy, are what indicate certain goals over others and certain teacher behaviors over others. The purpose/philosophy of a day care setting should be explicit and public, enabling parents to select the setting that best fits their philosophy and suits their needs. The statement can be distilled from several considerations: family values, urban/rural homes, condition of the children (e.g., mentally or physically handicapped), cultural values religious values, etc. Examples of key statements of purpose/philosophy include:

1. It is desirable for physically handicapped and physically normal children to interact in a social/educational setting to gain an appreciation and acceptance of one another.
2. Children who come from homes where the language spoken is not English should be encouraged to learn to use both their home language and English.
3. Children should be provided equal opportunities regardless of sex, race, or religion.
4. Children's development can be positively affected by an enriched environment and appropriate activities.

Each of the preceding examples would be amplified and possibly combined with others to create a more complete statement of purpose/philosophy that would indicate certain goals over others and certain teacher behaviors over others. Appendix A contains two examples of a statement of purpose/philosophy.

The purposes any day care setting attempts to serve and the philosophy that guides the selection of goals are matters of personal and group values. In a pluralistic society we would expect to find different purposes and philosophies, but all of them and all the goals and behaviors they indicate should reflect some understanding of children and how children develop. Accomplishing goals of child care is likewise dependent on understanding how children develop. Section Three contains several views of children that will provide a foundation for making decisions about purpose/philosophy and goals. But let us continue with our hypothetical model of parents, teachers, and director involved in curriculum development and offer two more examples of getting started.

Inventory of Goals

It was suggested that making an inventory of actions could serve as a beginning point for curriculum development. Another similar technique is called an inventory of goals. In the inventory of goals option, the reality base is the goals toward which the teachers are currently working. Rather than describing or inventorying their activities in the course of a day, the teachers could list the kinds of goals they are trying to achieve in a day, week, or year. It may be easier for teachers to think in terms of goals when they describe what it is they are doing now. If asked why they choose certain activities over others or why some may be avoided, teachers may answer in terms of the availability of supplies, time, and other constraints, but they may respond in terms of selecting certain goals over other goals. The purpose of the inventory of goals technique is to obtain an accurate picture of the kinds of goals currently being served.

A list of goals (see Appendix B) could be examined by the teachers to help them formulate the goals of their efforts. When a list of goals is compiled and the teachers agree the list includes all the goals they serve, there are at least two additional steps that can be taken. In one procedure, the teachers would indicate the relative emphasis each goal currently receives. In the other step, everyone would rank order the goals in terms of their perceptions of an ideal setting. These considerations of goals, of course, lead right to purpose and philosophy considerations. There is no way to avoid the purpose/philosophy considerations, but we believe approaching those deliberations through activities or goals is a useful way to proceed. These are not the only ways to proceed, but ways that have proved successful in the past.

Individual Efforts

In family day care homes curriculum development efforts are the responsibility of one person, working perhaps with an assistant and, ideally, with the parents. The relatively small number of children and parents served by a family day care home may tempt the director/teacher to proceed with the curriculum on his or her own. The primary obligation of the director/teacher in this instance would be to inform the parents of the purpose/philosophy and goals being served in that setting. Parents who entrust the care of their children to others deserve no less.

All the options previously discussed are open to the director/teacher of a family day care home. The particular procedure used is less important than either the concern for having a curriculum or the efforts to develop one. Lack of imagination and inventiveness are the primary obstacles to overcome in developing a curriculum.

It is possible that a day care center director and a majority of the teachers do not value having a curriculum. It may be that one teacher in such a setting does value the usefulness of a curriculum and wants to develop one for his or her own group of children. The teacher can, perhaps with the help of some of the parents, inventory the activities or goals, formulate a purpose/philosophy, and use the curriculum with the children. Other teachers may be intrigued by the process and follow suit. The director may see the positive effects using the curriculum has on the planning of activities and the attitudes of the teacher and parents. One teacher's efforts could lead to an entire center engaging in curriculum development, thereby making everybody more likely to be responsive to the needs of the children and parents they serve.

The Finished Product

The state of the art in the field of curriculum is such that a detailed description of a finished product in terms of a curriculum document would be an exaggeration at most and at least misleading. The components of a curriculum described in Chapter Two were found with mixed regularity in many such documents developed for school-age children. There is no model of a curriculum document that has worked successfully for all teachers and children in all settings. We have identified what we consider essential components of a curriculum: a statement of purpose/philosophy, goals, objectives, activities, and an evaluative scheme. It may be possible to have all these components contained in one comprehensive document. It is more likely, however, that the purpose/philosophy and goals may be written in one document, but that the objectives and activities, because they are so numerous, be contained in some kind of curriculum bank. This bank can take many forms. An example of one form can be found in Appendix D. The evaluative scheme may be a separate document as well. Ideally, the evaluation procedures will be considered when other curriculum decisions are made, but typically evaluation is thought of last, if at all, hence a separate plan may exist for evaluation.

Summary

Getting started in curriculum development requires some decisions about selecting and organizing people and procedures for formulating goals and purpose/philosophy.

There are no clear guidelines that apply well to all situations, consequently those interested in curriculum development may raise more questions than they can answer. In a hypothetical day care center, we suggested parents and teachers be involved in curriculum development. The most important guideline for organizing people was that the individuals themselves should decide how they want to organize and not feel compelled to follow some prescribed procedure. Four examples of options available to curriculum developers were discussed. Regardless of how people proceed in curriculum development, some understanding of children is necessary to writing a statement of purpose/philosophy and selecting goals, objectives, and activities. Finally, there is no model for the finished product in curriculum development. The form any document takes will be dependent on the needs and interests of the people it will serve.

NOTES

1. Evelyn Moore, "The Way It Is in Curriculum Development, Part I: A Note on the Need for Curriculum Development Studies," *Curriculum Theory Network* 7 (1971): 12-14.
2. J. Cecil Parker, "Guidelines for In-Service Education," *In-Service Education,* Fifty-sixth Yearbook of the National Society for the Study of Education, ed. Nelson B. Henry (Bloomington: The Society, 1957), pp. 103-28.
3. Ibid., pp. 104-13. Parker discusses twelve guidelines in all, but the four cited here are the most relevant for our purposes.
4. The hidden curriculum is discussed in Norman V. Overly, ed., *The Unstudied Curriculum: Its Impact on Children* (Washington, D.C.: Association for Supervision and Curriculum Development, NEA, 1970).

Suggested Readings

Grotberg, Edith H., ed. *Day Care: Resources for Decisions.* Washington, D.C.: Office of Economic Opportunity, 1971. An ambitious compilation of papers covering care in other countries, programs, adult involvement, ancillary services, and staff training.

Sale, June S. and Torres, Yolanda L. *I'm Not Just a Baby Sitter: A Descriptive Report of the Community Family Day Care Project.* Pasadena: Pacific Oaks College, 1971. A report of the first year's efforts of the Community Family Day Care Project that includes detailed discussions of the problems and potential of family day care homes.

White, Burton L. and Watts, Jean C. *Experience and Environment: Major Influences on the Development of the Young Child.* Englewood Cliffs, N.J.: Prentice-Hall, 1973. A study of young children that was designed to shed light on the impact experiential and environmental influences have on children's competencies.

Suggested Activities

1. List and discuss the advantages and disadvantages of involving parents in the process of curriculum development.
2. Select or create a list of goals and rank order them. See if others assign similar ranks.
3. If goals can be rank ordered and there is a consensus about their relative priority, what are the implications for the planning and evaluating of activities?

Chapter Four

Implementing, Evaluating, and Revising the Curriculum

... educational experiment, in the main, has been conducted and is being conducted in the dark—without feedback in useable form.

Jerome S. Bruner, Toward a Theory of Instruction
(New York: W. W. Norton Co., 1966), p. 30.

One generalization in the field of curriculum about which there is nearly universal agreement is that the process of curriculum development is a continuous one. A document called a curriculum that contains a statement of purpose/philosophy and a list of goals may be the end product of parents' and teachers' deliberations, but the process of implementing, evaluating, and revising the curriculum is an ongoing one.

This chapter is based on the assumption that a curriculum has been developed; that is, a statement of purpose/philosophy has been established, goals have been selected, and the teachers feel confident the goals will provide direction for planning daily experiences for the children. That confidence may stem from rich experiences and training that resulted in the accumulation of large repertoires of objectives and activities, or there may be actual banks of objectives and activities to which all the teachers have easy access. After this initial process of curriculum development has been successfully completed, attention must turn to the continuing processes of implementing, evaluating, and revising the curriculum.

Implementing the Curriculum

Previously we defined implementing as the use of the curriculum in guiding day-to-day planning. The curriculum can influence teaching, but our conception of curriculum is that the influence is in the form of a general framework as opposed to specific prescriptions. The connection between the curriculum and teaching is not always a clear one. For example, a curriculum might indicate certain goals clearly enough, but leave to the discretion of the teacher exactly how much he or she should interact with the children to achieve the goals. Indeed, teachers face the perennial problem of how much they should actually interact with the children in a teaching situation.

Graubard provides a cogent discussion of the dilemma teachers face when trying to plan how much or what kind of interaction with children is appropriate.[1] He suggests a continuum of learning models. On one end of the continuum is language development

43

that takes place without certified teachers and conscious teaching. On the other end of the continuum is learning to play a violin. Learning to play a violin requires a well-trained professional teacher, much practice and drill, and usually some force and displeasure. Traditional nursery school teachers appear to be on the language learning end of the continuum while high school and college teachers appear to reflect the violin learning model. Elementary school teachers are somewhere in between the two extremes. These characterizations obviously gloss over all the exceptions, but they are made to illustrate the choices teachers make at different levels of schooling.

Teachers and children of all ages may be at different places on the continuum, depending on their purposes, goals, skills, and other factors. How much a teacher should actively intervene with a child depends on that teacher's judgment of all the relevant information. We consider that judgment to be part of the latitude a teacher as a professional must have, given the paucity of useful instructional theories that might provide such guidance. A curriculum may provide guidance for the amount or kind of intervention, but we prefer to conceive of it as serving primarily as a point of departure for more specific planning. The curriculum can be helpful, but teachers have the final responsibility to decide the amount and kind of intervention that should occur.

Experienced teachers know that it is difficult, if not impossible, to achieve a one-to-one correspondence between plans for children and the actual behaviors of the children during an activity. Implementing a curriculum does not mean that such a correspondence should be the objective. It would be futile to try to anticipate exactly how the children will behave on any given day, nor should children be forced to fit into some preconceived mold. But these cautions should not be taken to mean that any kind of planning is unwise. It takes professional judgment to know when a specific activity should be modified or abandoned for something else. There are few guidelines for these kinds of decisions.

Another source of ambiguity related to implementing the curriculum is the assumption some teachers make that a single activity serves a single objective or goal. An excellent illustration of how one activity can serve many objectives and goals is provided by Hymes:

> A group of four year olds takes a trip to a farm to learn where milk comes from. If you make the teacher put one label on the experience, she will probably have to call it Science. Or if that isn't specific enough: Biology. Or if that is still too general: Animal Biology. But what about all the conversation that goes on in connection with the trip: before, during, after? That should be called the Language Arts. The stories before and after the trip are Literature. The singing—"Old MacDonald Had a Farm" is fated to be sung!—must be called Music. Rules for conduct are developed. This is what Civics and Government and Politics are all about. The teacher recalled what happened the last time the group took a trip: "You remember how we all crowded around and some people could not see." The lessons of the past are usually labelled History. A child misbehaves; the teacher's response is a lesson in Psychology. Someone counts the children to be sure no one is left at the farm: Arithmetic. The trip costs money; the minute that question comes up the four year olds take a brief course in Economics. The cow is probably pretty, even if the farmer and the highway are not. The presence of beauty and the absence of it are matters of Aesthetics. When the teacher soothes a disappointed child —"Things don't always work out the way we want"— the lesson is one in Philosophy. And if, on such a trip, the children drink some milk, that experience is labelled Nutrition! Yet the whole trip was labelled Science![2]

The reader should observe from the illustration that different objectives were used with different children. Teachers should not be lulled into thinking the total group of children is learning anything. Rather, the teacher must remember that learning is an individual affair, and to be effective a teacher must focus on the needs of individual children as much as possible.

Lesson Plans

The responsibility for implementing the curriculum rests with the teacher. Each teacher has the responsibility to demonstrate that the daily or weekly activities reflect the curriculum. The most obvious method of demonstration is through the use of lesson plans. The plans can be sketched for a week at a time and can later serve as a record of the kinds of goals, objectives, and activities that received attention. Using lesson plans enables the teacher to plan and maintain a balance and avoid an emphasis of certain goals over others.

Lesson plans can take many forms. They may be organized in terms of goals or objectives, themes or units, such as seasons of the year, or some combination of these. Lesson plans should contain the children's names and indicate in some manner the progress of each child vis-à-vis the goals. Separate records for the children can include each child's progress and needs, but making references to specific children in the lesson plans will increase the likelihood of the children receiving special attention. Over a three- or four-week period of time, the teacher can check the names of the children in the plans to see if any children are being systematically overlooked.

Classroom Observations

There are some sophisticated and systematic methods for observing behavior in a classroom. Most of these methods focus on the verbal interactions between the teacher and the children. Some techniques are designed to quantify the amount of talking on the part of the teacher and the children, while others focus on the kinds of questions the teacher asks. A description of the verbal interaction in a classroom can provide insights about the kinds of goals and objectives the teacher is or is not providing. The teacher may discover, for example, that he or she talks far more than the children. It may be that so much talking by the teacher precludes the children talking, thus the teacher's behavior may be in conflict with an objective concerning opportunities for the children to talk.

It is not unusual for parents, the director, and other teachers to make classroom observations of an informal nature. Ideally, such observations can yield information about the degree to which the curriculum is being implemented. There should be some connection, some correspondence, between the activities in which the children are engaged and the goals of the curriculum. Obviously, there can be no perfect correspondence between activities and goals all of the time. There will always be exceptions and unpredictable events when teachers interact and try to respond to the needs and interests of children; but if most of what goes on with a group of children shows no correspondence with the goals of the curriculum, then either the goals are unrealistic or the teacher needs assistance with implementing them.

Objective and Activity Banks

Two components or sections of a curriculum that may be organized in something other than a single document are the objectives and activities. The large number of objectives and activities precludes ever assembling an exhaustive list, but a collection of each can be contained in some kind of file or bank. Individual teachers may have their own, and/or a central resource, available to all teachers, can be established.

Implementing a curriculum involves selecting objectives and activities that are appropriate for the goals and children. Teachers who have worked with young children have some activities in their repertoire, but it would be unrealistic to expect teachers to generate a wide variety of activities without consulting some kind of resource. An objective bank and an activity bank can be useful resources for teachers who are implementing a curriculum.

There is no perfect system for organizing an objective or activity bank. One system that has been used successfully is the Curriculum Bank developed by Henry and Wanda Draper.[3] It consists of six goal areas broken down into objectives. For each objective there are implied activities. See Appendix D for more details of this system.

In-Service Training

In-service training can be a formal, planned program involving all the teachers or an informal, spontaneous self-help session involving only a few of the teachers. Each format has advantages and disadvantages; but some kind of in-service training is necessary, not only for teachers to acquire new skills, but also to share ideas and suggestions about implementing the curriculum. Specifically, it could be of value if time were spent on discussing activities that seemed to work well and those that seem to be difficult. Generating, collecting, and organizing activities according to the goals they serve can be an easier task when several teachers are engaged in it than when individual teachers are expected to accomplish all those tasks on their own.

There is no need to make sharp distinctions between in-service training and improving the teachers' skills of implementing the curriculum. In-service training may well serve other goals, but it should not be overlooked whenever teachers need assistance in using the curriculum.

Staff Selection

Another safeguard that can be taken to assure the curriculum will be implemented relates to the hiring of staff. When a prospective teacher applies for a position, he or she should be given a copy of the curriculum to become familiar with the purpose/philosophy and goals. The prospective teacher should be given an opportunity to work with children and be observed by the director, other teachers, or parents. There are many considerations that have to be made when hiring a teacher, and the prospective teacher's commitment to implement the curriculum should be one of them.

Infringement on Teachers' Rights

One connotation curriculum has had in the past is that of a plan imposed on teachers, thereby infringing on their rights as professionals to exercise their own judgment about appropriate activities for children. The use of a curriculum should not infringe on teachers' rights. A curriculum is a guide for teachers to use in planning their day-to-day and week-to-week activities. The curriculum enables teachers to use their judgment in carrying out activities with the children, structuring the environment, and organizing materials. The nature of the activities, structure of the environment, and use of materials can and will vary from teacher to teacher, depending on each teacher's knowledge, style, experience, and preference. It is important that the latitude the teacher has in making decisions about activities, environment, and materials be maintained. The teacher is dealing with human beings; and in order to effectively minister to their unpredictable needs, interests, and impulses, the teacher should not feel constrained or imposed upon by prescriptions that do not accommodate the dynamic quality of all human interactions. A curriculum, as we have described it, does not specify precisely the behavior of the teacher when interacting with children. Tyler put it well when he said, "A profession is an occupation that performs some tasks too complex to be guided by specific rules."[4]

The latitude teachers have can be a source of ambiguity for those concerned with implementing a curriculum. There is no easy answer to the question of what to do when a teacher chooses to ignore the goals or suggestions of a curriculum that has been developed for a center and justifies ignoring the curriculum on the grounds that it infringes on his or her professional judgment. Ideally, all the teachers should have had some involvement in the process of developing the curriculum. To date, involvement in the process is the best assurance we have that a teacher will work toward the goals. So little is known, however, about the best fit between goals and objectives, objectives and activities, and the whole field of teaching that everyone concerned about curriculum needs to keep an openness regarding its modifiability.

Evaluating the Curriculum

Evaluation serves several purposes, one of which is to examine the appropriateness of purpose/philosophy, goals, objectives, and activities of a curriculum. Evaluating a curriculum requires the collection of information that can be used in making decisions about the purpose/philosophy, goals, objectives, and activities.

Evaluation is typically thought about after a curriculum has been developed and implemented. Although the participants may not be aware of it, a kind of evaluation is taking place when the purpose/philosophy of a curriculum is being determined. The statement of purpose/philosophy is based on, among other things, the needs of the children and parents. Determining what those needs are is a form of evaluation. Determining children's needs can be a very specific endeavor, as in the case of administering a preschool inventory to each child; or it can be more general, as in the case of recommending that children interact with others of different ethnic backgrounds.

Formative evaluation has as its primary purpose the improvement of the curriculum and teaching. Summative evaluation is primarily concerned with the effects of the curriculum and teaching.[5] The difference between formative and summative evaluation is one of emphasis more than substance. Formative evaluation is what curriculum developers rely on to help improve the curriculum.

An excellent report of parents and staff working together in a formative evaluation of a Head Start Day Care Center is *Formative Evaluation: Parents and Staff Working Together to Build a Responsive Environment.*[6] The report describes how several parents were effectively enlisted to help the staff determine the needs of the children and parents, develop a curriculum that was responsive to those needs, and establish a communication link between the center and all the rest of the parents. One unique result of this center's efforts was the establishment of a cooperative evaluation procedure that included, for example, a goal statement, children's behavior that would indicate progress toward the goal, suggestions for helping the children at the center and in the home environment, and suggestions for checking on the children's progress. The overriding accomplishment of this evaluation project was the improvement of communication between and among the parents and staff. One of the several recommendations made in the report is to involve parents and teachers together in every place possible.

The relationship of evaluation to the other components of the curriculum is depicted in Figure 2.

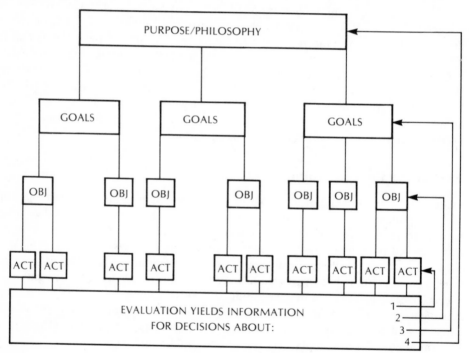

Figure 2   Relationship of Evaluation to Other Curriculum Components

The information provided by evaluation can be used to make decisions about the appropriateness of all the essential components of a curriculum. When the information indicates a change should be made, the curriculum or parts thereof are revised.

Revising the Curriculum

The central theme of this chapter is the continual process of curriculum development activities. Implementing and evaluating are activities that lead to revising. The curriculum should be a flexible aid to teachers, not a rigid set of prescriptions that somehow have to be filled. There is a relative stability in the purpose/philosophy statement and list of goals. The objectives and activities will be tried and tested on a daily basis, and, consequently, there will be more revising of these components than the others. Revising includes deleting, modifying, and adding individual items to the components.

The evaluation on which the revising is based may range from impressionistic data, informally collected by a teacher, to more sophisticated and systematic collections of data by specialists in the field of testing. Every time teachers select activities and use them, certain modifications or adjustments may be made. This relatively constant level of revising is part of the teacher's responsibility as a professional. Significant changes in activities, objectives, or goals will require the consensus of those responsible for curriculum development.

Revising the curriculum takes place at two levels: one is with the individual teacher who makes adjustments in activities or objectives to best fit the children, resources, and environment at that time; the other level is with a group of teachers and parents who have formal responsibility to revise the curriculum. This group's primary concern is to adjust the components of the curriculum to meet the changing needs of children, teachers, and parents. Monthly or bimonthly meetings of teachers and parents can be designed to collect information about the appropriateness and usefulness of the various parts of the curriculum. In the process of discussing the curriculum and how it might be revised, teachers and parents are continuing to provide one another with information about their needs, values, and practices. Exchanging this kind of information and making decisions in light of it help to ensure that the day care setting is providing the kinds of services to parents and children that the combined best thinking of parents and staff can provide. Nothing more can be expected of a service setting, and nothing less is tolerable.

Summary

Curriculum development is a continuous process. When teachers implement a curriculum, they have to make judgments about specific objectives and activities that the curriculum goals indicate. There will never be a perfect one-to-one correspondence between a planned activity and all the behaviors that may be elicited from the children. One activity may help achieve a multitude of goals. The use of lesson plans can help the teacher maintain a balance in implementing the curriculum. Classroom observations can provide useful feedback for teachers in their efforts to implement the curriculum. Objective and activity banks are important resources that should be available to all the teachers.

In-service training can provide opportunities for improving teachers' skills in meeting curricular goals, evaluating the curriculum, and revising the goals, objectives, and activities according to the evaluative data.

NOTES

1. Allen Graubard, *Free the Children: Radical Reform and the Free School Movement* (New York: Pantheon Books, 1972), pp. 234-36.
2. James L. Hymes, Jr., *Teaching the Child Under Six,* 2d. ed. (Columbus, Oh.: Charles E. Merrill Publishing Co., 1974), p. 86.
3. Henry Draper and Wanda Draper, *Horizons in Early Childhood: Education* (forthcoming).
4. Ralph W. Tyler, "Accountability and Teacher Performance: Self-Directed and External Directed Professional Improvement" (Paper presented at the National Symposium: Critical Issues in Teacher In-Service Education, Chicago, October 1975).
5. Benjamin S. Bloom, J. Thomas Hastings, and George Maddaus, *Handbook on Formative and Summative Evaluation of Student Learning* (New York: McGraw-Hill Book Co., 1971), p. 117.
6. Lucia Ann McSpadden, *Formative Evaluation: Parents and Staff Working Together to Build a Responsive Environment* (Salt Lake City: Headstart Day Care Center, n.d.).

Suggested Readings

Bloom, Benjamin S.; Hastings, J. T.; and Madaus, G. *Handbook on Formative and Summative Evaluation of Student Learning.* New York: McGraw-Hill Book Co., 1971. Chapters by Kamu and Cazden describe evaluation of goals derived from Piaget's view of development and language development.

McSpadden, Lucia Ann. *Formative Evaluation: Parents and Staff Working Together to Build a Responsive Environment.* Salt Lake City: Headstart Day Care Center, n.d. A report on the establishment of a formative evaluation procedure for children, classrooms, and entire center.

Palmer, Francis H.; Cagden, C.; and Glick, J. "Evaluation of Day Care Centers: Summative and Formative." In *Day Care: Resources for Decisions,* edited by Edith H. Grotberg, pp. 442-57. Washington, D.C.: Office of Economic Opportunity, 1971. A discussion of summative and formative evaluation that includes illustrations of the latter enabling revision of the curriculum.

Popham, W. James. *Educational Evaluation.* Englewood Cliffs, N.J.: Prentice-Hall, 1975. Chapter two contains an excellent overview and description of current evaluation models.

Suggested Activities

1. Visit any kind or level of school setting. What evidence do you find that suggests the teachers are continually engaged in revising the curriculum?
2. Try to determine how teachers feel about lesson plans and in-service training.
3. What kinds of evaluative procedures are used in early childhood programs in your community? What inferences can be drawn from your findings?

Section Three

Some Views of Children

The task of selecting goals, objectives, and activities for children will be much easier if one draws from what is currently known about children and how they develop. When day care personnel begin to think about goals and activities, they need to draw from organized bodies of knowledge that contain generalizations about children. Usually, those bodies of knowledge are broken down according to different aspects of behavior. Generalizations about intelligence and intellectual development as well as social, emotional, moral, and physical development can be found in the literature and research in the behavioral and social sciences.

It is important to make a note about theory and its usefulness. Simply put, a theory is an attempt to describe, explain, and predict a phenomenon. There are theories that do all three very well, and there are others that remain untested for now but do point, at least, to questions that need to be investigated. Research is simply testing questions that the theories indicate. Most theories in the behavioral and social sciences are not completely tested. All of them are subject to revision if they do not hold up to being adequate in description, explanation, and prediction.

Unfortunately, many people consider theory the opposite of practice. Thinking at the theoretical level is really very practical because it saves time and energy, if the theory is an adequate one, that would otherwise be spent trying out every individual instance related to the phenomenon the theory describes, explains, or predicts. Selecting information pertaining to what is known about children and their development and planning the curriculum accordingly are important enough activities that considering anything other than theoretical and research-based information is committing a kind of mindlessness of which we need no more. Theory and research will be discussed further in Chapter Thirteen.

There are two kinds of theories. Those that are written to describe and those that attempt to prescribe. Descriptive theories attempt to answer the question, What is? Prescriptive theories answer the question, What should be? Descriptive theories are not entirely value free, but prescriptive theories are heavily value laden. We will try to keep the two separate. Theories of child development are essentially descriptive in nature. Many theorists in this area have little or no concern with what should be, other than continuing their line of research. When we prescribe what should be done in day care settings, we will try to be clear that the prescription is based on our reading and interpretation of the descriptions. Whenever there is empirical support for a practice we will so indicate, but more importantly, we suggest a great deal of caution be used when reading any prescriptions that "ought" to be.

This section begins with a chapter containing a view of intelligence and selected descriptions of intellectual development. The second chapter contains views of psychological and social development, followed by a chapter on language, moral, physical, and motor development. The final chapter contains two integrated views of development.

The descriptions of the theories are cursory. Such abbreviated treatment invites error and misinterpretation, but the purpose of this section is more illustrative than exhaustive. The reader is encouraged to pursue the appropriate references at the end of each chapter for more elaboration on any one of the views.

Chapter Five

Intelligence and Intellectual Development

> For over half a century, the leading theory of man's nature has been dominated by the assumptions of fixed intelligence and predetermined development. . . . Recently, however, a transformation has been taking place in this traditional conception of intelligence and its relationship to experience. Evidence from various sources has been forcing a recognition of central processes in intelligence and of the crucial role of life experience in the development of these central processes.
>
> *J. McV. Hunt,* Intelligence and Experience
> *(New York: The Ronald Press, 1961), p.v.*

Entire books have been written about intelligence and intellectual development. The purpose of this chapter is to acquaint the reader with a few of the theorists who have made contributions in these areas. The selection is not exhaustive but represents a fair sample of contemporary views of intelligence and intellectual development.

Guilford's View of Intelligence

Guilford's theory of intelligence is included here for two reasons. First, it is a comprehensive and empirically based theory; that is, it attempts to describe all aspects of intelligence and has been developed on the basis of verifiable evidence. It has not been verified completely, but as previously mentioned, few theories in the behavioral sciences, particularly such comprehensive ones, are ever completely substantiated. The second reason for including a discussion here is that Guilford's view is a significant break from traditional conceptions of intelligence; conceptions, it might be noted, that were less comprehensive and enjoyed fewer substantiations.

Guilford introduced his theory of intelligence in 1958.[1] Based on analyzing tests that required different kinds of abilities, he devised a three-dimensional model that represented what he called the "structure of intellect" (see Figure 3). The three dimensions in the structure-of-intellect model are *content, operation,* and *product.*

The content dimension includes intellectual abilities that are related to kinds of information.[2] Figural information is information in which there is a direct correspondence between the perceived image and the actual form. Symbolic information includes symbols and signs that have no meaning in and of themselves but represent meanings to the individual. Letters, numbers, and other codes are examples of symbolic information. Semantic information is associated with verbal and nonverbal language. Words and gestures that represent meanings are examples of semantic information. Behavioral information is information that is nonverbal and involves human interactions in which awareness of perceptions, desires, moods, emotions, and actions of others and ourselves is important.

The second dimension of Guilford's model is *operation.* Included in this dimension are five different mental capabilities. The first one is *cognition.* Cognition is defined as

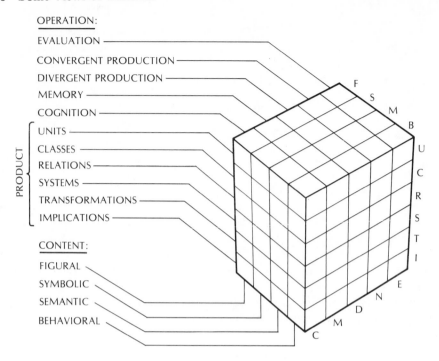

Figure 3   Guilford's Structure-of-Intellect Model

"awareness, immediate discovery or rediscovery, or recognition of information in various forms: comprehension or understanding."[3] The second capability along the operation dimension is *memory*. Memory is the retention of information in the same form in which it was originally learned. The third mental capability is *divergent production*. This capability is the production of information from given information, where the emphasis is upon variety and quantity of output from the same source. The fourth capability is *convergent production*. This is the area of logical deductions or prevailing inferences. Convergent production is used when enough information is available to indicate a specific answer. The final capability along the operation dimension is *evaluation*. Evaluation is the process of comparing information with other information according to criteria and reaching a decision about the degree to which the criteria are satisfied. These five operation capabilities are ways of functioning. It has been demonstrated by Guilford and others that each of these five kinds of operations are particular kinds of functions in which individuals differ.[4]

The third dimension in Guilford's model relates to the products of intellectual functioning. The concept *product* refers to the way in which any information occurs or is conceived. Included in the products are units, classes, relations, systems, transformations, and implications. Beginning with units as the simplest kind of product, the order becomes increasingly complex. Guilford defines the six products as follows:

1. Units are things, segregated wholes, figures on grounds;
2. Classes are sets of objects with one or more common properties;

3. Relations are connections or bridges between two things;
4. Systems are patterns or organizations of interdependent or interacting parts;
5. Transformations are changes, revisions, or redefinitions by which any product of information goes from one state into another state; and
6. Implications are expectations or predictions from given information.[5]

The three dimensions of Guilford's model and their respective categories interact with one another, thus potentially producing 120 separate and independent capabilities. As of 1967, 82 of these 120 had been empirically verified. With the invention of new tests, more may be verified. The significant thing about Guilford's view of intelligence is the multitude of verified separate and distinct intellectual capabilities. Contrasted with conventional thinking about IQ tests and the single scores they yield, Guilford's view drastically changes the kinds of generalizations we can make about intelligence.

There is no longer any justification for describing intelligence as being composed of a single or just two or three components. Guilford has demonstrated that learning is much more situation specific than previously believed. Teachers of children of all ages will have to recast their thinking about slow and fast or dull and bright children, particularly when only a few indicators have been used to make the judgment. The primary implication of Guilford's work is that intelligence is a many-faceted and complex resource, not easily measured or estimated by a few instruments or quick judgments.

Piaget's Theory of Intellectual Development

Whereas Guilford relied primarily on test scores and their analysis to develop his structure-of-intellect model, Piaget's work has drawn more from interacting with children while they were being tested. Most of Guilford's work has been necessarily, but not exclusively, drawn from children who are old enough to be tested in group settings. Piaget and his associates have worked primarily with younger children on a one-to-one basis. Although their sources of data and methods of collecting and analyzing them have some differences, there are many similarities between the two theorists. Both are trying to describe intelligence in a specific manner that can provide us with reliable knowledge to plan better environments and activities for children, at home or away from home, that will ensure full development of their human potential. Their respective theories are not incompatible. They are different mainly because they start from somewhat different questions. Guilford proceeds from wanting to know, What is intelligence? Piaget's primary question is, How does intelligence develop? Subsequent chapters will demonstrate that each contribution has important implications for day care.

Intelligence for Piaget characterizes a given stage of intellectual development. Intelligence is identical with knowledge.[6] The location of knowledge, or intelligence, according to Piaget, is neither out there in the objective world nor exclusively within the individual, rather it is "the mutual relation of the knower to the known."[7]

Piaget's stages of intellectual development encompass infancy to adulthood. A capsule overview of the development is provided by Furth:

If one attempts to picture what the world is like to an infant at birth and compares it to the knowledge of the world at the end of Stage VI, one realizes the immense change and veritable revolution that has taken place. Starting with a completely self-centered viewpoint where neither the self nor the world is recognized, there is a gradual transition from subjective body-centered activity to a practical separation of means and ends to a final stage where we can infer a "logic of action." The child is now able to organize reality on the basis of general schemes of actions. These schemes include the organization of space and time, of causality, and most importantly, of permanent objects, among which is found the self.[8]

The salient feature of Piaget's theory is its emphasis on stages of development. There are qualitative differences between and among the stages, but three important considerations must be kept in mind when studying the stages:

1. different children may pass through the stages at different rates;
2. each stage gets its name from the process that has most recently become operative, although others may be operating at the same time; and
3. each stage is the formation of a total structure that includes previous processes as necessary substructures.[9]

The processing of information is what Piaget calls assimilation. But when the processing itself is changed by the information, Piaget refers to it as accommodation. The changes in the processing or structures are brought about by the biological need for equilibrium. Assimilation and accommodation are both adaptations; the former is the child adapting incoming knowledge to a world view and view of self, and the latter is the child adopting a world view and view of self to new knowledge.

Phillips emphasizes the dynamic quality of equilibrium:

> The idea is that structures continually move toward a state of equilibrium, and when a state of relative equilibrium has been attained, the structure is sharper, more clearly delineated, than it had been previously. But that very sharpness points up inconsistencies and gaps in the structure that had never been salient before. Each equilibrium state therefore carries with it the seeds of its own destruction, for the child's activities are thenceforth directed toward reducing those inconsistencies and closing those gaps.[10]

Concepts such as equilibrium and adaptation can only be mentioned here. Further elaboration as well as discussion of other theory- relevant terms can be found in the suggested readings at the end of this chapter. In the interest of maintaining the rule of brevity for all theorists in this chapter, a short description of each of Piaget's periods and stages will follow.

The first period encompasses the ages zero to two.[11] This is called the *sensorimotor period* and is made up of six stages:

Stage 1 (Exercising the Inherited Schemata).   Zero to one month. During this first month of life, the infant makes responses to light and sound; objects placed in the palm are grasped; and sucking commences when the lips are touched. There is a transition from a passive to an active use of schemata.

Stage 2 (Primary Circular Reactions).   One to four months. Primary relates to reactions centering on the infant's body rather than on external objects; circular refers to their endless repetition. The child reaches for things he sees, looks at things he hears, and looks at things touching his hand. There is progress toward integration of the biologically given patterns of the infant into habits and perceptions.

Stage 3 (Secondary Circular Reactions).   Four to eight months. This stage includes further development of schemata that emerged earlier. Circular again refers to the repeating of behaviors, for example, continuous shaking of a rattle to hear its noise. There are signs of intentional movement and anticipation of effects. If a toy drops to the floor, the child looks for it. Certain objects are reached for while others are not, indicating the development of depth perception.

Stage 4 (Coordination of Learned Schemata).   Eight to twelve months. Further discrimination of means and ends takes place. The child will attack an obstacle that is in the way of an object. There is a greater departure from the extreme egocentrism present in earlier stages and a beginning of understanding for causality apart from the child.

Stage 5 (Tertiary Circular Reactions).   Twelve to eighteen months. Interest is in the effects and properties of objects and events. There is an interest, too, in novelty for its own sake.

Stage 6 (Representations of Schemata).   Eighteen to twenty-four months. Language development increases in this stage, thereby helping the child to represent objects and events without their presence. A more realistic conception of time and space continues to develop and with the use of language, a more refined sense of causality evolves.

The next period of development, according to Piaget covers the age span of two to eleven years. This period or stage is divided into *preoperational thought* (ages two to seven) and *concrete operational thought* (ages seven to eleven). Again, the ages and progress through the stages, though sequential, vary among individuals.

The preoperational stage is one where the child is capable within certain limitations of manipulating symbols that represent the environment. There is an increased internalization of symbols, but the child lacks the ability to decenter. During the sensorimotor period, the child moved from centering on the body (primary circular reactions) to decentering from the body (secondary and tertiary circular reactions). On the representational or symbol level then, the child develops the ability to change centers from objects, events, and those symbols representing them. An important ability related to the problem of centering for children in this preoperational stage is reversibility. Preoperational children cannot perform a reversible transformation. Piaget has developed a number of tests that discriminate between preoperational children and those at the next higher stage. A brief review of some of these tests will help describe the mental capabilities or limitations preoperational children have.

The conservation of quantities continuous problem involves the use of three containers, two of which are identical in shape and filled to the same level. The third can be either shorter and larger in diameter or taller and smaller in diameter than the first two. The child is shown that the first two containers have an equal amount of water. The child is satisfied this is true. Then the water from one container is poured into the third. The level will be different because of the different shape, and the child usually indicates the amount of water has changed, revealing a tendency to center attention on one detail of an event. In this experiment, if the child focuses attention on the height of the levels and the third container is taller and smaller in diameter than the original pair, he will equate the increased height with "more." If he centers upon width and the third container is shorter and larger in diameter, he will equate the increased width of water with "more." Other tests using solids, number concepts, and space have been developed and validated as effective separators of preoperational and operational thinkers.

Finally, preoperational children can be characterized by their concern for states of an event and lack of attention to intermediate or temporal states. The task of drawing or selecting from multiple choices the intermediate states of a vertical rod that falls to a horizontal position usually baffles preoperational children. They can center on the initial vertical state and depict or choose it and the final horizontal state and depict or choose it correctly, but seem oblivious to the intermediate states that transformed the initial to the final.[12]

The next stage of intellectual development is called concrete operational thought. Piaget defines operation as an "action that can return to its starting point, and that can be integrated with other actions also possessing this feature of reversibility."[13] The preoperational child is not capable of this reversibility, but the concrete operational child is, with the condition that such "thinking" be with concrete objects. Whereas the child at the sensorimotor levels is limited to physical, sensorimotor activities and the child at the preoperational level, even with the benefit of the representational nature of language, is still limited to egocentric and irreversible thinking, the child at the concrete operational level is capable of reversible thinking but dependent on concrete objects to aid and verify that higher level of thinking. The concrete operational child can successfully perform the tests previously mentioned. The primary limitation is the reliance this child makes on actual objects to supplement the process. It is not until about age twelve, according to Piaget, that concrete objects are no longer needed for thinking. He calls this last stage of intellectual development formal operations, wherein the child or adult can finally think about thinking and not need the actual experiences, events, or objects to verify it.

Kagan's View of Mental Functioning

Kagan's effort to explain intellectual development is based on the concept of schema. He maintains that the primary functional property of the mind is a schema. He further specifies:

> A schema is a cognitive representation of an event that preserves its spatial and temporal pattern of distinctive elements. and permits the organism to recognize aspects of past experience.[14]

The development of schemata (plural) is a continuous process that is affected by heredity and environment. Its product, simply put, is to help the individual keep uncertainty low. The more varied and developed schemata an individual has, the less likely it is that the individual will experience uncertainty and distress.

Whereas most developmental theorists like Piaget emphasize very definite stages in their theories of mental development, Kagan is more concerned about continuities and changes as well as differences between boys and girls and social classes. Kagan's interest is in testing the ways in which boys and girls from various social classes differ between the sexes and among the classes. His carefully controlled twenty-three-month study of ninety-one boys and eighty-nine girls from four different social classes has contributed significantly to what is known about sex and social class differences among children. He observed how children responded to different situations and made systematic observations of the mother-child relationship in the children's homes. Some of the generalizations supported by the data from Kagan's work are discussed below.

Kagan's work does not settle the question of how continuous certain aspects of a child's mental functioning are over time. Indeed, he has generated data about change and continuity that can be interpreted either as evidence of stable functioning over time or as evidence of significant changes in functioning. He notes:

> The cold, hard data are equivocal, and either group—those who champion stabilities or those who see the child as infinitely malleable—can feel validated.[15]

That may be a frustrating finding for those seeking a more definite answer to the question of how much children's intellectual development can be affected or impacted by the environment, but at least it keeps the question open to other investigations. Kagan's findings regarding sex and social class differences are more conclusive.

Girls showed a greater stability to vocalize as an accompaniment to an interesting event than did boys. Kagan suggests two possible explanations for this finding. One is the different way mothers react to sons and daughters. His observations of mother-child interactions suggest mothers engage in more face-to-face vocalizations with their daughters than with their sons. He found that the mothers he observed in his study seemed to have an implicit theory of tutoring their children. The theory for interacting with daughters appeared to emphasize verbal stimulation, whereas the theory that guided interacting with sons emphasized physical-motor play. Data collected in the study supported the generalization that mothers engaged in verbal stimulation more frequently with daughters than with sons and in more motor play with sons than with daughters.[16]

The other explanation of greater stability for girls' vocalization is related to differences in rates of maturation of central nervous systems in boys and girls. Kagan speculates:

> Since anatomical and physiological systems mature earlier in the girl than in the boy, perhaps the normal dominance relation of left over right hemisphere becomes established earlier and the association between information processing and vocal responsivity emerge earlier in the girl.[17]

Kagan allows that both the care-taking practices of mothers and the different rates of central nervous system organization may work together to explain the differences in vocalization of girls over boys.

Sex differences were related to social class differences. Social class was determined by the educational level of both parents. Growth and development of schemata were consistently stronger for girls than boys, depending on the social class of the parents. Boys' performance was relatively unaffected by the social class of the parents. Kagan suggests that mothers from different social classes have greater variability in their concern with proper behavioral and intellectual development in their daughters than in their sons.

Using educational level as an index of social class, Kagan found significant differences among children from different social classes by twenty-seven months of age. Such class differences in young children have not been found by Piaget tests. The differences were stronger for girls than boys but grew steadily in both as the children matured. Factors in which differences among social classes appeared included richness of vocabulary, duration of attention, and quality of performance. Kagan draws from his and other observational studies and interviews with parents for possible explanations of differences. He suggests:

> One of the major dimensions that differentiates lower- from middle-class parents is the parents' faith that they can influence the child's mental development. Excerpts from interviews with some lower- and middle-class mothers of ten-month-old, firstborn daughters capture the greater sense of fatalism and impotence of the lower-class mother, in contrast to the middle-class mother's belief that she has the power to shape her infant's mind.[18]

Social class does not explain anything and Kagan admits that. However, "the parents' feeling of effective power to control the environment . . . exerts a profound influence on broad classes of care-taking practices. . . ."[19] There was little effect of class at four months but clear effects at twenty-seven months. Kagan notes:

> The public effect (of social class) is subtle the first half year, but by age two, verbal competence, sustained attention, and inhibition—the hallmarks of white middle-class values— are more salient for the middle- than for the lower middle-class white child.[20]

Kagan is much less committed to a stages of development explanation of intellectual growth than is Piaget. Like Piaget, however, Kagan assumes the child actively tries to make sense of the environment. Both Kagan and Piaget can be contrasted with other theorists who assume the child is basically passive and simply reacts to the environment. Another comparison Kagan makes himself is that whereas Piaget is a developmental idealist—that is, Piaget believes the child is developing toward an ideal stage, formal operational thought, which might be likened to a car moving along a highway—Kagan has no idealized termination point. Rather than a specified destination for every child's development, Kagan likens the process of development to a small boat on a large pond.[21]

Bruner's View of Intellectual Growth

Bruner's study of intellectual growth has evolved into a view of growth that is called instrumental conceptualism. This view has two central tenets concerning the nature of knowing. The first is that "knowledge of the world is based on a constructed model of reality."[22] The ways through which models of reality are constructed are action, imagery, and symbolism. The second tenet of Bruner's theory is that the models of reality "develop as a function of the uses to which they have been put first by the culture and then by . . . (the individual)."[23]

Bruner's work is in many ways an extension of Piaget's, but there are at least two exceptions worth noting. One is that Bruner avoids the formulation of stages, preferring instead to consider intellectual growth as a gradual process. Bruner also questions Piaget's notion of disequillibrium. He states:

Overcoming "trouble" because of the bad fit to nature of one's models . . . is one aspect of seeking competence. The rub is that there are many cognitive conflicts of this kind that do *not* lead a child to grow.[24]

Knowing from Actions. During the first year of life (the first half of Piaget's sensorimotor stage), the child defines objects by the actions they evoke. The child is unable to differentiate between perceiving an object and acting on it. If a child holds a rattle and swings it, only to have it taken away, additional swinging without the rattle indicates that the child "sees" the rattle as part of the action of swinging. This dependence for meaning on motor representation does not disappear entirely, but is displaced gradually by the use of imagery to help build the models that represent reality.

Knowing from Imagery. By the end of the first year of life, the child is beginning to use imagery to represent the world. Action or manipulation of objects is still important for building meanings but in a somewhat different way. Manipulation of objects assists the child in establishing images. Bruner cites findings from previous research

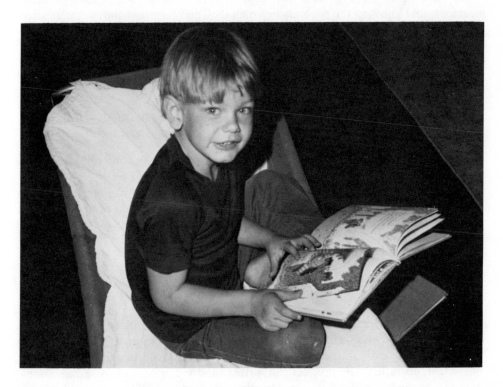

The images found in a picture book are more meaningful if the child has had personal experiences with similar objects, people, and events.

indicating motor activities, such as tracing with the finger when trying to recognize a complex picture of learning what a triangle is, enable children to form their images better. Recalling Piaget's investigations of the egocentricity of children in the concrete operational stage, Bruner underscores the same condition for children using imagery as a means of representing reality by stating that "the child characteristically is not able to view the world perceptually from other perspectives than his own."[25] Other traits of the child using imagery in making sense of the world include easy distractibility, relative inflexibility (what Piaget calls irreversibility) and undue concern for surface features, at the expense of looking deeper into pictures or problems. More positive descriptions of what young children can do will be seen in the section on sample applications and accounts of a typical day in a day care setting.

Symbolic Representation.   Bruner views symbolic representation as coming from:

> a form of primitive and innate symbolic activity that, through acculturation, gradually became specialized into different systems. The most specialized "natural" system of symbolic activity is, of course, language.[26]

There are other activities, both motor and imagery, that take on symbolic representation, but Bruner cites language as an illustration.

The learning of language is a slow process because many words have different meanings, and knowing the contexts in which they make sense requires many varied language experiences. Once single utterances or words are learned, however, and the child begins to learn the rules governing language, symbolic activity increases very quickly. Most children adhere to the basic rules of grammar at about age two. These rules provide the fundamental properties of sentences: verb-object, subject-predicate, and modification. Bruner notes:

> There are no human languages whose sentences do not contain rules for these three basic sentential structures, and there are no nonhuman languages that have them.[27]

Once these rules are learned, children become very effective producers of sentences. More effective, according to Bruner, than their conceptions of reality can manage. Bruner suggests language development outstrips mental development. Whereas children's use of language can indicate the use of categories arranged in hierarchies, their experiences are not so arranged. The point here is that thinking is not simply internalized language. Rather, the development of language precedes the development of thought.

Summary

The work of Guilford presents a view of intelligence that is a significant departure from the conventional view. Instead of an index of intelligence, often expressed as an IQ score with one or two subscores, Guilford, by separating intellectual functions in terms of content, operation, and product and further subdividing each of these dimensions, presents a model of intelligence depicting as many as 120 potential separate capabilities.

Piaget's view of intellectual development is one of periods or stages through which individuals progress. The sensorimotor period, made up of six steps, includes the time from birth to age two. The next periods are preoperational thought, ages two to seven, and concrete operational thought, ages seven to eleven. The final period of intellectual development is formal operations, and usually begins about age twelve. A number of tests have been devised to discriminate among children who are functioning at different periods or stages.

Kagan's view of intellectual development has focused on changes and continuities. His work leaves the question of heredity versus environment as primary contributors to intellectual capacity an open one. Kagan compared boys' and girls' intellectual functioning as well as their differences in terms of social class status. Kagan found girls to be somewhat ahead of boys in vocalizing and attributes it to the differentiated interaction they receive from their mothers and/or maturational differences in the central nervous system. Whereas girls' performances were affected in terms of social class, the boys tended to remain stable despite social class. In general, social class differences began to show at about age two with increased verbal competence, sustained attention, and inhibition emerging as distinguishing differences.

Bruner's view of intellectual development is not as stage oriented as Piaget's, but there are three major instruments through which individuals can demonstrate their intelligence. The instruments are action, imagery, and symbolic representation. Bruner views intelligence as a combination of innate and learned capabilities.

NOTES

1. J. P. Guilford, "Three Faces of Intellect," *American Psychologist* 14 (1959): 469-79.

2. J. P. Guilford, *The Nature of Human Intelligence* (New York: McGraw-Hill Book Co., 1967), p. 227.

3. Ibid., p. 71.

4. Ibid., p. 203.

5. Ibid., pp. 63-64.

6. Hans G. Furth, *Piaget and Knowledge: Theroretical Foundations* (Englewood Cliffs, N.J.: Prentice-Hall, 1969), p. 262.

7. Ibid., p. 44.

8. Ibid., pp. 50-51. Furth uses schemes for Piaget's schemata, the structural units that assimilate and process incoming data.

9. John L. Phillips, Jr., *The Origins of Intellect: Piaget's Theory* (San Francisco: W. H. Freeman and Co., Publishers, 1969), p. 18.

10. Ibid., p. 20.

11. The periods and stages are described by Piaget and others in a variety of sources. The discussion here draws from Guilford and Phillips. The suggested readings at the end of this chapter include these and other sources of more detail and explication.

12. See Philips, *Origins of Intellect,* for more information about this and other tests.

13. Adopted from Jean Piaget and B. Inhelder, *The Child's Conception of Space,* translated by F.J. Langdon and J.L. Lunzer (London: Routledge and Kagan Paul Ltd., 1956), p. 36. (Original French edition, 1948).

14. Jerome Kagan, *Change and Continuity in Infancy* (New York: John Wiley & Sons, 1971), p. 61.

15. Ibid., p. 177.

16. Ibid., p. 181.

17. Ibid., p. 182.

18. Ibid., p. 188.

19. Ibid., p. 190.

20. Ibid.

21. Ibid., p. 193.
22. Jerome Bruner et al., *Studies in Cognitive Growth* (New York: John Wiley & Sons, 1966), p. 319.
23. Ibid., p. 320.
24. Ibid., p. 4.
25. Ibid., pp. 24-25.
26. Ibid., p. 30.
27. Ibid., p. 33.

Suggested Readings

Bruner, Jerome et al. *Studies in Cognitive Growth.* New York: John Wiley & Sons, 1966. A collection of research reports that substantiate aspects of Bruner's theory of intellectual development.

Furth, Hans G. *Piaget and Knowledge: Theoretical Foundations.* Englewood Cliffs, N.J.: Prentice-Hall, 1969. A discussion of the theoretical underpinnings of Piaget's view of intellectual development.

Guilford, J. P. *The Nature of Human Intelligence.* New York: McGraw-Hill Book Co., 1967. A detailed description of the model of intellect as well as a review of other theories of intelligence.

Hunt, J. McV. *Intelligence and Experience.* New York: The Ronald Press, 1961. A comprehensive account of the assumptions underlying the idea of a fixed intelligence and the change to viewing intelligence as the product of an interaction between an individual and the environment.

Kagan, Jerome. *Change and Continuity in Infancy.* New York: John Wiley & Sons, 1971. A discussion of some variables of intellectual functioning and a description of the research investigating the variables in terms of gender and social class.

Lichtenberg, Philip and Norton, D. G. *Cognitive and Mental Development in the First Five Years of Life.* Rockville, Md.: National Institute of Mental Health, 1971. An overview and synthesis of hundreds of studies of intellectual development through age five.

Phillips, John L., Jr. *The Origins of Intellect: Piaget's Theory.* San Francisco: W. H. Freeman and Co., Publishers, 1969. An explication of Piaget's views of intellectual development and descriptions of many of the tests used by Piaget and his colleagues.

Suggested Activities

1. Discuss the ways in which some of the views of intelligence and intellectual development presented in this chapter and/or others are alike and different.
2. What are the implications for planning experiences for children if it is assumed that intelligence is modifiable?
3. Generate a list of goals that would be appropriate for helping children develop their intellectual capabilities.

Chapter Six

Psychological Social Views

> There is only one road to progress, in education as in other human affairs, and that is: Science wielded by love. Without science, love is powerless; without love, science is destructive.
>
> *Bertrand Russell,* Education and the Good Life
> *(New York: Avon Book, 1926), p. 142.*

The questions, What is the nature of the human organism? What basic psychological traits do all humans share? and What causes the differences that we find between members of the species? have plagued mankind for centuries. The field of psychology developed from inquiries and studies attempting to answer these and more specific questions related to the nature of humans. Psychology is currently divided into three major branches, each offering a different model of human nature. The three models are the psychoanalytic model, the behavioristic model, and the humanistic model. Each model contains numerous theories that vary somewhat, but the three basic models remain distinct.

The assumptions upon which the models are founded are different, therefore the views of human nature they present are different and somewhat contradictory. While each model has made a valuable contribution to the understanding of specific aspects of human needs and behaviors, none has been completely successful in presenting a complete explanation of human behavior.

Each model is represented in this chapter by one or two theories. The particular theories were selected as samples of the three models because they are current, and they all acknowledge the importance of the early years of life in total development. The authors do not hold a preference for one model over another. It is our belief that all of the theories presented view the nature of the species from a different perspective and they are all valuable in fostering an understanding of human development.

Erikson's Eight Ages of Man[1]

Erik H. Erikson has designed a theory of development entitled the "Eight Ages of Man." Erikson's theory is a stage theory consisting of eight psychosocial stages that encompass all of life from infancy to old age, and like most stage theories the stages are designed in a hierarchical fashion. His theory is heavily grounded in psychoanalytic psychology, and many of his constructs and much of his terminology are drawn from the work of Sigmund Freud. However, Erikson has considered not only Freud's areas of psychosexual development, but he has also incorporated considerations of intellectual development and social influences into his theory.

In his famous book, *Childhood and Society,* where Erikson first described his theory, he offers that there are many forces at work in the development of the personality. He mentions among others, internal conditions or readiness to develop, predetermined steps of development, interaction in society and societal conditions. Erikson characterizes the predetermined steps in personality development as a conflict or crisis that arises within the individual and demands resolution. A different conflict arises at each stage and stems from the struggle within the person to come to grips with two opposing attitudes. For example, the crisis in the infant arises from the conflict between the opposing attitudes of trust and mistrust. The crisis in the toddler arises from the conflict between the altering attitudes of autonomy versus shame and doubt. At every stage the person is forced out of equilibrium by internal forces and is required to make personal adjustment before equilibrium can be regained. This task is difficult, unsettling, and often requires a long period of time for resolution. Once the crisis is resolved, however, the person is relaxed, happy, and satisfied. Successful resolution of the conflict at any stage prepares the person to meet life's next crisis in the following stage with renewed vigor and confidence. It is in this way that the stages are hierarchical. The successful resolution of the crisis at one stage prepares the person for the crisis of the next. If the crisis in any stage is left unresolved, further development is impaired and the resolution of the next crisis is extremely difficult.

Erikson is critical of those who use his stages as a scale to measure emotional achievement. He cautions repeatedly that when the conflict of any stage is resolved, it has not been achieved for life. He is not talking about permanent character traits being developed in these stages. He is suggesting that a specific personality trait emerges at a specific stage and meets a crisis that must be resolved; but the personality continues to develop these traits throughout the rest of life, so we cannot say that an infant has achieved the personality trait of trust in any final sense of the word. We can only say that the infant has gained a sense of trust. The gains made at each stage add a new quality to the personality and a new strength to the person. Erikson defines the term *a sense of* to mean "ways of experiencing accessible to introspection; ways of behaving, observable by others."[2] Therefore, reference will be made to children who have gained a sense of initiative or a sense of autonomy.

Erikson also cautions us not to expect the resolution of the conflicts to develop a personality that has completely adopted either one trait or the other. An infant does not gain a sense of trust and then never again experience mistrust. A healthy balance of both traits is necessary. When put into a novel situation, an infant must be able to decide whom and what to trust and whom and what not to trust. Erikson uses the word *mistrust* to mean anticipation of danger or discomfort. Likewise, a toddler does not gain a sense of autonomy and never experience shame. It is difficult to imagine even the most autonomous of children who does not have the capacity to be ashamed if placed in an embarrassing situation. Children will never be completely free from feelings of mistrust or shame, but they must be assisted to gain a stronger sense of trust than mistrust and a stronger sense of autonomy than shame. Each of the altering attitudes to be discussed can be assigned positive and negative qualities. All personalities will possess some of the negative as well as the positive qualities of these attitudes after the resolution of the conflicts. The stronger the positive attitudes are, the more healthy the personality will be. The preceding discussion briefly describes what Erikson intended his theory to be and what he did not intend it to be. Erikson's eight stages are listed below and discussion of the first four stages follows.

Stage	Approximate Age
1. Trust vs. Mistrust	Birth - One
2. Autonomy vs. Shame and Doubt	One - Three
3. Initiative vs. Guilt	Three - Five
4. Industry vs. Inferiority	Six - Twelve
5. Identity vs. Role Confusion	Teen Years
6. Intimacy vs. Isolation	Young Adult
7. Generativity vs. Stagnation	Mature Adult
8. Ego Integrity vs. Despair	Older Adult

Basic Trust versus Basic Mistrust

The newborn baby has no way to experience the world except through the body and the senses. An infant's first physical feelings of hunger, comfort, elimination, and sleep are the first opportunities to experience social trust or mistrust. If the baby is fed when hungry, changed when diapers are wet or soiled, dressed in comfortable clothes for the temperature, and given a comfortable bed to sleep in, these first social experiences with the world have been ones that can be said to generate a sense of trust. If the infant is allowed to be hungry for long periods of time or is not kept comfortable in general, these first social experiences have been ones that will not lead to a sense of trust. During this stage the personality "crystallizes around the conviction 'I am what I am given.'"[3] In other words what a baby is given in the way of physical care and love is the basic beginning for a sense of trust or mistrust.

As the baby is awake for more time, the surroundings, familiar faces, and routines all become a source of comfort and predictability. If the baby's needs have been met regularly and consistently, hunger or gas pains can be endured for longer periods of time without a fear because the baby is confident that a familiar face will appear to eliminate or soothe the problem. A sense of trust is being developed. The development of trust does not depend entirely on food and physical care; it is also influenced by the quality of the relationships between the baby and significant adults in the baby's life. The baby must be talked to, loved, held, and hugged. If the infant's needs have been met regularly and sensitively, most frustrations can be endured. Finally, basic trust is not a hurdle to be cleared once and forgotten. The continuation and expansion of trust is a life-long quest.

Autonomy versus Shame and Doubt

As each of these stages is discussed, it will become apparent that the physical development of the child is closely interwoven into the crisis that occurs at each stage. The child of this age has just developed some degree of muscle control over most body parts: arms and legs, fingers and toes, anal muscles, and eyelids. The toddler is coming to possess many new abilities such as babbling then talking; creeping then crawling then walking then running; the ability to manipulate objects, to pull and to push, and to hold to things or to release them. Of all these new-found muscular abilities, perhaps the most influential in this stage is that of "holding on and letting go."[4] This holding on or letting go pervades all areas of the young child's life. It can be seen in the keeping or letting go of a toy that another child wants. It can be the holding on or letting go of mother when she leaves. It can be the holding on or letting go of a bowel movement. It might be the angry fighting or the peaceful resignation to nap at the end of a long morning.

With all this newly gained physical ability, the child quite naturally begins to use the body in heretofore unheard of ways and begins to insist on the right to decide what to do, how to do it, when to do it, and with whom. Children in this stage are often characterized as willful, demanding, stubborn, uncooperative, and insistent on making choices for themselves. Many exasperated parents and teachers have been heard to exclaim, "She is certainly developing a mind of her own." This is a healthy sign because Erikson says that the personality at this stage "crystallizes around the conviction 'I am what I will.'"[5] Children in this stage are even willing to risk the sense of trust gained in the previous stage to become self-willed individuals, to find out what they are and what they can will. They pit their wills against the world if necessary and against their parents and teachers particularly. Frustrated adults have been heard to vow, "I'm going to break his will." What a dangerous statement. A child without a will becomes an adult who feels helpless, who is easily manipulated, and who is unable to take a stand. Mature will power cannot develop in an adult unless the child's will is guided and allowed to develop. Adults without will power have a feeling of loss of direction and a sense that they have lost control over their own lives.

The danger faced by the child in this stage is developing a sense of shame. Adults often use shaming as a disciplinary technique with a child of this age. "Look at your new dress. It's all dirty. Aren't you ashamed of yourself?" or worse yet, "I'm ashamed of you." Shaming causes a child to become self-conscious and to lose self-esteem and pride.

Erikson cautions not to destroy a child's will but to guide and train it. Adult control at this stage is crucial. Guidance must be firm, consistent, and reassuring. Children slowly come to know what to expect of others and what others expect of them. Children who are carefully guided can maintain self-control and develop a sense of good will and pride. They are on the road to becoming autonomous individuals.

Initiative versus Guilt

"Initiative adds to autonomy the quality of undertaking, planning, and attacking a task for the sake of being active and on the move."[6] Initiative is a necessary part of everything a child learns and does. Children of this age are rapid and avid learners and are capable of sharing and working cooperatively. They are actively seeking information about themselves and the world in which they live. They are forcing their way into the world, attacking it, and demanding to know what it is all about. Aggression which implies forcing and attacking becomes a function of initiative. Children are trying to find their purposes in the world. They do this by trying on life to see what it feels like to be someone else. *Curious* and *imaginative* are appropriate words for describing children in this stage. Imaginative play serves children in the same way that planning and thinking serve adults. Children play out their past failures and successes in order to understand how they occurred. They play out their dreams, fantasies, and expectations for the future. Erikson explains that the personality of this phase "crystallizes around the conviction 'I am what I can imagine I will be.'"[7]

This is the stage where the conscience, or to use the psychoanalytic term, the *superego,* is developed. Children internalize the desires and commands of parents and society. They feel guilty when their behaviors or even their fantasies do not meet with the approval of their conscience. "The superego of the child can be primitive, cruel, and uncompromising, as may be observed in instances where children over control and over constrict themselves to the point of self-obliteration; where they develop an over-obedience more literal than the one the parent has wished to exact."[8] The danger of this stage is a sense of guilt over one's acts, fantasies, and goals.

In this stage the forces of imagination, curiosity, and creativity battle the internalized forces of social control. The process of gaining a healthy sense of initiative means that children can question, explore, discover, and interact in their own creative and unique ways under the direction of a firm and guiding but not punishing conscience.

Industry versus Inferiority

At this stage children easily step from the world of make-believe into the world of reality and perform in ways that give them a sense of accomplishment and competence. They can now use their minds and bodies to perform work alone or cooperatively. They want to be shown how to get busy with things. Children enjoy watching how things are done and being taught things they could never have thought of on their own, "things which owe their attractiveness to the very fact that they are not the product of play and fantasy but the product of reality, practicality, and logic; things which thus provide a token sense of participation in the world of adults."[9] Children at this stage have a strong desire to complete what they start even if the task involved is work. Through social learning children of this age are taught to enjoy productive tasks and are taught to be diligent and to persevere in their work efforts. In all cultures children in this stage are given instructions in the technology, skills, and traditions of their society. Some cultures meet this need through organized educational systems such as public schools, while others perform this task through informal instruction, apprenticeships, and learning from older children. Regardless of how the task is handled, this is the stage where skills are acquired. Erikson contends that the personality in this stage "crystallizes around the conviction 'I am what I learn.'"[10] Children are now ready to become producers and to gain recognition through the production of things. They are also ready to work cooperatively in a productive situation. The danger children face in this stage is in developing feelings of inadequacy and inferiority. If children do not feel secure with the tools and skills of their culture or if they feel inadequate when comparing their skills to those of their peers, then a sense of inadequacy and inferiority can develop. It is at this point that society's role is important. The home, school, and community must all strive to help all children understand the technology and economy of their culture and to assist them to feel that they are useful members of society.

Maslow's Theory of Motivation

The field of psychology has traditionally been dominated by psychoanalysis and behaviorism. There were of course efforts in the field outside of these two areas, but until recently none that had made any lasting impact. In an effort to integrate into one theory segments of the works of many others such as Freud, Adler, Goldstein, Jung, Levy, Fromm, and Horney, Abraham Maslow developed a theory of motivation and presented it to a psychoanalytic society in 1942. In 1954 his book, *Motivation and Personality,* appeared outlining in detail his motivation theory. While Maslow was attempting to build on both psychoanalytic and behavioristic works and theories, he could accept neither totally. He felt that man has a higher nature that was not being considered by either of the psychologies of the day. His theory of motivation was an effort to expand the image of man. Maslow had no intention of creating a new branch of psychology, but that is exactly what happened. His theory laid the foundation for a third force to be formed in psychology; a force that has come to be called humanistic psychology.

There are two key concepts in Maslow's theory of motivation. The first concept is that human beings are never satisfied except temporarily. They are always wanting or desiring something. The second is that the needs or desires that humans have seem to arrange themselves in a hierarchy of prepotency. Maslow is critical of other theorists who formulate long lists of drives or desires that motivate humans. Rather, he has approached the study of motivation by constructing a classification of motives based on the fundamental needs or desires of mankind. The most basic of all human needs are the physiological needs. When these are satisfactorily met, the safety needs emerge, then the love and belonging needs, the esteem needs, and finally the need for self-actualization. These needs are not exclusive or single determiners of behavior. Most behaviors are multi-motivational. One behavior can be determined by several or all of the basic needs at the same time. Maslow contends that the fundamental desires of all humans are similar across cultures. The means to achieve these desires are vastly different, but the underlying needs are the same. He quickly admits though that this premise has not been researched well enough to be stated conclusively.

Humans are often not consciously aware of many of their needs, desires, or goals. Conscious desires are usually only symptoms of more basic needs. Superficial desires cannot be taken at face value, but must be understood through an appreciation of the unconscious needs of the individual. Many of the conscious desires of humans are really only a means to an end. For example a young girl, Mary Jane, wants to save twenty dollars. She wants the money to buy a new dress so that she will be pretty and well dressed at the school party. She wants to look pretty and be well dressed to try to gain acceptance into a group of girls who are all attractive, well dressed and who have never quite accepted Mary Jane as one of the "in crowd." The underlying need here is acceptance by the group of girls, but Mary Jane is probably not conscious of this need. She thinks she wants the money just so she can have a new dress and look pretty. Money and the new dress are the means to the end, acceptance. Even though humans are not always consciously aware of the needs underlying their desires, they usually desire that which is conceivable or possible. In other words, we have a tendency to be realistic about our wishes. This is an important point to remember when attempting to understand the differences in motivation between various socioeconomic levels of people in our country and in other countries.

The first key concept of Maslow's theory is that humans are never satisfied except temporarily. Initially this may sound like a statement of human greed and selfishness, but on the contrary, it is one of the very qualities of humans that lift us above the other animals. Humans are not satisfied with having only the physical needs met. Once physical needs are achieved, more is wanted. A good life that is based on higher needs is desired. A world without war, enough food for all of the people in the world, or a happy life for all children can all be desired. Maslow says that we as humans seem to "function best when we are striving for something that we lack, when we wish for something that we do not have, and when we organize our powers in the service of striving toward the gratification of that wish."[11] This is the way humans grow and develop. One need is satisfied and happiness follows for a short time only to be replaced by another source of discontentment at a higher level of needs. Needs do not have to be 100 percent satisfied for the next need to emerge. Partial satisfaction of any need gives room for the next higher need to gradually emerge.

Maslow's second concept is that human needs arrange themselves in a hierarchy of prepotency. The first needs, the physiological needs, are the most potent. Until these are met, none of the other needs will arise.

Need gratification is closely connected with the development of character traits. Gratification of any need helps determine the formation of the person's character by improving and strengthening the person. Frustration of the basic needs leads to personality traits that are not healthy. Consistent gratification of the safety needs leads to the development of a person who is secure and assured, who has confidence in the future, and who is not nervous or apprehensive. A frustration or nongratification of the safety needs leads to nervousness, suspiciousness, anxiety, tension, fear, and dread. Maslow says that "it seems quite clear that many traits characteristic of the healthy adult are positive consequences of childhood gratification of the love needs, for example, ability to allow independence to the loved one, the ability to withstand lack of love, the ability to love without giving up autonomy, etc."[12] The surest way to create an adult who craves love and physical attention and who will go to all lengths to get love is to deny that person love as a child.

With the satiation of one need and the emergence of another, there are changes in human values. What was once important is no longer important and goals that previously had little importance come to be highly valued. The interests of people change as these needs are gratified or fail to be gratified. As lower needs are gratified and higher needs emerge, we also see changes in the cognitive capacities of the individual. Attention, learning, and thinking are all directed toward the new interests and values of the person.

Before each of the five levels of basic needs is examined, one other key point must be stressed. When basic needs are gratified, they are not satisfied forever. The level at which any person is operating is dependent on the present situation. For instance, a young man whose physiological, safety, love, belonging, and esteem needs are met and who is striving for self-actualization can be shipwrecked on a jungle island. His level of needs will quickly revert back to physiological needs. In more typical settings people often take the gratification of their basic needs for granted and value them lightly, especially if they have always been easily gratified. Food, comfort, safety, friendship, and love are often accepted in a rather nonchalant way and are even devalued and mocked. In most people this lack of appreciation is quickly reversed when the need is deprived of gratification and the person experiences hunger, poverty, loneliness, or rejection. Maslow points out that one of the characteristics of self-actualized people is their ability to remain gracious, to be conscious of their blessings always, and to appreciate what they have.

With this introduction, Maslow's five levels of basic needs as they appear in the hierarchy of prepotency will be examined.

The Physiological Needs

It is impossible to list all of the physiological needs, but this level includes needs such as food, liquids, sleep, safe temperatures, activity, exercise, and the use of the senses such as smelling and hearing. These physiological needs are the most prepotent of all. "What this means specifically is that in the human being who is missing everything in life in extreme fashion, it is most likely that the major motivation would be the physiological needs rather than any others."[13] If all needs are unsatisfied, the person is dominated by the physiological needs and all other needs are forgotten, ignored, or become nonexistent. If a person is dying of hunger, nothing else is important except obtaining food. All of the mental and physical capacities are called on to meet this need. The person dreams of food, thinks of food, remembers food, tries to get food, etc. Only during instances of extreme physiological deprivation can we talk of a pure hunger drive or thirst drive.

During these instances of severe physiological deprivation, the entire future outlook of the person changes. For a person deprived of food, the dreams, wishes, and desires for the future all center around having enough food. Food and only food will bring gratification and happiness. Higher levels of aspiration such as love, freedom, and respect are no longer meaningful. When any physiological need is not met, its gratification becomes an all-encompassing, all-consuming task; but when the physiological needs are met with some degree of regularity, new and higher needs emerge immediately to replace the physiological needs in dominating the person. When these new needs are satisfied, other still higher needs arise and demand to be fulfilled. It is in this way that the basic needs emerge in a hierarchy of prepotency.

Gratification is a key word in Maslow's theory, for only through gratification of lower level needs can higher level needs emerge and be dealt with. Once the physiological needs are gratified, they are no longer active determinants of behavior. A desire that is met is no longer a desire. A satisfied need is not a motivator. The organism is dominated and its behavior influenced only by unsatisfied needs. If physiological needs are met, they become unimportant as active determiners of behavior and are important only as a potential influence. If they become unfulfilled, they can emerge again as the most dominant of all needs.

The Safety Needs

When physiological needs are reasonably well satisfied, the safety needs emerge. Included in the safety needs are a need for safety from bodily harm; a need for structure, order, law, limits; a feeling of security and stability; and a freedom from fear, anxiety, and chaos. Physical safety is crucial but mental or psychological safety also occupies a large portion of the safety needs.

All that has been said about the physiological needs applies in a lesser degree to the safety needs. The organism can be completely dominated by these needs with all mental and physical resources being expended to gratify these needs. Most of the behaviors of the organism are efforts to gratify these needs and the person's primary goal is safety seeking. Again, the person's outlook on life and the future is altered by current needs and the primary goal is safety.

For most healthy, fortunate adults in our society, the needs for safety are generally met and are not a dominant determiner of behavior. Only in real emergencies such as war, crime waves, natural disasters, disease, societal disorganization, or breakdown of the government do the safety needs emerge again to dominate the organism. However, as our society experiences social chaos and stress, the safety needs are again becoming the most dominant of the needs in the lives of many citizens. Social conditions such as riots in the streets; mass murders; increasing numbers of assaults, thefts, and rapes; wiretapping and record keeping on government officials and private citizens; assassinations and attempted assassinations all have a direct effect on the loss of a feeling of safety for many adults in our country today.

Unlike the adult who is dominated by the safety needs only during emergencies or social upheavel, the child is often dominated by the safety needs. Infants fear the loss of safety when they are disturbed or dropped suddenly, startled by loud noises or bright lights, submitted to unusual sensory stimulation, or handled roughly. Most people and especially children prefer the familiar to the unfamiliar. Strange, unusual situations such as getting lost or separated from parents, confronting new faces and new tasks or unfamiliar objects, or suddenly becoming ill can elicit fear in children. Children exhibit a need for safety in their preference for routine and regularity. They seem to appreciate a system that has a "skeletal outline of rigidity, in which there is a schedule of a kind, some sort of routine, something that can be counted upon."[14] Children also want an environment that is predictable. Injustice, unfairness, unpredictability or inconsistency in the environment or in the adults in the environment make children feel anxious and unsafe because the world looks unreliable and unsafe.

Maslow feels that adult rage against children, threats of punishment, speaking harshly, name calling, rough physical treatment, or actual physical punishment often elicit total panic and fear in children. More is involved in the fear than fear of physical pain alone. These children are fearful of their very safety. In many children, abusive and neglectful treatment is still followed by clinging to and crying for the parent or other adult who abused them because these children fear for their safety and the parent is still seen as their protector.

The Belongingness and Love Needs

When both the physiological and the safety needs are reasonably well gratified, the love and belongingness needs emerge. Physical safety demands no longer seem very important to the individual. What does matter now is being accepted and loved. A place among family, close friendships, and love relationships are all desired. The love need involves both giving and receiving love. People at this level in the needs hierarchy need contact with other people and intimate relationships. They can now experience loneliness when they are away from loved ones, rejection when they do not feel welcome by their chosen group, friendlessness when no friends are available, and rootlessness when they feel no ties to other people or familiar places.

With their physiological and safety needs regularly met, toddlers are free to given and accept love and feel secure as members of the group.

When the love and belongingness needs are not met the resulting feelings are alienation, aloneness, strangeness, and loneliness. Maslow contends that the rapid mobility of our society and the scattering of families can have a destructive effect on children. Children who are moved too often can become disoriented and experience feelings of being without roots and of being torn from family, friends, homes, and neighbors.

The Esteem Needs

The esteem needs fall into two categories. The first is a desire for competence, mastery, achievement, strength, confidence, independence, and freedom. These needs are personal and are based on one's own evaluation or opinion of oneself. This is called self-esteem. The second category is a desire for reputation or prestige. These needs involve the opinions of other people and are usually based on status, fame, glory, attention, importance, dignity, and appreciation. When these needs are met, one has a feeling of self-confidence, worth, strength, capacity, of being useful, and of being necessary. Thwarting of these needs produces feelings of inferiority, weakness, and helplessness. Maslow cautions that a sense of accomplishment is crucial for young children as early as the age of three for healthy self-esteem to develop.

The Need for Self-actualization

This term refers to the human desire for self-fulfillment or the tendency to strive to achieve one's potential. To be self-actualized is to become everything that one is capable of becoming. The emergence of the need for self-actualization clearly rests on prior satisfaction of all of the other needs. The specific form that self-actualization takes varies greatly from individual to individual just as our capabilities vary, but all of the people that Maslow labelled as self-actualizers had many common characteristics. Self-actualized people had found a personal identity and were autonomous. They had developed patience and compassion for themselves and others, and they were prepared for death. This is the one need that cannot emerge in the young. It only arises in those who have successfully met the other needs over an extended period and who have had good conditions in their lives to develop a need for self-actualization slowly.

Maslow assumes that at birth practically every baby has the ability to grow and develop into a psychologically healthy, self-actualizing human being. In reality very few adults achieve self-actualization. The environmental and interpersonal conditions that are necessary to meet all of the other needs and prepare a person to become a feeling, actualized adult human are woefully lacking in the world today. It is the responsibility of all adults to try to provide an environment that has good conditions for each child. Maslow says the goal of education should be the development of each child to the fullest height that that individual can attain, to help "the person to become the best that he is able to become."[15]

Maslow makes no claim to have a complete theory of determinants of behavior nor of character structure and human development. He advises that his theory be combined with other theories of frustration, learning, values, discipline, will, psychological health, and others in order to have a complete theory of the psychological determinants of behavior. He claims only that his theory of need gratification is one part of the answer to the complex question, What causes people to act as they do? Maslow offers a warning to parents and educators who have taken his theory as a recipe for child rearing. He cautions that gratification of the basic needs is not enough in rearing children. Children must have limits and discipline. They also need to have experience with firmness, toughness, and frustration. Children who have had all of their basic needs easily gratified and who have not been disciplined or experienced frustration can become overindulged, overprotected, selfish, and demanding. "Permissiveness within limits, rather than unrestricted permissiveness, is preferred as well as needed by children."[16] Maslow also warns that "gratification of all the basic needs does not automatically solve the problem of identity, of a value system, of a calling in life, of the meaning of life. For some people at least, especially young people, these are separate and additional life tasks beyond the gratification of basic needs."[17]

Maslow discusses two other areas of needs that he says should be viewed as interrelated and synergistic with the basic needs. They are not a part of the hierarchy of prepotency, but they play an essential role in motivation theory and should not be isolated from the basic needs. These other two areas of needs are the desire to know and understand, and the aesthetic needs.

Desire to Know and Understand

One of the uses of our cognitive capacities is to work toward the satisfaction of our basic needs. We use our cognitive abilities to reason, hypothesize, question, search, and invent in order to meet our basic needs. Any blocking of our cognitive capacities is also indirectly a threat to our basic needs. The need to know and understand is seen in late infancy and childhood, perhaps even more strongly than in adulthood. This seems to be a spontaneous product of maturation rather than of learning. "Children do not have to be taught to be curious. But they may be taught . . . not to be curious."[18] There is no question that curiosity motivates people to learn, experiment, and philosophize. From the desire to know emerges the desire to understand, organize, analyze, and look for relations and meanings.

Aesthetic Needs

In some people there is a basic aesthetic need. Ugliness affects them in a negative way. They crave beautiful surroundings. This need is seen universally in healthy children. The needs for order, symmetry, closure, completion of the act, system, and structure may be assigned to aesthetic needs.

Apparent Exceptions

Maslow acknowledges that even though the needs of most people arise in the order discussed, it is possible that there are exceptions to this hierarchy. There are some people for whom self-esteem seems to be more important than love. But unconsciously these people may be seeking love through self-esteem. There are also some highly creative people whose drive toward creativeness or self-actualization emerges in spite of rather than because of gratification of more basic needs. Other people, who have been forced to live at one of the lower levels for long periods of time, will remain satisfied when this need is met regularly and not advance to a higher level need. The reversal of this is also possible. If a basic need has been met regularly for a long time and higher needs have been met and valued, the basic needs may be jeopardized and neglected for the sake of maintaining the valued higher need. One possible explanation of these apparent reversals of the hierarchy comes from the fact that the hierarchy deals with desires or needs and not with actions or behaviors. A person may want safety but reject it and act upon the need for self-actualization. Some people will give up everything for the sake of an ideal or value. These people are often called martyrs. We can understand these people through an understanding of the concept of increased frustration tolerance through early gratification. Maslow suggests:

> People who have been satisfied in their basic needs throughout their lives, particularly their earlier years, seem to develop exceptional power to withstand present or future thwarting of these needs simply because they have strong healthy character structure as a result of basic satisfaction. . . . In respect of this phenomenon of increased frustration tolerance, it seems probable that the most important gratifications come in the first few years of life. That is to say, people who have been made secure and strong in the earliest years tend to remain secure and strong thereafter in the face of whatever threatens.[19]

This statement should certainly have some far-reaching implications for the care that children receive during their early years.

Skinner's Operant Conditioning

The area of psychology called behaviorism does not consist of a single theory agreed on by all behavioral psychologists. Rather, there are numerous scientists who have conducted research within the field of behaviorism and have set forth different theories or laws in an attempt to explain human behavior. The theories or laws of behaviorism are based on carefully controlled research with much data to support them. The difference between the theories is often just a difference in interpretation of the data. Perhaps the strongest binding element among all the theories is the belief that all behavior is learned; thus behavioral theories are commonly referred to as learning theories. Within the framework of learning theories, many cognitive processes such as learning, remembering, forgetting, abstracting, and attending can be accounted for without referring to any internal mental or conceptual apparatus. Therefore, learning theories do not include reference to such constructs as the superego or unconscious motives; they are concerned with the actual behaviors of a person or organism as viewed from the outside.

Another term that is often used to refer to behavioral theory is *stimulus-response* or *S-R theory*. The stimulus is a part of the environment or modification of part of the environment, and the response is the behavior that is elicited by the stimulus. For example, if a particle of dust blows in a person's eye and causes the eye to water, the dust could be labelled as the stimulus that elicited the response of watering. Any behavior that can be correlated with a specific stimulus is called a respondent behavior because there is a direct cause and effect relationship between the environmental stimulus and the behavior.

Skinner accepts the concept of respondent behaviors, but he views the explanation of a specific stimulus eliciting a specific response as limited in explaining all behaviors. He maintains that while some behaviors are elicited by stimuli in the environment, most behaviors are emitted by the organism without any identifiable stimulus being present in the environment. Skinner calls any behavior that is not under the control of a specific stimulus an operant behavior. Operant behaviors may eventually come under the control of stimuli, but it is not necessary; and it is often impossible to determine what stimulus precedes a response.

Skinner adds a third term to the traditional S-R paradigm, and this term is *reinforcement*. For Skinner the key relationship in operant behaviors is the relationship between the response and the reinforcement that follows the response, whereas the key relationship in respondent behavior is between the stimulus and the response. Based on laboratory studies, Skinner has advanced a Law of Operant Conditioning: If the occurrence of an operant behavior is followed by presentation of a reinforcement, the strength of the behavior is increased.[20] Here the word *strength* relates to making a response more probable or more frequent. The following example will clarify the concept of operant conditioning. This example is one of Skinner's well-known experiments. A rat is placed in a cage equipped with a lever that the rat can reach and press. When the rat presses the lever a pellet of food is released in a food box near the lever. The first press of the lever by the rat is accidental and meaningless, but after receiving food, the rat presses the lever again and again until the rat is satiated with food. The key concept of this experiment is that the lever-pressing response is reinforced or rewarded with food and the occurrence of this response has been strengthened because of the reinforcement. Skinner calls this type of learning instrumental conditioning because the correct response (lever pressing) is instrumental in gaining reinforcement (food pellets). Other psychologists have referred to this process as operant conditioning because the response of pressing the lever was a spontaneous move by the rat and was not a response to any specific stimulus. Therefore, the lever-pressing behavior is operant rather than respondent.

Reinforcement

Reinforcement is the consequence following any particular behavior that increases the probability of that behavior reoccuring in the future. Reinforcement is always contingent upon a response. Skinner has indentified two types of reinforcement: positive and negative. The effect of both types is the same. Positive reinforcement is the presentation of something pleasant or desirable following a response that increases the probability of that response reoccuring. For example if Dana's mother praises her for making her bed and this results in more frequent bed-making behavior, then praise is serving as a positive reinforcer. Negative reinforcement is the withdrawing of something unpleasant or undesirable following a response that increases the probability of that response reoccuring.

The only defining characteristic Skinner has for a reinforcer is that it increases the probability or frequency of the response it follows. Reinforcers are not the same for everyone. What may be reinforcing to one person may not be to another. In unusual circumstances what appears to be punishment can actually be reinforcing to some people. Any event which strengthens a behavior is called reinforcement.

Extinction

Extinction is the process of undoing operant conditioning. Skinner has advanced a law called The Law of Extinction of an Operant Behavior: If the occurrence of an operant behavior already strengthened through conditioning is not followed by reinforcement, the strength of the behavior is decreased.[21]

If reinforcement is no longer received after a response is given, the response will be given less and less until it finally disappears. Even though operant extinction is a much

A teacher's attention often serves as reinforcement for a child.

slower process than operant conditioning, it can be an effective method for eliminating or changing undesirable behavior in children. Skinner maintains that all behaviors that persist are reinforced in some way. To extinguish a behavior in a child the reinforcer must be identified and withheld. This has been called the process of nonreward. Nonreward is especially effective if a behavior that is incompatible with the undesirable behavior is reinforced during the extinction process. This method eliminates an undesirable behavior and strengthens an alternate desirable behavior at the same time. For instance, Jill and Kerry Adams bicker and fuss a great deal when they are in the presence of their mother. She was unknowingly reinforcing their behavior by intervening and thus focusing her attention on their behavior. Their mother's attention was the reinforcer for Jill and Kerry. By using the technique of nonreward, their mother ignored their quarreling and would not respond to their bickering in any way. Mrs. Adams waited for the opportunity and immediately focused her attention on her daughters when they began to play cooperatively. She continued to reward cooperative play and not reward quarreling. Before long friendly cooperative play was Jill and Kerry's usual behavior, and their mother ensured its continuance by frequent reinforcement.

Occasionally a behavior will suddenly reappear after it appears to be extinguished. This phenomenon is referred to as spontaneous recovery. Jill and Kerry may suddenly quarrel and fight during play. If the behavior is reinforced at this point, the extinction process must begin again. If the behavior is not reinforced after spontaneous recovery, it will disappear completely.

Schedules of Reinforcement

The wise administration of reinforcement leads to rapid acquisition of desired behaviors. Once behaviors have been learned, however, their maintenance over time is explained by the effects of the schedule of reinforcement under which they were acquired. If a behavior has been reinforced continuously, it is acquired rapidly; but once the reinforcement is withheld, the behavior is easily extinguished. In fact, it may even go below its original level. Ryan is given a cookie after each meal if he has finished his milk. Ryan does not like milk, but he does like cookies, so he drinks his milk without complaint to get the reward. After several days of drinking his milk and not receiving his cookie, Ryan's milk-drinking behavior quickly stops. Behaviors are more resistant to extinction when they are reinforced on an intermittent schedule when they are being acquired. There are several intermittent schedules introduced by Skinner. The four most basic schedules will be explored below.

Fixed Ratio.   Reinforcement is received after a specific number of responses. For example, Beth is given a nickel every third time she remembers to feed her cat without being reminded. Initially this kind of schedule produces rapid responses because any increase in the rate of responding increases the frequency of reinforcement. This is the schedule commonly used in school settings. After a certain number of problems are worked, the student gets a check mark; more problems earn another mark. Eventually behaviors reinforced on this kind of schedule show a low response just after receiving reinforcement because the person knows that many responses are required before reinforcement comes again. Terry is rewarded for each book he reads. He begins to read rapidly and avidly as he nears the end of his book; but when the book is completed and the reinforcement is received, his reading responses decrease because he knows that he has much reading to do before he is rewarded again.

Variable Ratio.   Reinforcement is not given after a specific number of responses, but is given around some average number. Instead of being reinforced every third time for feeding her cat, Beth is rewarded after two feedings and then after four, then after one, then after five. The number of times she must feed the cat to get her nickel averages three, but it is not necessarily three each time. According to this schedule, the reinforcement can be received at any moment, so the organism adjusts and responds at a constant rate.

Fixed Interval.   Reinforcement is received after a specific length of time. Bobby is given an allowance every Friday if his behavior during the week has been acceptable. A child soon learns that responses that follow reinforcement are not rewarded, so the rate of responding becomes low for a time after each reinforcement.

Variable Interval.   Reinforcement is given around some average period of time. Reinforcement is always possible, so performance is stable and uniform and extinction is difficult if this schedule had been used during conditioning.

Intermittent schedules of reinforcement are more resistant to extinction than are continuous schedules and variable intermittent schedules are even more resistant than fixed intermittent schedules. Many social reinforcers are dispensed on schedules that are a combination of variable ratio and variable interval, and this combination is even more resistant to extinction. Through an understanding of these principles of reinforcement, many behaviors can be understood. Often the persistence of a behavior that appears to be unrewarded can be traced to a highly intermittent schedule of reinforcement.

Shaping

Most behaviors do not appear complete and refined in the behavior of an organism. For instance, after listening to someone play the piano, a young child does not become a skilled pianist. The child first makes crude attempts at the keyboard and is reinforced and gradually becomes more and more accomplished. Skinner says that "by reinforcing a series of successive approximations we bring a rare response to a very high probability in a short time."[22] Through the process of shaping, the final behavior can be vastly different from the behavior originally emitted. This is a crucial concept for parents and teachers. Reinforcement must be given for behaviors that are approximations to the final behavior that is desired. Most behavior that requires some degree of skill such as drawing, writing, reading, or riding a bicycle are all gradually shaped as each attempt gets closer to the desired behavior. It would be difficult for three-year-old Gerald to clean up his cluttered room if he had had no previous cleaning experience. But if he is reinforced for just picking up the blocks at first and then for picking up the blocks and the balls and the next time for the blocks, the balls, and the stuffed animals, soon he will be able to straighten up his room without assistance. His behavior has been shaped by reinforcing closer and closer approximations to the desired behavior.

Stimulus Control

Most operant behaviors acquire important connections with the environment of the organism. Stimuli in the environment do not elicit behaviors in operant conditioning, but they do set the stage for behaviors to be emitted and reinforced. For instance, bedtime for Sharon and Carlos is 8:30, but when Grandmother is visiting, they are usually successful in extending their bedtime to 9:30. Grandmother's presence sets the stage for a particular behavior from Sharon and Carlos that enables them to stay up an additional hour. Sharon and Carlos' behavior has come under stimulus control with Grandmother serving as the discriminative stimulus. When behavior is under stimulus control, the stimulus is present prior to a response being given but it does not elicit the response. It simply modifies the probability that a response will occur. If the response is reinforced, the probability that the response will reoccur in the future in the presence of the stimulus is strengthened.

Understanding the concept of stimulus control can assist adults in the control of children's behavior. Erin's behavior at story time is disruptive to the rest of the class. Even though Phillip does not participate in the disruptive behavior, it is his presence next to Erin that serves as the discriminative stimulus for her behavior. The teacher rearranges the group so that Erin and Phillip are separated by the rest of the children, and her disruptive behavior ceases because the discriminative stimulus has been removed.

Generalization and Discrimination

If new behaviors had to be learned every time a new situation occurred, each new situation would be met with trial-and-error attempts. This is not the case, however, because responses learned during one situation are called on and used again in similar situations. This phenomenon is referred to as generalization. Generalization is the tendency for a behavior that has been conditioned to one stimulus to be emitted in the presence of similar stimuli. For instance, once a child has learned appropriate responses for spending the day at Grandmother's house, these same behaviors can be applied at Aunt Mary or Mr. Smith's house.

Not only is generalization necessary for social learning to occur but adequate discriminations are also needed. Suzie loves animals and has been rewarded by her parents for her uninhibited and gentle manner with family and neighborhood pets. On a trip to the zoo it is helpful to Suzie to be able to generalize that these are nice animals who eat, drink, sleep, and often sound like the animals at home, but she must also be able to discriminate that there is a difference. The cats, for example, have dangerously sharp claws and teeth and are not meant to be hugged and petted. Children learn to discriminate through the reinforcements or lack of reinforcements that their behaviors gain for them and they learn to distinguish between similar stimuli and respond to one but not another. If Suzie tried to get inside one of the cages containing a large cat, she would probably be pulled back and firmly told not to get in the cage because the large cats could hurt her. If discrimination is not learned, then generalization from one situation to another may be based on irrelevant stimuli; and inappropriate behaviors may be emitted.

Conditioned Reinforcers and Generalized Reinforcers

Secondary conditioning is the process where neutral stimuli can acquire reinforcing properties by being presented simultaneously with a reinforcer. After the rat in a previous example learned to press the lever and receive food, a light was turned on each time the food was presented and remained on for a few seconds while the rat ate the food. After repeated pairings of the light and the food, the light alone became reinforcing to the rat and by itself maintained the response of pressing the lever. The light became a conditioned reinforcer. Most human behavior is reinforced by conditioned reinforcers such as toys, money, grades, and attention rather than by primary reinforcers such as food, water, and sleep.

When a stimulus has been associated with several reinforcers, it can become a type of conditioned reinforcer known as a generalized reinforcer. Money is the most common generalized reinforcer because it can be exchanged for many other primary and conditioned reinforcers. Tokens can be used as effectively with children as money is with adults. Token economies have been successfully used in some day care centers and schools. Children are rewarded immediately for good behavior, cooperation, good work, etc. The tokens take the form of punches on computer cards, poker chips, check marks, or gold stars. At specified times the tokens can be spent for free time, a field trip, an extra snack, or anything else agreed to by the child and the teacher. A token system is effective for several reasons: it allows for immediate reinforcement; behaviors that will gain tokens are clear to the children and the teachers; and the children are given choices in what reinforcers they will receive. Tokens like money can quickly lose their value, however, if they can no longer be used to purchase valued reinforcers.

Aversive Control

Punishment can be defined as the removal of a positive reinforcer such as taking away privileges or withholding attention, or the presentation of an unpleasant stimulus such as a spanking or the assignment of extra chores. It was once believed that punishment had the opposite effect of positive reinforcement and that if behaviors were punished, they would disappear. Based on extensive laboratory studies, Skinner maintains that punishment will temporarily suppress or inhibit an undesired behavior, but it will not extinguish the behavior. An inhibited behavior is capable of reoccuring at any time. In addition to its inhibitory effect on behavior, punishment also has numerous other side effects.

One possible result of punishment is escape learning. A child or other organism learns to make a specific response in order to escape from a noxious situation. A rat is put in a cage and shocked by an electric grid on the floor. The press of the lever turns off the shock. The rat quickly learns to press the lever to escape from the pain of the electric shock. Escape learning is commonly seen in children. Laura has just taken a toy away from Jason and pushed him down. Jason relays the incident to the teacher, and the teacher instructs Laura to sit in a chair away from the other children. After being in the chair a short time, Laura approaches the teacher and says, "I'm sorry, I won't do it again." The teacher allows Laura to return to the group. Laura has learned that an "I'm sorry" response will allow her to escape from the noxious situation.

Avoidance learning is another possible result of punishment. Avoidance learning is similar to escape learning except the subject may avoid the punishment entirely by responding before the punishment is given. The rat in the electrified cage is now given a buzzer warning ten seconds before the shock comes on. After receiving the shock a few times, the rat learns to press the lever at the sound of the buzzer and completely avoid the painful shock. When the electric shock is disconnected, the rat will still press the lever at the sound of the buzzer because there is no way for the rat to know that the painful stimulus is no longer present. Laura learns to avoid the teacher's punishment by beating Jason to the draw. She approaches the teacher before Jason does and says, "I pushed Jason but it was an accident, I'm sorry." The teacher cautions Laura to be more careful and sends her back to play without any punishment. Laura has learned a behavior that enables her to completely avoid the punishment she might have received. Avoidance learning is common in children and adults, and once learned it is extremely difficult to extinguish.

Another undesirable effect of punishment is that it may be generalized to nonpunished behavior. For instance, Keith is punished each day at nap time because he will not stay in his crib. He may become conditioned not only to fear punishment at nap time but also to fear other behaviors associated with the punishment such as sleeping or staying in his room alone. It is difficult to precisely control the effects that punishment may have on a person's behavior. Punishment may also create such pain or anxiety that the child tries to avoid or withdraw from the environment in which the punishment was administered. For example, a child who is punished regularly for misbehaving at swimming lessons will try to withdraw from the lessons entirely. Older children who have been regularly punished at home try to withdraw from the home environment by running away.

In spite of the disadvantages of punishment, there may be occasions where it is useful and effective in quickly suppressing undesirable behavior. Punishment can even be an effective way of changing behavior if desirable behavior is elicited and rewarded while the undesirable behavior is suppressed. In years past punishment was thought of as the sole means of changing a child's behavior. However, Skinner has introduced other techniques that have proven to be more effective than punishment in altering behavior without the undesirable side effects that often accompany punishment. The alternatives have already been discussed, but in summary they include extinguishing undesirable behavior through nonreward, conditioning acceptable behaviors that are incompatible with undesirable behaviors, and modifying the stimuli in the environment that set the stage for undesirable behaviors.

Bandura and Walters' Social Learning Theory

Albert Bandura and Richard Walters are behavioral psychologists whose theory differs from that of traditional behaviorism in one important way. They have introduced into behaviorism the role of social phenomena as an influence on personality development. Bandura and Walters call theirs a "socio-behavioristic approach."[23] They are critical of learning theorists who ignore social variables in personality development. They contend that most learning theories are inadequate to account for the acquisition of new behaviors. Bandura and Walters, like most behavioral scientists, have conducted extensive, well-controlled research from which their theory has emerged. They have integrated their own research results with the findings of other researchers in the fields of child development, social psychology, experimental psychology, and cultural anthropology.

According to their social learning theory, the same principles that govern the acquisition and maintenance of socially acceptable behavior also govern the acquisition and maintenance of socially deviant behavior. Other learning theories have not been rejected by Bandura and Walters; rather, they have accepted and built upon the work of many other behavioral theorists. Their work is an addition to and an extension and modification of existing learning theories.

They have suggested additional learning principles that more completely account for the development and modification of human behavior. They have attempted "to explain the development of all forms of social behavior in terms of antecedent social stimulus events."[24] *Antecedent stimulus* is the behaviorist term for environmental factors that occurred in a person's life prior to the performance of some behavior that had an influence on that behavior being performed. Examples of antecedent stimuli are child training practices that have been used to develop desired behaviors in the child, social models that the child has observed, and the conditions that have been necessary for the child to receive reinforcement. Several of the learning principles offered in this theory are contained in Skinner's theory and have already been discussed. These include the principles of reinforcement, punishment, inhibition, nonreward, generalization, and discrimination. Bandura and Walters have done extensive research in the area of observational learning and imitation and have established other learning principles that offer observational learning as an explanation for the acquisition of novel responses, for the displacement of aggressive feelings, and for regressive behaviors. The five learning principles described below have resulted from this research.

The Acquisition of Novel Responses
through Observational Learning

Many learning theories fail to account for the acquisition of new behaviors or novel responses. They generally assume that a repertoire of possible behaviors is present and the particular behavior that is performed is determined by expected reinforcement and the value of the reinforcers to the person. Bandura and Walters question this limited explanation of behavior, and attempt to account for the acquisition of new behaviors through observational learning. For example, Jimmy is given a tool that he has never seen before and has never heard of. He is asked to name the tool and use it correctly, and he will be given a favorite treat. Jimmy wants the reward and wants to perform well, but he cannot because he has had no previous experience with this object or similar objects. How can Jimmy learn the behavior that was requested? He calls on his older sister who labels the tool for him and demonstrates its proper use. In a short time, after watching his sister and listening to her labels and explanations, Jimmy can identify the tool and use it properly. In many instances throughout life, especially during childhood, imitation is an indispensable aspect of learning.

Reinforcement often accompanies imitation. For instance, Mother rolls the ball to Sally. When Sally imitates her mother and pushes the ball back, she is rewarded with praise and a hug. Bandura and Walters acknowledge the importance of reinforcement in observational learning, but they present evidence that learning can occur from observation of the behavior of others without any reinforcement being given. For instance, five-year-old Kathy observes her teen-age cousin apply eye make-up and lipstick. When Kathy is left alone in the room with the make-up, she imitates her cousin's behavior and liberally uses the make-up on her own face. Bandura and Walters also include vicarious reinforcement in their social learning theory. Vicarious reinforcement occurs when the behavior of the observer is influenced because of the reinforcement received by the model. Patrick is rewarded with fifty cents for taking the initiative and cleaning up his own room. His younger sister Lynn imitates his behavior and cleans up her room.

Effects of Prior Learning and Situational
Factors on Social Influence Procedures

Bandura and Walters have isolated numerous situational factors that have an influence on the effectiveness of reinforcement and modeling to effect a change in a child's behavior. Some that appear to be especially important for young children are listed below:

1. Children who are highly dependent are influenced more by social reinforcers and imitate modeled behavior more readily than children who are not highly dependent.

2. Children do not as readily imitate the behavior of a model of the opposite sex as they imitate the behavior of a model of the same sex.

3. Children who have experienced failure regularly are prone to imitative behavior and are more influenced by social reinforcers than are children who have regularly experienced success.

4. Reinforcement is more effective when it is given by a person who is prestigious in the eyes of the child than by a person who has low prestige to the child.

5. The behavior of high-prestige models is more likely to be imitated than the behavior of low-prestige models.

Conflict and Displacement

When a child has learned a certain behavior through previous positive reinforcement and the behavior is suddenly paired with an unpleasant stimulus, a conflict situation is developed and the child becomes frustrated. Many psychologists and psychiatrists accept aggression as the natural, unlearned reaction to frustration. They believe if the child's normal behavior is blocked or frustrated, the child will behave in an aggressive manner. If this aggression cannot be directed at the frustrating agent for social or other reasons, then the aggression is displaced and directed toward someone or something else.

Bandura and Walters take issue with this theory. They contend that specific social training plays an important role in fostering displacement of aggression. If children have been taught or have witnessed their parents displace their aggressive behaviors to others not responsible for the frustration, then it is likely that they will learn this kind of behavior. It is like the old story of the man who was severly reprimanded by his boss at work. The man came home and displaced his aggressive feelings by shouting at his wife. The wife in turn became angry and spanked Johnny. Johnny went outside and kicked the dog. Bandura and Walters contend that this kind of displacement is not a predetermined human characteristic but is one that is learned through social reinforcement and modeling.

Parents often determine the types of displaced responses that a child will exhibit through modeling, giving examples and control of reinforcement. "Social training consists largely in teaching a child to express aggression, dependency, and other social responses only in certain ways."[25] Bandura and Walters use the term *response displacement* for the substitute of more socially acceptable responses for less acceptable ones. When parents and other adults use aggressive methods to control children's aggression, they are often defeating themselves. The adults are providing a model for the very behavior that they wish to stop in the child.

Personality Development and the Concept of Regression

As a result of the child-training procedures that Bandura and Walters have outlined—reinforcement, nonreward, punishment, modeling, and displacement—the child learns a variety of behaviors for specific social situations. The behaviors that have been learned best are the dominant behaviors for that child and are the ones that will be seen most often. Nondominant responses are ones that have been learned weakly or have been strongly learned at an earlier age but are no longer appropriate. When a behavior that is no longer appropriate for the child's age emerges, regression has occurred.

> Regressive behavior is often elicited in children through their observing a younger sibling rewarded for behavior which is appropriate for a younger, but not an older child. Imitation of the younger sibling may then occur because the older child mistakenly anticipates reward for matching the sibling's behavior. In such cases, the anticipation of reward . . . is the important factor in eliciting the age inappropriate response.[26]

Continuities in Social Development

Stage theories developed by Erikson, Freud, Gesell, Piaget, and others all assume that social behaviors develop in a discontinuous manner with individuals passing through a series of prefixed sequences or stages. These stage theories accept the variability within an individual over a period of time but emphasize similarities of all individuals at specific ages in life. Bandura and Walters are critical of these theorists and maintain that they minimize the variability in behavior of individuals of the same age "due to biological, socioeconomic, ethnic, and cultural differences and to variations in the child-training practices or socialization agents."[27] Children from different backgrounds are exposed to different social models and are reinforced for different behaviors. As a result of this social learning, we see great group differences at any age level. In addition, because biological, familial, and subculture factors are important determinants in social training and these factors usually remain constant throughout early childhood, continuity rather than discontinuity should be expected for each child at successive age periods. Thus, the focus of the social learning approach is on the developmental differences between individuals and the developmental continuities within each individual.

The research done in the area of imitation or observational learning has been one of Bandura and Walters' most important contributions to the field of behavioral psychology, and indeed it should be of prime importance to the person who will be working with young children. The research findings of Bandura and Walters, their associates, and their students have given us a new understanding of how children learn social behavior and how their personalities are developed.

Role of Imitation

All cultures use social models to transmit desirable social behavior. Children are told, "Watch and I'll show you how." "Listen and you'll learn." "Brush your teeth like Daddy." "Try to act nice like your brother." etc. Models are used to accelerate the learning process. Early in life children are provided with child-sized replicas of tools and equipment used by adults. They are given brooms, irons, dishes, dolls, firemen's hats, doctors' bags, cowboy hats, construction toys, jeeps, cars, and guns. While using these toys children exhibit attitudes, mannerisms, language, voice inflections, and gestures that have never been taught directly. The children learned how to behave as an adult by watching and listening to adults they have seen and heard. In our society real-life models are still prevalent, but we also depend heavily on symbolic models that employ written or audiovisual means of communication. In our technical society verbal instructions that tell us how to do things and when to do them are common and are a means of symbolic modeling. Five-year-old Jenny asks permission to make a

Children adopt an active role and an enthusiastic attitude when an admired teacher displays these same behaviors.

batch of cookies. Her mother reads the directions to her, so she knows what to do and the proper sequence of each step.

When she is older, she can read the recipe herself. The written recipe and verbal directions serve as a symbolic model for Jenny.

Visually presented models are common on television and the movies. Even though these models give no direct instructions to the child who is viewing, they are powerful models in shaping and modifying behavior. Because of the large amounts of time that many children view television, it has a strong influence on the social norms and behaviors adopted by children and adolescents. Actual performances of a behavior as seen on television are more easily remembered and clearer to children than are verbal instructions and descriptions given by adults, therefore television can be a more influential model than parents or teachers.

The use of exemplary models is another method used by parents and teachers to elicit desired behavior from children. An exemplary model is another person who possesses the characteristics that are desired in the child. This model is described to the child, or the child is asked to watch the model. If the child is familiar with the model, he or she can simply refer to the model's characteristics. This type of modeling is common with young children. "All good football players go to bed early to get plenty of rest." "If you want your hair to be pretty and shiny like Patty's, we have to brush it twice each day." Exemplary modeling can be positive when children are encouraged to emulate a model and adopt acceptable behaviors. However, negative exemplary modeling is also possible. This occurs when the undesirable characteristics of a model are pointed out and the child is warned not to reproduce these behaviors. This kind of modeling is accompanied by a reminder of the consequences that usually follow the undesirable behavior. This kind of modeling has one unfortunate side effect. The attention of the child has to be directed to undesirable behaviors that otherwise might never have been considered.

Laboratory research studies indicate that when a model is observed, three different effects might occur:

1. The child may acquire a new response or learn a new behavior that was previously unknown. In an experiment by Bandura, Ross, and Ross, children observed real-life and filmed models performing physically aggressive activities. There was no reward offered for any particular behavior. The children were simply placed in the same environment in which they saw the model's behavior occur. The children imitated the model's aggressive behavior and performed the novel activities. Experimentally, the acquisition of aggressive responses is the only type of behavior that has been studied, but field studies indicate that children acquire other personality traits by modeling the behavior of parents. Children also acquire socially deviant behavior from observation and modeling of others. This has been documented in numerous clinical cases of children with severe personality problems.

2. If the child already knows the observed behavior or a similar behavior, the observation can have an inhibitory or disinhibitory effect on the occurrence of the behavior in the future. After observation of a specific response, the observer may not only perform the observed behavior but may perform other similar behaviors as well. In a number of studies children were shown cartoons that contained aggressive behaviors. After viewing the cartoons the children imitated the aggressive actions on the film and they also performed other aggressive acts that had been previously learned but were not contained on the film. The aggressiveness of the cartoon models had a disinhibitory effect for a general class of aggressive behaviors.

3. Observation of the model's behavior serves to elicit similar behaviors from the child that are neither entirely novel nor inhibited. "The role of a model as an eliciting stimulus can be most clearly seen when the behavior that is imitated is not likely to have incurred punishment."[28]

When appropriate models are present socially accepted behaviors such as giving money or time or sharing or helping are easily elicited.

Bandura and Walters identify two other variables that determine the effect of the model on the behavior of the child.

Influence of Response Consequences to the Model. The responses that a model receives after performing a specific behavior have a direct influence on whether or not the behavior will be imitated by the observer. Bandura, Ross, and Ross report that children in an experimental situation who saw an aggressive model rewarded "showed more imitative physical and verbal aggression than children who saw the model punished."[29] Using these and other studies as supportive evidence, Bandura and Walters maintain that the consequences a model receives has an influence on whether or not the behavior will be imitated. If the model is rewarded, the behavior is more likely to be imitated, whereas punishment seems to have an inhibitory influence on the behavior being performed.

Influence of Observer Characteristics. (1) Children who have a poor self-concept or who are incompetent are more likely to imitate a successful model. (2) Children who have been previously rewarded for model imitation are especially prone to imitate a successful model. (3) Children who believe that they are like the model in some characteristic or belief are more likely to imitate the model than children who believe that they are different from the model.

Bandura and Walters have presented substantial evidence in support of observational learning, but they readily admit that the entire social learning process is not accounted for by imitation of observed responses. Once the observed behavior is performed by the child, the consequences to the child will influence whether the behavior will be maintained or not. Once new behaviors are acquired, they are subject to reinforcement and punishment that will increase or decrease respectively the likelihood of a specific response.

Summary

Erikson's view of psychological and social development is based on eight stages that correspond to stages of an entire life span. Conflicts related to trust, autonomy, initiative, and industry must be resolved by children as they develop into their teen years. An explanation for what motivates people is offered by Maslow's hierarchy of needs model. He suggests gratification of basic needs such as physiological needs, safety, and love must precede the higher level needs of esteem and self-actualization.

Behavioral theory, amply represented by Skinner, has as one of its main tenets the generalization that all behavior is learned. As a learning theory, behaviorism focuses on reinforcements, generalization, and discrimination. A greater emphasis on the social context in which learning takes place is what distinguishes Bandura and Walter's social learning theory from other behaviorists. Bandura and Walters concern themselves with imitation and modeling in explaining children's behavior.

NOTES

1. Erik H. Erikson, *Childhood and Society,* 2d. ed. (New York: W. W. Norton & Company, 1963).
2. Ibid., p. 251.
3. Erik H. Erikson, "Industry versus Inferiority," in *Human Development,* ed. Morris L. Haimourtz and N. R. Haimourtz (New York: Thomas Y. Crowell Co., 1966), p. 301.
4. Erikson, *Childhood and Society,* p. 251.
5. Erikson, "Industry versus Inferiority," p. 301.

6. Erikson, *Childhood and Society*, p. 255.
7. Erikson, "Industry versus Inferiority," p. 301.
8. Erikson, *Childhood and Society*, p. 257.
9. Erikson, "Industry versus Inferiority," p. 302.
10. Ibid., p. 301.
11. Abraham H. Maslow, *Motivation and Personality*, 2d ed. (New York: Harper & Row, Publishers, 1970), p. xv.
12. Ibid., p. 65.
13. Ibid., p. 37.
14. Ibid., p. 40.
15. Abraham H. Maslow, *The Farther Reaches of Human Nature* (New York: The Viking Press, 1971), p. 169.
16. Maslow, *Motivation and Personality*, p. 40.
17. Ibid., p. 71.
18. Ibid., p. 50.
19. Ibid., p. 53.
20. B. F. Skinner, *Behavior of Organisms* (New York: Appleton- Century-Crofts, 1938), p. 21.
21. Ibid.
22. B. F. Skinner, *Science and Human Behavior* (New York: The Macmillan Co., 1953), p. 92.
23. Albert Bandura and Richard H. Walters, *Social Learning and Personality Development* (New York: Holt, Rinehart and Winston, 1963), p. vii.
24. Ibid., p. 44.
25. Ibid., p. 20.
26. Ibid., p. 23.
27. Ibid., p. 24.
28. Ibid., p. 79
29. Ibid., p. 82.

Suggested Readings

Bandura, Albert and Walters, Richard H. *Social Learning and Personality Development*. New York: Holt, Rinehart and Winston, 1963. A synthesis of the learning principles that guide human behavior and descriptions of research that support the principles that new behaviors are commonly acquired through modeling or imitating.

Erikson, Erik. *Childhood and Society*. 2d ed. New York: W. W. Norton & Co., 1963. A presentation of the Eight Stages of Man and a discussion of the relationship between internal and social forces on emotional and social development.

Maslow, Abraham H. *Motivation and Personality*. 2d. ed. New York: Harper & Row, Publishers, 1970. An introduction to his theory of motivation and hierarchy of needs that influence human behavior.

Reynolds, G. S. *A Primer of Operant Conditioning*. Glenville, Ill.: Scott Foresman and Co., 1968. An elementary explanation of the vocabulary and basic concepts of operant conditioning.

Skinner, B. F. *Science and Human Behavior*. New York: The Macmillan Co., 1953. A comprehensive treatment of the scientific and social philosophy of behaviorism with a detailed description of the theory of operant conditioning.

Suggested Activities

1. Observe some young children in a school or day care setting. If you had to describe or explain the behavior you observed, would one of the four points of view in this chapter be easier for you to use in such a description or explanation? Compare your response to others.

2. In what ways are the views presented in this chapter complementary to one another? Are any, or parts thereof, mutually exclusive to one another? Discuss your answers.

3. How do you differentiate between and among such words as *teach, learn, train,* and *educate?* What are some implications of the different definitions in terms of actual practice?

Chapter Seven

Language, Moral, Physical, and Motor Development

It has been said that scientific investigation begins and ends with theory; also that it begins and ends with observation. It has also been said that the scientific investigator in any particular field starts with a theory that is quite different from the theory which (s)he later develops.

F. J. Roethlisberger, "Contributions of the Behavioral Sciences to a General Theory of Management," in Readings in Managerial Psychology, *ed. Harold J. Leavitt and L. R. Pondy (Chicago: The University of Chicago Press, 1964), p. 523.*

The scientific study of language and physical development predates the study of moral development, but all three have grown to be relatively specialized areas of investigation. By specialized, we mean that compared to other areas of development discussed elsewhere in this section, the limits of their focus are narrower and technical language is encountered more quickly. The latter is especially true of the literature in language and physical development. The psycholinguists, in an effort to be precise and exact in their descriptions of young children's speech, utilize the technical language of syntax and grammar. Studies of physical and motor development frequently involve physiological/anatomical considerations replete with appropriately technical vocabulary.

The discussions in this chapter will avoid the technical language of each area as much as possible and stay, instead, on a more general level of description. The purpose is to introduce the reader to these areas of study by gleaning generalizations from each. For more specific detail of each area of development, the reader is referred to the Suggested Reading list at the end of the chapter.

Language Development

The fundamental properties of sentences—verb-object, subject-predicate, and modification—that Bruner referred to in his reference to language development form grammatical rules that are found in all languages.

Between the ages of twelve and twenty-four months, children produce mainly one-word sentences. Most often these are nouns, but sometimes verbs and adjectives appear. A child's vocabulary increases from 1 or 2 words at a year old to approximately 200 words at two years of age. By age six, children's vocabularies are in the thousands. Speech that adheres to grammatical rules seldom appears before one-and-one-half years of age, but the basic process of being able to understand the intricate competence of adult grammar is nearly accomplished by three-and-one-half years of age.[1]

The first two- or three-word sentences in a young child's speech take the form of what is called telegraphic speech. These sentences are reduced in almost the same way adults reduce sentences when sending telegrams. A child's telegraphic speech generally leaves out articles, prepositions, auxiliary verbs, and inflections on verbs and nouns. The important point is that even such abbreviated speech follows simple grammatical rules. The set of grammatical rules is the knowledge a child has about the language. The knowledge is the measure of language competence. Competence precedes performance and is part of the mental equipment of the language user. Performance is the actual behavior. Language performance is affected by memory, fatigue, and distraction.[2]

The child practices speaking within grammatical rules and develops language competence by applying and refining the rules to fit the rapidly growing variety of meanings encountered through interaction with others. McNeill, a developmental psycholinguist, assigns these basic grammatical relations a place in the child's linguistic endowment:

> Since all languages have this general structure and since all children seem able to acquire its local manifestation in their own communities, we assume that this ability (developing language) is part of a child's natural endowment as a human being.[3]

This assignment of language development to a child's natural endowment runs counter to the "blank slate" notion many people have embraced for years. The traditional view among educators has been that language is learned primarily from imitating or modeling others. The "language as a learned behavior" point of view has more implications for structuring a learning environment than the psycholinguist's view of language development as a natural process for which learning—that is, imitating or modeling—is of secondary, if not incidental, importance.

The social learning theorist's view of language development places more emphasis on learning through imitation or modeling.[4] Neither the social learning point of view nor the psycholinguistic one entirely discounts the contributions of the other, but each can substantiate its own position with research findings. The fact that children use grammatical rules they themselves form is evident from their speech samples that include such words as *comed* for *come, bringed* for *brought,* and *runed* for *ran;* words unlikely to have been heard from the adults around them. These awkward-sounding words are examples of the child's application of rules of grammar inferred from the speech of others. Simple imitation or modeling does not explain the inappropriate past tense used by children. Imitation and modeling undoubtedly explain, however, that children use the language of those around them, including dialect and accent. The controversy will continue until some kind of synthesis of the viewpoints or other breakthroughs in the study of language development can be made.

Children cannot speak a language when they are born, but they develop, or acquire, the fundamental grammatical structures of adult language by about age 3½. The complete explanation of this phenomenon eludes us now, but enough is known from both points of view that can provide some direction for those interested in helping children's language development. An example comes from McNeill's discussion of parental expansions:

Quite often adults repeat the speech of small children and, in so doing, change the children's sentences into the nearest well-formed adult equivalent. . . . It is a kind of imitation in reverse, in which the parent echoes the child and, at the same time, supplies features that are missing from the child's sentences.[5]

The role of parental expansions is to help a child acquire more refined speech by presenting models tailor-made to the child's utterances. A verbally rich environment in which children are given many opportunities to listen and speak will promote language development.

The sequence of language development proceeds from listening, to speaking, to reading and writing. But the sequence is not passed through just once. As the child increases his or her language skills, the sequence is repeated; and many times simultaneous learning takes place.

Moral Development

The levels of moral development postulated by John Dewey and the stages of moral reasoning researched by Jean Piaget have been refined, modified, redefined, and validated by Kohlberg to form his stage theory of moral reasoning. Kohlberg's model of the development of moral reasoning consists of three levels, each containing two stages. Research by Kohlberg and his associates has been interpreted to indicate that this is a natural series of stages through which all children's moral reasoning must pass. Kohlberg offers evidence that this theory applies across cultures. He calls his a cognitive-developmental approach to moral reasoning. It is cognitive in that it recognizes the role of active thinking and questioning in making moral judgments. Kohlberg offers that the level of moral reasoning is not highly correlated with verbal intelligence or IQ, but that children's cognitive abilities or inabilities to make logical inferences, reason abstractly, and form hypotheses have an influence on the stage of moral reasoning they can attain. Using Piaget's stages of cognitive development as a guide Kohlberg states that:

> since moral reasoning clearly is reasoning, advanced moral reasoning depends upon advanced logical reasoning; a person's logical stage puts a certain ceiling on the moral stage he can attain. A person whose logical stage is only concrete operational is limited to the preconventional moral stages. A person whose logical stage is only partially formal operational is limited to the conventional moral stages.[6]

Kohlberg's theory is developmental in that the six stages are sequential and hierarchical. Movement through the stages is always a forward process, never a backward one and no stage can be skipped because each stage builds on the previous stage and prepares the way for the next. The moral reasoning found at each stage includes within it all the thinking of the lower stages.

Movement from one stage to the next is not an abrupt process. A person's level of moral reasoning can be partially in one stage and partially in the next higher stage. Each higher stage of development represents an improvement in moral reasoning and an improvement in cognitive organization over the previous stage. Movement from one stage to the next is not an automatic maturational process. Children must be helped to achieve the level of reasoning at the next higher stage. Research indicates that children are particularly responsive to attempts to influence their thinking in the direction of the stage above that at which they most typically respond. Moral conflict and imbalance are a precondition for development from one stage to the next. Adults can assist children to move from one stage to the next by:

1. Exposing children to situations that pose problems and contradictions to their current level of reasoning;
2. Exposing children to situations where there is a conflict of moral values and no obvious "right" answer;
3. Encouraging children to exchange and defend conflicting solutions to moral dilemmas; and
4. Exposing children to the next higher stage of moral reasoning.

Kohlberg cautions that moral reasoning is not to be equated with moral behavior. There are many factors that determine a person's moral actions. Moral reasoning is only one of the factors involved, but it is a highly influential one.

The first two levels of Kohlberg's theory are discussed below.

Level I: Preconventional Level

Children at this level respond to the rules and labels of the culture. They react to what is labelled good or bad and right or wrong in terms of the physical consequences of the action or in terms of the physical power of those who make the rules. At this level value resides in physical happenings and physical needs rather than in persons or standards.

Stage 1: The Punishment and Obedience Orientation.   The physical consequences of an action determine whether it is right or wrong regardless of the value of the consequences or the intention of the performer of the act. Children at this stage avoid punishment and trouble by obeying the person in authority, not by following rules. Respect is seen as obedience. Deference to superior powers and avoidance of punishment are valued in their own right. People are valued because of their power and possessions. A child at this stage talks about:

1. Being punished or rewarded;
2. Being labelled good or bad; and
3. How authority figures will react.

Stage 2: Instrumental-Relativist Orientation.   At this stage the right action is the one that is satisfying to personal needs and occasionally to the needs of others. Human relations are viewed in terms of fairness and reciprocity in a physical, pragmatic way. Reciprocity is not a matter of loyalty, gratitude, or justice, but is oriented to barter and exchange. "You push me and I'll push you." The sense of fairness is a narrow, naive one: "The same for you as for me." Duty does not exist and rules do not have to be obeyed if one is willing to suffer the consequences. A child at this stage talks about:

1. Needs and motives of others;

2. People not being fair;

3. One good (or bad) deed deserving another; and

4. My way is the best way.

Level II: Conventional Level

This level has been called the generalized conformity level. At this level the individual actively maintains the expectations of family, peers, and the culture as a value in itself. Level II individuals are also concerned with maintaining, supporting, and justifying the social order to which they conform.

Stage 3: Good Boy-Nice Girl Orientation.   A person at this stage is capable of "putting himself in the other fellow's shoes" and seeing things from another person's perspective. The person at this stage is concerned with what other people think and wants to help and please them. The person seeks approval and acts to get it. Approval is earned by being a "nice" person. There is much conforming to stereotypical images of what is "right" and "good" behavior. For the first time behavior can be judged by intention rather than the consequences of the act. A person at this stage talks about:

1. Pleasing others;

2. The welfare of others and ways to help them;

3. Being liked by others; and

4. What others expect and approve.

Stage 4: The Law and Order Orientation.   The right behavior is seen as doing one's duty, showing respect for authority, and maintaining the social order for its own sake. There is a clear delineation between right and wrong. The stage four individual verbally sticks to the rules regardless of the situation. Authorities have a legal claim to be respected because they maintain the social order. One earns respect by dutifully conforming to the rules of society. A person at stage four talks about:

1. Doing one's duty;

2. Showing respect for authority; and

3. Obeying rules.

Level III is called the postconventional or principled level. At this level, there is an effort to define values apart from authority. There is a thrust toward autonomous moral principles that are universally valid and applicable apart from a given social system.

The rate of movement from one stage to the next is highly variable. Some individuals move quickly, while others move slowly. Only about 20 percent of the adult population ever moves beyond stage four.

Physical and Motor Development

Physical and motor development follow two directional sequences. The first is cephalocaudal: Physical and motor development proceeds from head to feet. The head forms first, then arms before legs in early development. The nervous system also develops from the brain downward, thus the child gains control of muscles that support the head before gaining control of those muscles in the trunk and legs.

The second direction in which physical and motor growth proceeds is proximodistal. Whereas the first direction was from the head down, the second direction is from the center of the body out toward the periphery. Control proceeds from the trunk to the arms, then the hands, and finally the fingers. Likewise, control begins at the hips and extends to the legs, feet, and toes.

All children's physical and motor development follow the directional patterns mentioned, but children will vary in their rates of development because of each child's unique hereditary endowment and early experiences with the environment. Growth and development, especially during the early stages, are usually attributed to maturation, the unfolding of innate processes, and are unaffected, for the most part, by direct experiences with the environment. Maturation is differentiated from learning in that learning occurs through experiences with the environment. Maturation and learning, though easily separated for discussion purposes, are interwoven and difficult to isolate or explain in the growth and development of children.

Descriptions of the physical and motor development of children typically follow an age and stage sequence. The ages are rather arbitrary points used for convenience of discussion only. That is, a child moves progressively through the stages and does not make significant leaps from one to another. Convenient stages for descriptions of physical and motor development are the neonate, from birth to one month; babyhood, one month to two years; and early childhood, two years to six years.[7]

The Neonate

The newborn baby is approximately twenty inches long and weighs about 7½ pounds. The head is disproportionately large in comparison to the rest of the body. The baby has a number of reflex responses during this stage. There is some dispute over whether or not responses can be conditioned during this first month, but it is indisputable that the infant has many responses in his repertoire.

The neonate exhibits a startle reflex. This involves throwing the arms outward from the body. A grasping reflex, the closing of the fingers when the palm is pressed, is present also. A rooting reflex is exhibited when the hungry infant is touched on the face. The response includes quick jerky movements of the arms and a directional movement of the mouth toward the stimulation.

The neonate has a great deal of adjusting to do in this more varied environment. The infant is less restricted and begins to explore the surroundings and exercise all the senses. Both maturation and learning will inspire the continuous physical and motor development.

Babyhood

Babyhood includes the time from one month to two years. Upright locomotion is achieved during this period and the child continues to exhibit both maturation and learning in physical and motor development.

The reflex grasping of the neonate gradually disappears and is replaced by voluntary prehensive grasping. This newly acquired skill corresponds to the baby's increased ability to raise the head and peer about. Initial voluntary grasping efforts, beginning at about twenty weeks, do not involve the thumb. It is not until about forty weeks that the thumb is used and not until about fifty-two weeks is the thumb used proficiently. The entire act of reaching, grasping, and manipulation is relatively smooth and automatic by eighteen months.

During babyhood the child attains the upright position that leads to walking, running, and other skills. The upright position requires strengthening of the muscles that control the neck and head. By four months most babies can lift the head and turn it from side to side while in the prone position. At around six months, sufficient control exists in the trunk and arms to enable the baby to begin crawling and creeping.

Being able to sit up alone without support takes place at about seven months. Between seven and ten months enough strength is in the trunk and legs to permit the baby to stand while holding onto something for support. Independent walking can be achieved anywhere from seven to eighteen months, with thirteen to fourteen months being the average.

Prehension, grasping with the use of the thumb, and locomotion in the form of crawling, creeping, and walking enable the child to learn a host of different skills. Feeding oneself, scribbling with pencils and crayons, building with large and small blocks, and a myriad of other motor skills are part of the child's repertoire by the age of two.

Physical skills acquired during babyhood are developed and refined during early childhood.

Early Childhood

The period from two to six years is a time when basic skills, such as walking, are refined and other abilities, such as bladder control and dressing oneself, are first learned.

The progressive development of motor skills is best seen in the refinement and extension of walking, first learned in babyhood. Running and jumping require more strength and coordination than walking. The body must be propelled off the ground in both skills, requiring leg muscles stronger than those used for walking. Jumping with both feet and maintaining balance requires more physical coordination than walking.

Hopping, a skill similar to jumping but more difficult in that it requires a one-foot takeoff and landing on the same foot, is a progressively more complicated task for young children. Balancing on one foot is usually not achieved until about twenty-nine months. Success in hopping and jumping, as well as proficiency in running and walking, are extremely variable within and among individual children. Age norms for average attainment of these and other skills are readily available, but such charts and tables should be used cautiously in that normalcy is often mistakenly inferred. Normal physical and motor development occurs within a range of time periods, and centering on an average can be misleading when observing and comparing individual children.

Other motor skills often achieved by middle-class Western children before age six are throwing, catching, and ball bouncing. Tricycles and bicycles can be mastered by age six, and some children even learn to swim with minimal proficiency. In all these motor developments the natural unfolding of innate abilities (maturation) is blended with learning from the environment. A great deal of variation exists relative to when children gain proficiency in these motor skills.

Summary

Language development is best understood by considering both an inborn propensity to speak and learn rules of grammar as well as imitating and modeling others' speech. By 3½ years of age, most children are capable of understanding adult speech patterns and are well on their way to amassing a vocabulary that will be in the thousands by the time they are six.

Moral development, according to Kohlberg, follows a sequence of stages that is related to the child's level of intellectual development. Children's moral development can be promoted by discussing moral dilemmas and providing children opportunities to encounter points of view from stages higher than their own.

There is a great deal of variability in children's physical and motor development. All of the development follows the patterns of trunk to extremeties and gross motor to fine motor skills, but the exact roles played by heredity (maturation) and experience (learning) in contributing to physical and motor development have not been discovered.

NOTES

1. David McNeill, "Developmental Psycholinguistics," in *The Genesis of Language*, ed. Frank Smith and G.A. Miller, (Cambridge: The MIT Press, 1966), p. 2. More recent findings indicate full competence with all structures is not reached until later childhood. See Francis J. Divesta and D. S. Palermo, "Language Development," in *Review of Research in Education 2*, ed. Fred N. Kerlinger (Itasca, Ill.: F. E. Peacock Publishers, 1974), p. 81.

2. Francis J. DiVesta and D. C. Palermo, "Language Development," in *Review of Research in Education 2*, ed. Fred N. Kerlinger (Itasca, Ill.: F. E. Peacock Publishers, 1974), p. 64.

3. McNeill, "Developmental Psycholinguistics," p. 65.

4. Alfred L. Baldwin, "Social Learning," *Review of Research in Education 1*, ed. Fred N. Kerlinger (Itasca, Ill.: F. E. Peacock Publishers, 1973), p. 45.

5. McNeill, Developmental Psycholinguistics," p. 73.

6. Lawrence Kohlberg, "The Cognitive-Developmental Approach to Moral Education," *Phi Delta Kappan* 56 (June): 671.

7. William L. Hottinger, "Motor Development: Conception to Age Five," in *A Textbook of Motor Development*, ed. Charles B. Corbin (Dubuque: William C. Brown Co., 1973), p. 10.

Suggested Readings

Corbin, Charles B. A *Textbook of Motor Development*. Dubuque: William C. Brown Co., 1973. An elementary overview of physical and motor development of young children.

DiVesta, Francis J. and Palermo, D. S. "Language Development," In *Review of Research in Education 2*, ed. Fred N. Kerlinger. Itasca, Ill.: F. E. Peacock Publishers, 1974, pp. 55-107. A review of research in language development supporting the social learning view of language development.

Kohlberg, Lawrence. "The Cognitive-Developmental Approach to Moral Education." *Phi Delta Kappan* 56 (1975): 670-77. An overview of the stages of moral reasoning.

McNeill, David. "Developmental Psycholinguistics." In *The Genesis of Language*, ed. Frank Smith and G. A. Miller. Cambridge: The MIT Press, 1966, pp. 15-84. A comprehensive treatment of the psycholinguists' view of language development.

Suggested Activities

1. Listen to a group of two- and three-year-old children and record some of their speech. Select samples of the speech that reflect applications of grammatical rules. Select samples that indicate social learning of language. Discuss your results.

2. Listen to four and five year olds respond to a moral dilemma. Try to classify the responses according to Kohlberg's hierarchy. Can you find different levels of moral reasoning among the children?

3. Observe a day care or other early childhood setting. What evidence is there that the environment provides opportunities for physical exercise? See Appendix C for specific objectives in gross and fine motor skills to aid your observations.

Chapter Eight

Integrated Views

It is almost impossible to portray in words the functioning of a system in which every part is related to every other in such a way that each has a causal influence on the others.

Konrad Lorenz, On Aggression, *trans. Majorie Kerr Wilson (New York: A Bantam Book, 1971), p. xi.*

Educators and child development workers have often lamented that there is not a comprehensive theory of child development. There are well-researched theories on the ways children develop physically, mentally, emotionally, and morally, and there are theories that explain how they learn and acquire speech. What has yet to be developed is a theory that considers all of these aspects of development as interrelated parts of the whole organism.

Havighurst and Muller have not developed comprehensive theories of human development, but each has incorporated key concepts from other theories into a single framework that considers many aspects of development. The concept of developmental tasks, introduced by Havighurst, is useful in viewing the child as a complete person. Havighurst offers this definition: "A developmental task is a task which arises at or about a certain period in the life of the individual, successful achievement of which leads to his happiness and to success with later tasks, while failure leads to unhappiness in the individual, disapproval by the society and difficulty with later tasks."[1] Muller sees the successful accomplishment of each childhood task as a hurdle that must be overcome on the way to maturity. Throughout childhood skills are gained and abilities are acquired that slowly make the child no longer a child. Muller adds, "If the task is not accomplished . . . the child will remain in some way incomplete, unexpressed, and frustrated. The tasks which follow will be more difficult to master, the final product less complete and perfect maturity more difficult to achieve, if not completely impossible."[2]

Developmental tasks arise from three sources: physical maturation, societal expectations, and personal goals and values. Many tasks arise from a combination of these three influences. Some tasks, such as walking and talking, appear to be universal and are primarily influenced by maturation. Other tasks such as learning to read are specific to certain cultures. Lists of developmental tasks will vary from culture to culture and from time to time. The tasks given by Havighurst were written in 1948 and were based on the American middle-class culture with consideration being given to the

111

lower-class culture. The tasks offered by Muller were written in 1969 and pertain primarily to children in modern industrialized societies. Lists of developmental tasks will have to change just as the world changes.

The tasks listed for each age are closely interwoven. No task can be ignored, for its achievement or failure affects the achievement or failure of other current tasks. Developmental tasks are presented in a hierarchical manner. Successful achievement of early tasks prepares the individual to achieve tasks at the next stage, while failure to achieve a task causes partial or complete failure of tasks yet to come.

The concept of developmental tasks implies that there is an appropriate time for each task to be accomplished. There is a critical period in life for each task to be achieved. If the task is delayed for too long, it may never be successfully accomplished. This can be seen in the development of speech in the young child. If the basics for speech are not acquired during the critical period, future speech development is difficult and tedious. Likewise, until the critical period has arisen for a task, it is often frustrating if not impossible to accomplish the task. This can be seen when overzealous parents push their young child to learn to read before the child is physically or mentally ready for the task. The critical period when the mind and body are ready to accomplish a task and when society demands that the task be achieved is called the "teachable moment" by Havighurst.[3] Research in child development is useful to determine when to expect the teachable moment to arise for specific tasks. It is the responsibility of mature, helping adults to be alert to these critical periods and to provide an appropriate environment at the right time to assist children in the achievement of these tasks.

Havighurst's Developmental Tasks

Havighurst has divided the life cycle into six age periods.

	Stage	Ages
1.	Infancy and Early Childhood	Birth - Six
2.	Middle Childhood	Six - Twelve
3.	Adolescence	Twelve - Eighteen
4.	Early Adulthood	Eighteen - Thirty
5.	Middle Age	Thirty - Fifty-Five
6.	Later Maturity	Fifty-Five - Death

He has described from six to ten developmental tasks for each age. He readily concedes that the number of developmental tasks in each age is arbitrary and is dependent on the specificity of the tasks and the social situation in which one lives. The tasks that are given are defined broadly and could be subdivided into many smaller, more specific tasks. The developmental tasks given for the first two stages of life are most relevant for our purposes and will be described below.

Infancy and Early Childhood

Learning to Walk.   Usually between the ages of nine and fifteen months, the body has developed so that children are ready to walk. Once this basic skill is achieved, children learn to run, climb, skip, and jump.

Learning to Take Solid Food.   The importance of this task lies as much on the technique that is used to wean the baby from the breast or the bottle as on the baby's ability to chew and digest solid food. The treatment children receive during weaning and their age and feeding schedule all have an influence on their personality. Toddlers can usually handle solid foods sometime during the second year.

Learning to Talk.   Havighurst offers that babies are born with the physical ability to make many sounds that are used in speech, so children are biologically capable of speech long before they actually begin to talk. He further explains that the people in the babies' lives teach them to attach meanings to the sounds they make. For most children speech arrives between twelve and eighteen months. Research indicates that this period of time is the critical period for human speech. Even though there is still much to be learned at the end of the second year, if the child has not achieved the basic elements of speech, the task becomes extremely difficult and may never be accomplished well. If it is not accomplished here, it will present a problem in the future for achieving other tasks that are dependent on language. During this stage, children usually utter one-word sentences to let others know their needs. "Ba" means I want my bottle. "Mama" means where is my mother? Children's speech progresses during the first six years to include new sounds, especially consonants and blends of letters that make new sounds. At this time children are rapidly increasing their vocabularies, making longer sentences, and learning grammar.

Learning to Control the Elimination of Body Waste.   In defining the nature of this task, Havighurst says the child must "learn to urinate and defecate at socially acceptable times and places."4 Many American families attempt to toilet train their children at an early age and punish them rather severely for accidents. Biological evidence indicates, however, that the muscles and nerves in children's bodies that regulate voluntary elimination are not fully developed until the age of two to four or later. Psychologically, children seldom recognize a need to control their elimination before the age of two or two and one-half, therefore the teachable moment for toilet training will probably not occur until two to three years.

Learning Sex Differences and Sexual Modesty.   This is perhaps one of the most obvious areas where the societal demands for personality development in 1948 were different from what they are today. Havighurst states, "He (the young child) observes behavior differences between the sexes and very early is taught to behave like a boy or a girl, as the case may be."5 Today there are many in the early childhood field who believe that young children should be provided with warm, understanding, interesting, and competent role models of both sexes. These adults should be charged with guiding and encouraging each child to develop behaviors that are personally comfortable and compatible with the expectations that the child holds for the present and future regardless of his sex. Children should not be directed into adopting behaviors based on society's stereotypes of what "good little girls" or "tough little boys" should be.

Havighurst adds that children learn that there are anatomical differences between the sexes at an early age. This discovery is important and is the first step in developing a sexual identity. Children become interested in the physical differences between the sexes and often become fascinated with their own and others' sexual organs. "The kinds of sexual behavior he learns and the attitudes and feelings he develops about sex in these early years probably have an abiding effect upon his sexuality throughout his life."6

Achieving Physiological Stability.   This task is purely biological and is not affected by societal demands or cultural environments. Children's bodies are not physiologically stable like adults. Usually by the time the child is five, such things as the heart rate, the basal metabolic rate, the water content of the body, and the sugar and salt content of the blood have become stabilized.

Forming Simple Concepts of Social and Physical Reality.   Children during these early years learn to see similarities and regularities and come to make generalizations about things, events, and people. Children develop the ability to categorize and discriminate, and they learn labels for their concepts. "These are all good." "I just want the round ones." Much of a child's mental development is based on these concepts that are learned in early life.

Learning to Relate Oneself Emotionally to Parents, Siblings, and Other People.   Using language and physical gestures, children are able to share their joys, sorrows, frustrations, and accomplishments with others. Children identify with parents, siblings, and other people who are viewed as prestigious and imitate their behaviors. The way children in turn are viewed and treated by these important people is crucial to their emotional development.

Learning to Distinguish Right and Wrong and Developing a Conscience.   During this period children internalize the cautioning, warning, scolding voice of their parents and begin to distinguish good from bad and right from wrong as defined by their parents. This is the beginning of a child's conscience.

Middle Childhood

Learning Physical Skills Necessary for Ordinary Games.   The muscles and bones of children in this stage are developing in such a way that new physical skills are now possible. Swimming, jumping, running, kicking, throwing, and catching are now all possible. The muscles have become coordinated and skills developed in early childhood can now become more refined. Large muscle control precedes small muscle control, therefore success in the skills already mentioned will precede the ability to cut with ease, play an instrument, type, or perform any other task that requires control of fine muscles.

Building Wholesome Attitudes Toward Oneself as a Growing Organism.   The nature of this task is to learn to care for the body, to enjoy using the body, and to keep oneself safe. Included in this task is learning and applying rules of good health care such as cleanliness, good posture, proper diet, well-kept teeth, exercise, fresh air, and adequate sleep. This is also the age where children should be educated about sex in regard to reproduction and should be assisted to develop wholesome attitudes about sex to prevent feelings of inhibition or obsession in later life.

Learning to Get Along with Age-Mates.   This is the period when children begin to depend on their peers rather than on their families for approval and acceptance. The child must learn to make friends and get along with people who are not friends. During this age social habits are being developed such as being polite, playing fair, helping others, and working cooperatively. This task consumes a great deal of the child's energies.

Children need to develop the physical skills necessary to enjoy the games of childhood.

Learning an Appropriate Masculine or Feminine Role.   Again at this period of life Havighurst states that the nature of this task is "to learn to be a boy or a girl—to act the role that is expected and rewarded."[7] However, he adds that "the actual anatomical differences between boys and girls do not require a difference in sex role during middle childhood."[8] Rather than forcing or molding children into predetermined sex-typed personalities, perhaps this is the period in life when all children should be encouraged to be themselves, to explore many possible alternate roles, and to develop personalities and goals that are uniquely their own.

This rejection of reinforcing traditional male and female roles should not be confused with each child's need to develop a healthy sexual identity. Boys and girls should certainly know what their sex is and should be proud of their sex. Children need role models of their same sex as well as the opposite sex and should be taught through literature, history, and social experiences the accomplishments of both women and men.

Developing Fundamental Skills in Reading, Writing, and Calculating.   These are crucial skills to be learned if a person is to function in our society. The teachable moment for these skills is still a matter of debate. Many children are clamoring to learn to read as early as four or five years of age, while others seem to learn much more rapidly and easily if they wait until they are seven or eight. Achieving this task, as all other developmental tasks, is highly variable among individuals. All of the tasks need to be accomplished, but the exact time that the teachable moment arrives for any given individual and any given aspect of a task will vary greatly.

Developing Concepts Necessary for Everyday Living.   A concept is an abstract idea generalized from particular instances. During this age the task is to acquire many concepts, so that thinking is facilitated. The most successful and meaningful way for children to gain concepts is through personal experiences using concrete objects. Many children develop faulty concepts because they have not learned through actual experiences. As children reach the end of middle childhood, they should have a storehouse of concepts to draw upon, so they can generalize better and abstract more. By the end of middle childhood, they are prepared to learn more from reading than ever before.

Developing Conscience, Morality, and a Scale of Values.   The conscience began to be developed in early childhood with the internalization of the parents' warnings, rewards, and punishments. During middle childhood the conscience expands and the child learns the rules for socially acceptable behavior. This is also the period when children begin to establish their values.

Achieving Personal Independence.   The child becomes independent from family and adults by becoming a knowledgeable person who is capable of questioning parents or teachers. Children also become independent by turning to peers for friendship, encouragement, and reinforcement rather than to family for fulfillment of these needs. To become independent, children must have choices. They will be small at first and slowly become more important. Children should be allowed to plan part of their activities at school and home and profit from both successes and failures.

Developing Attitudes Toward Social Groups and Institutions.   "Middle childhood is the period when the basic social attitudes are learned, such as attitudes toward religion, toward social groups, toward political and economic groups. These attitudes may be changed by later experiences, but they do not change easily."[9] These social attitudes are learned from family, peers, teachers, and the rest of society. It is during these years that every society passes on to its children its most important social attitudes. In America children are often taught to favor democracy, public education for all, freedom of speech and religion, and the right of every person to improve his station in life through personal efforts. In addition, most families are training their children in their choices of religion, racial attitude, educational attitude, and attitude toward their fellow man.

Muller's Tasks of Childhood

Muller maintains that there are many legitimate ways to divide childhood, depending upon what factors of growth, development, or societal conditions are considered and that none of the divisions is superior over the others when total development is considered. He has therefore arbitrarily divided childhood into three main stages—infancy, school age, and adolescence—and has subdivided each stage into three ages with appropriate developmental tasks for each age. The childhood tasks of infancy and school age will be described.

Tasks of Infancy[10]

Age	Developmental Tasks
Age of the newborn	Still entirely physiological
Age of the young baby	1. Coordination of eyes and movements, the first "action"
	2. Ingestion of solid food
Age of early language	1. Acquisition of language
	2. Toilet training

The Age of the Newborn

During this age there is no specific developmental task. The developmental process is still entirely physiological. The birth process is the first educational experience encountered by babies. All babies show marked individual differences from birth, and there is evidence that indicates babies have unique personalities by the age of one month. There is little agreement on the length of this first period of life. Muller suggests using milestones that measure the movement from one age to the next rather than an arbitrary chronological age. The baby's first smile is the milestone that indicates the baby is leaving this age and entering the next.

The Age of the Young Baby

Coordination of Eyes and Movements, the First "Action." This task appears to be dependent only on maturation; it involves the achievement of motor competence. Perception is a necessary part of this action, but it cannot be separated from the movement provoked by the perception. The first perceptual process can be analyzed as four phases.

1. A stimulus in the environment provokes physiological change in the infant without causing any change in behavior.
2. Then the baby fixates on the stimulus. This is possible when eye-motor coordination is achieved.
3. Fixation affects all motor activity. The stimulus is followed by the eyes, the head, and sometimes the entire body; but all other motor activity is blocked momentarily, then released.
4. After fixation the baby moves the arm and sometimes the whole body toward the stimulus and tries to grasp it, often with success.

Throughout the first year of life, these movements become more decisive and precise, and many external stimuli are neutralized and no longer elicit actions from the baby. Babies gain more control over their movements and over their responses to the environment.

Ingestion of Solid Food. The eating of solid foods is the baby's first step toward independence. The abruptness of the transition from the breast or bottle to solid food and the attitude of the mother or teacher regarding this transition have an important influence on the baby's behavior. This task must be met satisfactorily because it provides the foundation for other tasks that lead to autonomy and provides the basis for a positive relationship with significant adults.

The Age of Early Language

Acquisition of Language.   Muller offers five stages of language development:

1. The prelinguistic stage—Included in this stage are all the sounds made by babies which do not function as language. These sounds include crying and babbling. Even though babies communicate with these sounds, they are not considered language because they lack intention. By the age of eleven months, the babbling repertoires of most babies contain all the sounds used by adults as well as other sounds that will in time disappear.

2. Passive control—At this stage sounds are meaningful to the baby, but they are not yet fully understood by others. Children react to the sound of words and to the situation in terms of past experience.

3. The first word—There are many conflicting theories about this stage of language acquisition. Babies attach meaning to sounds and understand some language that is spoken to them. They make sounds that begin to have meanings to others in their environment. A baby's first word is difficult to recognize because it is usually a part of the baby's babbling. Children first make their own words and then later imitate the words suggested by adults.

4. The first sentence—The first word and first sentence serve the same function, but a sentence exists when the baby recognizes the different functions of a series of words. There are two possible explanations for the structure of the baby's first sentence. First, the sentence may follow a certain word order commonly found in the language so that the sentence appears to be a telegraphic version of an adult sentence; "ball gone" means "the ball is gone." Another explanation of the structure of the first sentence is the pivot word. Many words a baby learns are fixed in the first position and serve as pivot words for other words in the vocabulary. "Bye-bye boy. Bye-bye dog. Bye-bye water." Bye-bye serves as a pivot word in combination with many other words.

5. Master of language—The first sentence discussed above marks the beginning of the mastery of language. There is little understanding of how language is learned past this point. Language is acquired rapidly, and complex grammar is learned. The ability to use plurals, possessions, prepositions, suffixes, and past and future tense are all acquired rather matter of factly by children. Even though the explanation of how language is learned is incomplete, comparative studies indicate that children who have had the most adult verbal stimulation are the most advanced in the mastery of language.

Toilet Training.   This is a complicated task that modern society demands be accomplished early in life. If maturation were the sole influence for the task, many additional years would be required before the task would be met. This difficult task demands that the child "substitute *voluntary* control for what was previously a reflex activity . . . (and) submit a source of intimate satisfaction to *social* control."[11] The child's ability to meet these expectations is usually met with rewards such as praise, attention, a hug, or a special treat. Lack of adaptation to these demands often brings punishment such as a show of disgust or disappointment by adults, harsh language, isolation, withdrawal of love, or a spanking. Children learn that they must give the demanding adults what they want every time, and this is elimination in an acceptable place in an acceptable way. When the task is accomplished, the child has a new feeling of autonomy and is ready to move to the next stage.

Tasks of the School Child[12]

Age	Developmental Tasks
Early childhood	1. The growth of self-awareness
	2. The attainment of physiological stability
	3. The formation of simple concepts related to physical and social reality
	4. The formation of the concepts of good and evil, appearance of the conscience
Childhood realism	1. Learning social communication in the peer group
	2. Learning the appropriate sexual role
	3. Achieving a healthy attitude to his own development
	4. Mastery of the physical skills necessary in games
	5. Learning reading, writing, and arithmetic
	6. Acquiring the concepts necessary in everyday life
The age of the first choices	1. The change of logic

The Age of Early Childhood

The Growth of Self-Awareness.   Muller describes the following stages of self-awareness:

1. Babies cannot distinguish between external objects and parts of their own bodies. They do not recognize themselves in a mirror. The visual image of self has not been unified with physical sensations felt all over the body. During infancy children still center on themselves and their relationship to the environment is poorly defined.

2. Children discover themselves through the actions of adults and peers toward them: Actions such as calling the baby by name and showing physical love. Children's names are their first source of identity in relation to others. Children also discover themselves by resisting and insisting on doing things for themselves.

3. Up until this point infants have reacted to others. Now they can form relationships with adults and peers. Relationships formed with peers enables children to place themselves in respect to others, and this enables them to form many varied relationships. The consistency of these relationships helps children acquire self-awareness.

4. In this stage the image of "self" is expanded to include one's name, habits, possessions, family, home, and friends. And children now recognize that each part of their body belongs to them and their total body is theirs.

The Attainment of Physiological Stability.   This task is purely biological. In children "emotion is known to cause physical effects which persist long after the original cause. The very small child is at the mercy of his emotions and they shake him to his foundations."[13] By the age of four or five, the child's body matures and begins to regulate against extreme changes in temperature and against the physical effects of emotions.

The Formation of Simple Concepts Related to Physical and Social Reality.   This task refers to the cognitive development of preoperational children discussed by Piaget. Representative thought begins, and the use of symbols is dramatic. Children's language skills become more complex and their vocabularies increase rapidly. Concepts about their physical and social worlds are gained through experience. Children's first moral concepts are also formed at this age.

The Formation of the Concepts of Good and Evil, Appearance of the Conscience.   Even though there is general agreement that the conscience is acquired, there is little agreement on how it is acquired. Freud explained the conscience as the adoption by the child of the rules imposed by parents and society. Behavioral scientists explain conscience in terms of operant conditioning. This theory maintains that the behavior that will be given is dependent on the situation and that certain behaviors are regularly given to avoid punishment or receive reward. Experiments by Piaget show that a child's morality progresses from an early morality that is authoritative to a more flexible and subjective type. At this early age research indicates that children's moral codes are oriented to obedience and punishment, and rules are rigid, absolute, arbitrary, and little respected.

The Age of Childhood Realism

Learning Social Communication in the Peer Group.   This task has to be mastered so that children can be educated in groups. Children must give up dependency behaviors and learn new responses of cooperation and obeying the instructions of teachers. They must learn to restrict their aggressive behaviors in order to strengthen positive social relations. And they must learn to share the time and attention of the teacher with other children and respond to the intellectual tasks presented by the teacher. Children do not adapt their behaviors to group situations all at once, but over the course of a few years these skills should be well in hand. A child who does not make these adaptations may develop antisocial attitudes or become isolated and withdrawn. In either case the future intellectual tasks may be seriously affected.

Learning the Appropriate Sexual Role. Children must recognize and assume behaviors appropriate to their sex. These behaviors have previously been suggested by parents and society. When parents or society create rigid divisions between acceptable behaviors for the two sexes, adapting to these expectations can be difficult and present problems for some children. However, in the United States and other industrial countries, the social differences between the sexes are slowly disappearing. This should provide a wider range of acceptable behaviors for children. Success in this task gives children a sense of security among peers.

Achieving a Healthy Attitude to His Own Development. The child begins to accept a certain amount of responsibility for personal hygiene and good health. This is also the age during which children compare their abilities and interests with those of peers instead of with those of adults and older children, and can accept age-appropriate activities and interests.

Mastery of the Physical Skills Necessary in Games. The field of games is the area where primary-school children excell, both in games of skill and strength. It is important for later development that the child feel secure and successful in these activities.

Learning Reading, Writing, and Arithmetic. These are the intellectual skills that must be mastered by all children for successful participation in an industrial society. Universal agreement does not exist on the age at which children should be taught these skills, nor is there agreement on the methods that should be used to teach them. Muller simply contends that many schools are failing to help children accomplish these tasks.

Acquiring the Concepts Necessary in Everyday Life. Based on Piaget's framework the child has now reached the stage of concrete operations. The concepts of reversibility and conservation have been achieved, and the child has learned two new logical rules that are important for success in school: inclusion of classes and serial ordination. Inclusion of classes enables the child to consider the parts of a whole separate from the whole itself. Serial ordination allows the child to arrange a series in ascending or descending order on the basis of size, length, weight, color, quantity, height, etc.

The Age of First Choices

The Change of Logic. The achievement of formal logic is a turning point in mental development. With formal logic children have control of their own thoughts, can think theoretically, and can reason deductively. They do not cling to concrete things as before and can consider abstract hypotheses. Thought is logical and reversible. Success at this task is dependent on the intellectual level of the child, but environmental factors can be influential in helping a child master this skill. The accomplishment of this task is necessary to all the rest of education.

Summary

Both Havighurst and Muller present theories that attempt to embrace all aspects of behavior. Their developmental tasks are arranged in a hierarchical manner, thus requiring successful completion of one before the next can be fully mastered. While each of their theories lacks specific detail, this is compensated for by a comprehensiveness that other theories discussed earlier do not achieve.

NOTES

1. Robert J. Havighurst, *Developmental Tasks and Education,* 2d ed. (New York: Longmans, Green and Co., 1952), p. 2.
2. Phillippe Muller, *The Tasks of Childhood* (New York: McGraw-Hill Book Co., 1969), p. 145.
3. Havighurst, *Developmental Tasks and Education,* p. 5.
4. Ibid., p. 11.
5. Ibid., p. 12.
6. Ibid.
7. Ibid., p. 19.
8. Ibid.
9. Ibid., p. 27.
10. Muller, *The Tasks of Childhood,* p. 147.
11. Ibid., p. 181.
12. Ibid., p. 184.
13. Ibid., p. 193.

Suggested Readings

Havighurst, Robert J. *Developmental Tasks and Education.* 2d ed. New York: Longmans, Green and Co., 1952. The concept of developmental tasks is introduced in this book. Havighurst offers his six stages of life. Each of the developmental tasks appropriate for each stage is discussed in detail.

_____. *Human Development and Education.* New York: Longman, 1953. The developmental tasks are discussed. Havighurst defines the role of the schools as an instrument to help children accomplish these tasks. He makes recommendations that involve the schools as a major influence in assisting children to accomplish the tasks.

Muller, Phillippe. *The Tasks of Childhood.* New York: McGraw-Hill Book Co., 1969. The tasks discussed in this book were written as appropriate for children in industrial societies. The concept was adapted from Havighurst. Muller has drawn heavily from both European and American theorists to formulate the tasks.

Suggested Activities

1. Discuss the advantages an integrated theory of child development has for planning educational activities. What are the disadvantages?
2. Observe a group of young children and try to determine the developmental tasks at which they are working. Are the children working at several tasks or only one?
3. Describe one child in terms of his or her success at achieving one developmental task.

Section Four

Sample Applications

The chapters in this section are samples of curriculum development and implementation with four different groups of children. The children in the examples have been divided into four groups based primarily on their ages. This is a common procedure in many day care centers and other early childhood programs. It is a reasonable practice because grouping children by age helps narrow the range of abilities within a group and makes planning appropriate activities and preparing the environment a simpler task. However, grouping by age is not always possible or desirable. Many view the mixed age groupings often found in family day care homes and small centers as a strength of these settings. Children of different ages can be together; younger children learn from older ones, and older children learn to accept some of the responsibility for the younger ones. Mixed age grouping is often called family grouping because children of varying ages play, interact, and learn from each other as they would in a home/neighborhood setting. Both of these ways of grouping children have advantages. The children in our samples were grouped by age to simplify the task of discussing appropriate goals, objectives, and activities for each age group. We do not have a preference for grouping children. The decision of how to group children will be determined by the physical setting, purpose/philosophy, and goals of the group. Regardless of how children are grouped, the procedures for curriculum implementation are the same.

The next four chapters are an attempt to select goals appropriate for four different age groups of children and to demonstrate how the choice of goals influences what objectives are selected and what activities are planned. The goals selected for elaboration are in no way the "right" goals for children's programs, nor are they the only ones that could be chosen. They simply reflect the authors' interpretation of the theories in Section Three and previous experience in working with children of these ages in day care settings.

The theories explored in Section Three invite other interpretations that may suggest different goals. And there are other developmental theories and other child development studies not discussed in this book that would offer a basis for selecting different goals. The right set of goals for a day care setting will be those selected by well-informed adults with a particular group of children in mind. Goals also will vary depending on the needs of the children. A center that is set up to accommodate a large number of physically handicapped children will probably have goals somewhat different from those of a center that enrolls physically normal children.

The selection of a set of goals is not an easy task and should not be taken lightly. Many factors must be considered: the individual needs of the children, theories of child development, and the purpose/philosophy of the setting. Stating goals can be a difficult process even though a group of adults has reached agreement on an area of concern that they would like to see included as a goal. Goals can be looked upon as something to be completed or accomplished, or goals can be viewed as an ongoing process that is never complete. For instance, if the area of social development is a concern, a goal might be stated as, "The children show respect for each other and are able to share and cooperate." This goal is written in the form of the desired finished product. It can be achieved and measured. Social development is a process that continues from childhood into adulthood and remains a part of human development throughout life. Therefore, a goal might be stated as "To provide opportunities for optimum social development to occur." This goal will never be completed. It can only be worked toward. Goals may be stated as a final product or as a continuing process. Thinking about goals from these two perspectives should help in the final writing. Goals have been written in both ways in this section. Once goals are chosen and carefully stated, they should become the backbone of the program, providing direction for selecting objectives and activities, selecting equipment, arranging the room, and planning the daily schedule.

As was stated in Chapter Two, a goal is a broad global statement, whereas an objective is a more precise statement that pertains to only a part of the goal. For instance, the goal "To provide the children with opportunities to develop language skills" might be broken down into numerous specific objectives. A few objectives that could be appropriate are: responds to own name, follows a familiar direction, can identify fifteen familiar objects, can retell a short story. These objectives are written from the perspective of what skills we want to see the children develop; that is, babies learn to respond to their own names and follow a familiar direction. Some educators insist that all objectives be written in a form that states specific expectations of the child that can be achieved and measured. Many objectives can be written in this way, but others are more appropriately written from the perspective of what is expected of the teacher in relation to the children. Throughout this section we will be writing objectives from both the perspective of the child's behavior and the teacher's behavior.

Goal statements are often appropriate for children of varying ages, but objectives are more specific and focus on the developmental level of each child. A review of the theories in Section Three reminds us that many areas of children's development occur hierarchically. The objectives that are written to meet the goals should reflect the hierarchies in development. If language development is a goal for children from birth to age ten in a particular setting, then the objectives for the younger children will likely be different from those for the older children. The differences in these objectives should reflect an understanding of how language develops, an awareness of what skills each child has already accomplished, and a knowledge of what other tasks would be reasonable current objectives for each child.

Once a goal has been subdivided into appropriate objectives, the next steps in curriculum implementation are to create an environment, select equipment, plan a schedule, and devise activities that will assist the children in accomplishing the objectives. It is at this point that many programs that embrace the same goals and objectives can differ in how the goals are reached. You will remember from Chapter Three that the purpose/philosophy of a setting will be reflected in the techniques, attitudes, and behaviors of the teachers. Even though two programs hold the same goals and objectives, their purpose/philosophies can dictate different methods to accomplish the goals. Many techniques can be used to accomplish the same objective, and it is important to remember that there is no best or right way. The key is in finding the methods and techniques that are best suited to the children, the teachers, and the families being served.

These next chapters should serve as sample applications of goals, objectives, and activities. It was noted earlier that the goals for these chapters were based on the authors' interpretation of child development theories and previous experience in day care settings. They are also influenced by the authors' purpose/philosophy of a day care setting with which they are associated. This philosophy is offered here not as a model but as the starting point to understand the reasoning for the choices throughout the chapters. The purpose/philosophy that guided the rest of this section includes:

1. The early years of life are important for all areas of development.
2. No area of development is more important than any other area. Day care programs should reflect a concern for the child as a total being.
3. Children are modifiable and capable of being guided and directed.
4. High-quality child care can have positive effects on the development of the child.
5. Equal opportunity is important for all children regardless of sex, race, or creed.
6. Interaction and cooperation between the day care staff and the child's family is crucial.

Chapter Nine

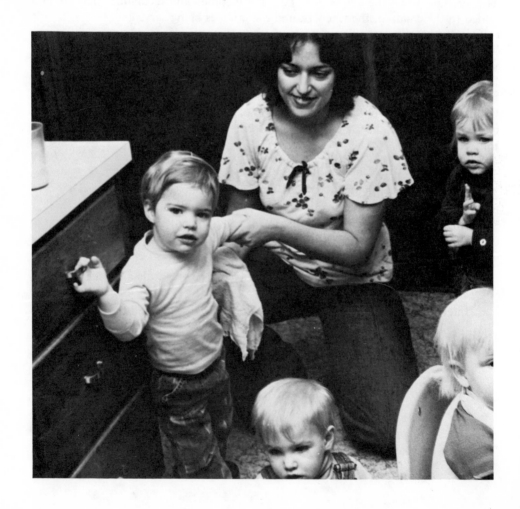

Infants through Eighteen Months

We are born feeble and need strength; possessing nothing, we need assistance; beginning without intelligence, we need judgment. All that we lack at birth and need when grown up is given us by education.

>*Jean Jacque Rousseau,* The Emile of Jean Jacques Rousseau, trans. and ed. William Boyd *(New York: Bureau of Publications, Teachers College, Columbia University, 1962), p. 11.*

Providing care for infants in groups is one of the pressing concerns of professionals involved in day care. Only in the last decade have infant programs received attention as legitimate services for families and babies. The increasing demand by families for infant care coupled with research findings that point to the importance of the first years of life in future development have given new prestige to the area of day care for infants. The challenge to all who are involved in infant care is to ensure that the available settings are designed to provide quality care that meets the many needs of the infants and families enrolled.

Goals for an Infant Program

Day care settings designed for infants are unique in that a major portion of each day must be devoted to the physical care and safety of each baby. Adults working with infants should not feel hampered or limited by the lack of free time; rather, they should capitalize on the time spent in routine care to meet the goals of the program. Indeed, the accomplishment of many goals selected for infants is dependent on the total day care environment and cannot be limited to morning activity time. The needs of infants are numerous and complex; and although goals are written as individual statements, the day care environment should reflect an integration of the goals with each serving as a guide to optimum total development for each child. The goals that follow represent one way of viewing the needs of infants and suggestions for planning the environment to meet those needs.

Meet the Physiological Needs of Each Infant

Infants come into the world as totally helpless organisms. They are dependent on adults for food, shelter, clothing, and safety, and unlike any other animal this dependency continues for many years. Whether the adults caring for an infant are the parents at home or the teachers in a day care setting, the physical care of an infant is a high priority. As Maslow has indicated, the most basic of all needs are those that pertain to the physical body. Until these needs are met, there is no room in the baby's life for other needs. What are the physiological needs of a baby? The most obvious is food. Babies cannot hold large amounts of food at one time, so they must be fed often and given food that is appropriate for their sensitive digestive systems. When a baby feels hunger, he experiences an all-encompassing feeling. Nothing else will satisfy the baby except food. Waiting for food seems intolerable to an infant. Long waits for food can cause the baby to become anxious and fearful and can lead to a sense of mistrust of the world. As babies grow older and larger, they can usually accept a delay in receiving their food if they are given reassurance from a loving adult. In group care where there may be as many as three or four infants per adult individual, eating needs can be met with planning. Often by the time babies are eight or nine months old, their eating schedules are not unlike those of older children and mealtimes need not be as frequent as they are for younger babies. The food that babies receive must be given careful consideration, so each infant receives a well-balanced, nutritious diet.

Another physiological need of infants is bodily comfort. This need includes frequent diaper changes to prevent chafing and to keep the infant free from bacteria. Every center that enrolls infants should be equipped with a diapering area that is safe and sanitary. Keeping the baby clean is also a part of this need. Babies should be given frequent tub baths. Sponge baths will keep the babies fresh and clean between tub baths, and the babies' hands, faces, noses, and ears should be kept clean throughout the day. Clothing that does not bind the body or inhibit movement is a necessity for comfort, and the clothes worn by babies should be appropriate for the weather.

Adequate sleep is another of the physiological needs of infants to which teachers must attend. Safe, clean, comfortable sleeping quarters are necessary, and a quiet, relaxed atmosphere that is conducive to sleep should be created. Infants who sleep when others are playing must be isolated from the group, so they can sleep without being disturbed.

A sanitary environment should be a goal for all day care settings, but it is of prime importance when infants are cared for in groups. Infants and toddlers chew indiscriminately on toys and furniture, and their fingers are often in their mouths. Germs and contagious diseases can spread easily in a group of infants if preventive measures are not taken. The floor, cribs, and furniture should be disinfected every day, and the toys should be disinfected periodically throughout the day. Babies' hands and faces should be washed well before each meal, and teachers must keep their own hands free from germs after diapering and bathing the babies.

One extremely important preventive measure that must be undertaken for infants is a complete immunization program to prevent disease. Parents usually assume the primary responsibility for this program, but records must be kept in the center to ensure that children receive this necessary protection. In many locations public health nurses will visit a center regularly to keep the children's immunizations current. Parents and staff members should cooperate to ensure that children are tested for other diseases such as tuberculosis and sickle cell anemia. If these or other diseases are diagnosed, proper steps can be taken to help the child regain normal health.

The age from birth to eighteen months is a period of rapid growth and development. Many developmental milestones are reached during this period. Infants learn to crawl and walk, they utter their first words, they smile and laugh, and they get their first teeth. This is the age during which the intellectual, social, physical, and emotional foundations for the rest of life are being built. This is therefore the age where children must be watched critically for any sign of developmental deficiency. Teachers can be trained to observe the infants for signs of physical problems or developmental lags. Pediatric nurses, physicians, and speech, hearing, and vision specialists from local agencies should be called on to assist the teachers to detect any present or potential problem. Early detection of handicapping problems can lead to correction and improvement. If problems are not detected until later in childhood, remediation can be much more difficult.

Create an Environment of Trust, Security, Happiness, and Safety

This goal provides for sound emotional development through a positive, supportive environment. There is a degree of overlap between this goal and the one previously discussed, but the meeting of the physiological needs alone will not guarantee that this goal is met because it requires additional support and encouragement from adults and the environment. However, if the physiological needs have not been met regularly, accomplishing this goal is extremely difficult. Even though meeting the physiological needs of the infant plays a crucial role in meeting this goal, we will assume that these needs have been met and concern ourselves with additional ways to accomplish this goal.

Developing a feeling of trust is the first emotional challenge for infants according to Erikson. Babies must learn to trust before they can develop other positive emotions. A sense of trust can be developed in infants if their physical needs are met regularly and they are shown love and acceptance. The behaviors of teachers and parents have an immediate effect on the babies' emotional development. For instance, if during the course of feeding, bathing, and diapering, babies are handled roughly, ignored, or spoken to harshly, feelings of mistrust may develop. If babies are taken from the crib only long enough to be fed and diapered and are never held and hugged, feelings of rejection may develop. Feelings of mistrust can also be developed if infants are allowed to cry for long periods of time without being attended.

Many of the objectives for meeting this goal will refer to the adults' behavior and attitude in caring for the babies. For instance, "Each baby shall be held and loved frequently throughout the day" is a realistic expectation. This objective implies that the teachers will treat the babies gently and demonstrate affection by patting, hugging, talking, and smiling. This is the manner in which the babies should be treated every time they encounter the teachers. Another possible objective that can help develop a sense of trust is "Each baby is greeted upon arrival and made to feel welcome." All the infants should be called by name and welcomed verbally. Young infants should be held for a few minutes to reassure them as they are separated from parents. Older infants may also need to be held or reassured with a pat or hug. There are many other objectives that teachers will want to consider. Developing a sense of trust in an infant must be a constant, continuous effort.

According to Maslow's hierarchy of needs, when the physiological needs are met the safety needs arise. He included both physical and mental safety in this category. A safe physical environment should be a matter of routine for all day care settings regardless of the age of the children. Equipment should be well maintained to prevent accidents. Inside rooms as well as the outside play area should be checked throughout the day for objects that could injure a child. Day care staff should take precautions against all possible sources of danger such as a heating system that could burn a child, an open stairwell, or unscreened high windows. Physical safety of the children must be the concern of all adults in the day care setting.

The safety needs that pertain to emotional well-being require a different set of objectives. "A familiar environment is maintained" is an appropriate expectation. Babies prefer the familiar to the unfamiliar. They are often frightened by new faces, new surroundings, and new routines. The adults in a baby's life should remain as stable as possible. Frequent replacement of teachers should be avoided with a group of infants. The routine that is established with a group of infants serves as a source of security and predictability. It, too, should remain stable. The schedule should not be so rigid that new activities or special events cannot occur, but it should be regular enough that it is a source of comfort rather than confusion. Twelve-month-old Shannon knows that soon after she awakens from her nap, she will get an afternoon snack. She wakes up, sits up in her crib, rubs her eyes, pats her hands, and says, "Cookie." This is the kind of security a routine should give to babies.

"Infants should be comforted and reassured when they are frightened or anxious." The most conscientious teachers cannot totally prevent the babies in their care from experiencing feelings of fear and anxiety. Situations arise daily in the lives of infants that can be frightening to them. For instance, when fourteen-month-old Suzie suddenly became ill and threw up her lunch, she was frightened. When the local fire station conducted a test of the sirens during nap time, all the babies were startled and frightened. Teachers must respond to babies' fright by comforting and reassuring them. Babies might need to be held close for a while before they feel safe again, or they might simply need a kiss on a bumped arm. Whatever the situation, babies should not have to handle fear and anxiety without the support of a loving, caring adult.

Although the objectives illustrated pertain to the teachers' behaviors, the result of meeting these and similar objectives should be reflected in the infants' behavior. An infant who is happy, trusting, and secure will behave very differently from one who is unhappy, not trusting, and insecure. A list of behaviors that reflect healthy emotional development in babies could easily be formulated. This list could be used as a check to ensure that the bahaviors exhibited by the teachers are having the desired effect on the babies.

Provide Opportunities for the Development of Language Skills

When we refer to the development of language skills in young children, an image of a baby who is learning to talk usually comes to mind. Indeed, learning to talk is an important part in language development, but it is not the only step nor the first step involved. Infants develop receptive language such as attending, responding, discriminating, and following directions before they develop expressive language. Therefore, when specific objectives are selected in the area of language development, all of the components of language must be considered.

One objective that appears very simple is "To provide the infants with many occasions to hear speech every day." No matter which language development theory one accepts, it is quite certain that children will not learn a language if they do not hear it. It is almost as certain that children will learn a language to some extent if they do hear it. This objective does not require a special time set aside to talk to the babies. It is an ongoing process. When babies are being diapered, they should be talked to. They can be talked to at mealtime, playtime, outside time as well as when they arrive and when they leave. There are unlimited opportunities during the day for the babies to hear speech from their teachers. For instance, it is time to go outside and play. A teacher who realizes the value of talking to the babies might say, "Now it is time to go outside. Are you all ready? Let's get your sweaters on. Here is Billy's sweater and here is Kristen's. Where is your sweater, Juan? Oh, here it is. I am going to open the door now. What a sunny day." Infants slowly learn that speech has meaning by hearing it in many situations. Talking to the infants in this casual way, the teacher labels objects such as sweater and door. Children must have labels for things in their environment before they can communicate. "Providing labels for common objects" is a worthy objective for language development of infants. Having a label for things such as mama, ball, bottle, bed, snow, grass, and fish enables the child to more fully comprehend speech that is heard. It is usually these common labels that the infant first attempts to speak.

Another objective in developing receptive language might be "The babies can respond to their own names by turning, smiling, or cooing." Again, this objective, as many in the area of language development, does not necessarily require a special activity time. The infants can be called by name and be referred to by name many times during the day. "Gordon, do you want more milk? Let me check your diaper, Sylvia. Where is Buckskin? Peekaboo." When the babies can sit up, games that include their names can be a source of real fun. "Here's the ball for Elita, and here is the ball for Dawn. Can you roll the ball to me Elita? Now I am going to roll it back to you. Here is the ball for Elita."

An appropriate objective for older infants could be "The babies can respond to a simple direction." They will only be able to do this if they have labels for objects and comprehend the meaning of some verbs. "Roll the ball, David. Rachel, bring the book to me. Zachary, sit down in the chair." If the infant cannot or does not follow the direction, the teacher can provide assistance as a means of explanation. If Zachary does not sit down in the chair, the teacher can pick him up and place him in a sitting position in the chair and repeat, "Zachary, sit down in the chair."

Havighurst tells us that babies usually begin to talk between the ages of twelve and eighteen months. He calls this the crucial period for the development of speech. An appropriate objective might be "The baby can say five or more words by the age of eighteen months." During this period babies usually say one word at a time that represents a complete thought. "More" usually means "I want more." Teachers can assist the baby to develop more complex speech by expanding what the child has said. "You want more milk." Again, this is done throughout the day whenever the infant speaks. When babies are capable of one-word statements, they can be encouraged to talk by being asked questions that can be answered in one word. "What do you want?" "More." "What is this?" "Dog." There are numerous other objectives that are appropriate for infant language development, and there are many activities that can be helpful to accomplish the objectives. The teacher's role is to subdivide the goals of the curriculum and select or create specific objectives and activities to assist the infants in accomplishing the objectives and reaching the goals.

Provide for Optimum Motor Development

From birth when infants are unable to lift their own heads until the age of eighteen months when most can walk, climb stairs, grasp, and throw, tremendous motor development occurs. Young babies are characterized by global movement. They lack the control to move one part of their body without moving all over. As

A well-equipped outside play area can provide many opportunities for motor development in infants and toddlers.

babies develop, their movements become more particularized and they gain the ability to move specific parts of their body without moving other parts. Motor development is a gradual process that usually occurs in a sequential fashion. Each accomplishment serves as a stepping stone to new and more complex skills. Motor development progresses from the large muscles to the small muscles and from the trunk of the body to the extremities. For example, babies develop control of large arm muscles before they develop control of smaller finger muscles, and they develop control of back muscles (trunk) that are used in sitting before they develop control of leg muscles (extremities) for crawling. Objectives that are selected for each infant should reflect a knowledge of the infant's present motoric abilities and a knowledge of what additional motor skills the infant is physically capable of achieving. For instance, most infants cannot roll from their stomach to their back until they can first raise their shoulders and chest off the crib by lifting their head and pushing with their arms. "The baby can roll over from the stomach to the back" would be a realistic objective for four-month-old Jason who has head control and can elevate his chest by using his arms. This same objective would be premature for four-month-old Wally who also has head control but cannot yet successfully elevate his shoulders and chest with his arms.

Motor development during infancy encompasses many specific skills that will require numerous specific objectives. The ability to grasp, crawl, roll over, stand, sit, walk, scoot, climb, pull, and hold are all areas of concern in motor development. Each of these broad areas can be subdivided into numerous objectives. For instance, the skill of sitting up can easily be divided into six or more specific objectives. "Can sit erect with support." "Can sit alone momentarily." "Can sit alone when placed in a sitting position." "Can lean forward and sideways from a sitting position to retrieve objects." "Can change from a prone to a sitting position." "Can pivot in a sitting position." Each of these objectives will be the most appropriate at some point in the babies' development.

When the appropriate objectives are selected for each baby, a special environment can be created that is conducive to motor development and specific activities can then be planned to accomplish these objectives. If one of the current objectives for nine-month-old Celeste is "She can pivot in a sitting position," there are several activities that can be conducted to help her meet the objective. The teacher could place Celeste's favorite toy to the side and slightly out of her reach and then verbally encourage her to pivot around to reach it. Whether or not Celeste is successful in her attempt to obtain the toy, the teacher should smile and pat or hug her and verbally reinforce her for her efforts. Skinner's theory tells us that children are more likely to repeat behaviors for which they have been rewarded. The next time the teacher places a toy out of reach so that a pivot is required to reach it, Celeste will probably make a noble attempt to reach the toy. After a short time, being able to reach desired toys will become the reinforcement for pivoting. Another activity that would encourage pivoting would be to play a hiding game with Celeste. The teacher could station himself directly behind Celeste and then call her by name. "Where is Celeste? Oh, here she is," the teacher could say as he or she peeks around the side of Celeste and then draws back out of sight. The teacher could continue to peek around and draw back out of sight laughing and playing, enticing Celeste to pivot around. These two activities performed several times over a period of a few weeks might be all that is needed to help Celeste learn to pivot in a sitting position. When this same objective is selected for Alfonso, these two activities might not interest him at all. To be prepared to meet the interests and the needs of each baby, teachers should have knowledge of many possible activities that would help in accomplishing each objective.

Provide an Environment Leading to Intellectual Development and Stimulation

Infants are born only with reflex abilities to react to their environment. They respond to sound and light, grasp objects that touch their palm, cry to signal distress, and suck when something touches their lips. Infants are not born with well-developed cognitive structures, but during infancy intellectual development is a rapid process. By the age of eighteen months, most infants can use objects correctly, follow directions, remember events, solve problems, understand some spatial relationships, make visual discriminations, classify objects by form, and understand simple concepts. The development of these abilities is not automatic. The infant must have a stimulating environment and numerous experiences to develop these skills.

Before babies are intellectually ready for an objective and activities that involve abstract concepts such as spatial relationships, other basic skills must be acquired. Piaget tells us that during the first stage of development infants are not aware of the separateness of their own bodies apart from the rest of the environment, nor are they aware that objects in the environment are separate from one another. They are not able to distinguish figures from the background. For instance, a young infant does not realize that a doll in the corner of the crib is a separate object from the crib. Bruner's theory maintains that a baby is only able to confer reality on these objects through interaction with them. The doll will never be separate from the crib until the baby experiences the doll and the crib as two different objects. Babies learn that their bodies are separate from the surroundings and learn to distinguish objects through experiences that involve the body, the senses, and the environment. Babies must be given many daily experiences to explore and become familiar with their surroundings. A time should be set aside each day during which the babies are provided with interesting toys and other objects for exploration and interaction. The structure of intellect indicates that the first way a child has to conceive information is as a segregated unit. Before children can form classes, relationships, or implications, they must first understand the single unit. The only way a baby can comprehend that the ball is a unit apart from the rug it lays on is to experience the ball and the rug as two separate things. Many varied experiences with the environment enable babies to understand and comprehend the objects that comprise their world.

The intellectual abilities can be used as objectives. For instance, an objective related to understanding simple spatial relationships might be stated as "The infant is able to demonstrate by action the comprehension of two or more spatial concepts such as in, out, up, down, or under." From Guilford's structure of intellect, we see that cognition is one of the most basic and first-acquired intellectual skills. Cognition is the ability to understand or comprehend. It is the ability to recognize information in various forms. Comprehension of such abstract concepts as spatial relations will take time and many varied experiences. First the baby must hear these words over and over in everyday situations: "I'm going to take you out of your crib." "The bird is up in the sky." "Let us blow the bubbles up in the air. Oh, they are coming down." "The doll is under your blanket."While hearing these words, the baby should be shown where the bird, bubbles, and doll are. The baby should have an active role in blowing the bubbles and looking for the doll.

Infants should be given opportunities to experience these spatial relationships with their own bodies. "Sam, let's get in the box." After this Sam and the teacher crawl into a large box. "Sam is in the box. Are you ready to get out? Now we are out of the box. Look, Becky is on the box." Infants can also experience these spatial relationships with parts of their bodies. "Put your foot in your shoe." "Take your hand out of the bag." "I am putting the hat on your head." Toys that are given to infants can also help reinforce these concepts. "Jack is in the box; oops, he popped out." "You put the boy in the car." "Can you take the puzzle pieces out? Good. Now can you put them back in the puzzle?"

Piaget's label for the first stage of cognitive development is sensorimotor. This word indicates that infants develop intellectually through the use of their senses and through physical or motor involvement. Activities that are planned to foster the comprehension of spatial relationships or any other intellectual skills should include the child's senses and motor experiences. In the previous examples the senses of sight, hearing, and touch were used as were motor activities of crawling in and out, putting in and taking out, and blowing and lifting.

Another important objective in intellectual development is "The baby can demonstrate an understanding of simple concepts." Babies cannot form concepts until they recognize individual objects. In infancy concept formation involves the ability to recognize new objects based on attributes that are held in common with other familiar objects. When asked to identify a familiar fuzzy green tennis ball, fifteen-month-old Sarah says, "Ball." If she understands the concept "ball" she should be able to identify a Ping-Pong ball, a basketball, and a beach ball that she has never before seen. She makes the identifications based on common attributes such as the ability to roll, the ability to bounce, and the familiar shape of all the balls. If Sarah cannot identify the new balls, then her understanding of the word *ball* applies only to her green tennis ball and she does not understand the concept.

There are several activities that can be planned to help infants develop concepts. The teacher can play a "bring me game." "Luke is through with the book. Luke, can you bring me your book? Now can you get Edna's book? Good, now we have two books. I will help you get Larry's book. His is a big one. Look at all the different books." Or the teacher can help the babies recognize common attributes of objects. In the above example if Sarah did not understand the concept "ball" the teacher could introduce a new ball to her and say, "Sarah, do you want to play with this big ball? I will roll it to you. Can you roll it to me? This one rolls like your ball. Can you roll your ball? Good! Now, can you roll the big ball? Great, Sarah, you did it. Now we have two balls."

Infancy is a time when remarkable intellectual growth can take place. Teachers must be alert to the accomplishments and needs of each child and should be conscious of preparing an environment, activities, and interactions with the infants that will promote optimum intellectual development.

Typical Day in an Infant Center

Lisa is seven months old and has been attending the West Side Day Care Center for four months. Her mother selected West Side after much searching for a center that offered quality care for infants. It appeared that this staff gave the babies good physical care and created a warm, loving, stimulating environment. Let's see what a typical day is like for Lisa and the others in the infant area.

Lisa's mother is a conscientious parent who is aware of the needs of a small baby. Before they leave for the center in the morning, Lisa is given a sponge bath and dressed in comfortable clothes for the day. She is also given a bottle of juice to prevent hunger until she is fed breakfast at the center at 7:30 A.M.

On the door of the infants' area is posted a schedule of the activities for the day. It is important for parents to know what their children do during the day. This schedule is only a general one that lets parents know what times the babies are fed, when they nap, when they go outside, when they play, etc. A much more specific plan for the day is kept in the room and used by the staff.

As Lisa's mother opens the door to the infant room, she hears babies laughing, playing, babbling, and even one whimpering. The baby in distress is fifteen-month-old Jeff. He has just returned to the center from a week at home with a cold, and he is experiencing some anxiety at having his mother leave him. One of the teachers is holding Jeff, talking to him, and reassuring him that he is safe and that his mother will return. Three other babies are in a large corral, adapted from Russian day care centers. The corral gives the babies room to crawl, creep, pull up, and play; but at the same time it confines them somewhat as other infants are arriving and adults are entering and leaving the room. The corral contains many toys including rattles of all kinds, balls, soft animals, small boxes, dolls, and soft cardboard blocks. The room appears bright and attractive to Lisa and her mother. The room is painted a bright, sunny yellow, and there are colorful prints on the walls and lively curtains at the windows. There are open shelves with toys for the children, and above each baby's crib is a lively mobile and an exercise bar with rings and pulleys. These teachers are aware of Maslow's findings that a need for an aesthetically pleasing environment is extremely important in young children. They attempt to fulfill this need in every possible way.

When Lisa and her mother enter the room, they are greeted warmly by the second teacher. She takes Lisa's diapers, clothes, and formula; labels them; and puts them away. She quickly jots down on Lisa's daily sheet any instructions or information from Lisa's mother. These notes might include information about a restless night, a need for a hat when the babies go outside, or simply a report of a new food that Lisa had eaten the evening before. Having this information in written form enables all the teachers as well as the director to accommodate the particular needs of each infant. A teacher who arrives after Lisa and quickly reads the daily sheets is then able to say, "Oh, I know why you're so sleepy this morning. You didn't sleep well last night." Then Lisa can be fed a little early and put down for her nap before the scheduled time. On this same daily sheet, information is recorded throughout the day that is of importance to the baby's development and well-being. Notes are made on daily accomplishments, eating and napping, elimination, attitude, symptoms of illness, accidents, etc. With these sheets as a reference, the development of each infant can be watched carefully and parents can be given accurate reports about their baby's daily progress. A teacher is able to greet Lisa's mother in the afternoon with a statement such as "Lisa didn't eat much lunch. She seemed to be too cross and sleepy, but when she woke up she had a whole jar of applesauce and a full bottle for an afternoon snack. And do you know what else she did today? She crawled up the low stair platform all by herself."

In less than five minutes Lisa has been welcomed, her things have been put away, and necessary notes have been made. She has also had a chance to look around the room and spot all of the familiar cues that help her recognize this as her safe place away from home. She sees the smiling, familiar faces of her teachers and recognizes them as people she likes and can trust to care for her. She has been coming to the West Side Center long enough to have developed trust in her mother to return at the end of the day, so Lisa goes happily from her mother to her teacher. Her mother says good-bye for the day, and Lisa experiences little distress at being left. The teacher talks to Lisa, holds her for a time, casually checks for any symptoms of illness, checks her diaper, changes it if necessary, and does anything else that is necessary to keep Lisa comfortable and content. Then the teacher either places her in the corral with the other three babies and interests her with a toy or some motor activity or places her in her crib to rest if she still seems sleepy. Lisa sleeps in the same crib every day, and the crib is kept in the same place to keep the surroundings as familiar as possible.

Soon after Lisa begins to play, the door opens again and Barbara and her mother enter. Barbara looks sleepy and she is still dressed in her pajamas and has on her diaper from the night before. Her mother overslept, as she regularly does, and did not have time to dress or feed Barbara, but she did remember to bring in a long-overdue supply of disposable diapers. She loves Barbara, but she simply does not know much about caring for a ten-month-old baby. After working all day, she often leaves Barbara with unfamiliar babysitters while she goes out in the evening. Barbara shows great apprehension when her mother leaves. She cries and struggles after her mother as if she is afraid her mother will not return. She is hugged, comforted, and talked to by the loving teacher. It is the day care center, its staff, its routine, and its pleasing environment that Barbara can look to for physiological care, trust, and security. The teacher undresses her, bathes her, dresses her for the day, brushes her hair, gives her a drink, and makes her comfortable. The teacher sits down and holds Barbara, talks to her, points to objects and names them, smiles at her, and plays peekaboo or pat-a-cake. Barbara is given more time today than Lisa, but this is one way that the teacher meets the individual needs of each of the babies. According to Erikson, the first crisis in the life of all humans is the conflict between a feeling of trust versus mistrust. Lisa entered the center this morning with a feeling of trust. She is developing trust in her mother to care for her physical needs, to love her, and to return to her every day. It is a simple step for Lisa to trust her day care environment that is filled with predictable events, familiar surroundings, and loving adults. Barbara, on the other hand, is struggling much harder to be able to trust the world. It is the responsibility of the teachers in Barbara's life to assist her to develop a sense of trust in her daily environment even if this need requires more time than some of the other babies receive.

By now Jeff feels secure and content and is squirming to join the other children. He is placed in the corral and the first teacher is free to welcome the next baby, while the second teacher cares for Barbara. And so it goes as the infants arrive. The teachers work as a team to ensure that each child's arrival is as smooth as possible. It is an absolute necessity that there always be at least two adults with each group of children. Not only does this requirement enable the adults to meet the children's needs more effectively, but it is crucial from the standpoint of safety. If a child is injured or suddenly becomes ill, the total attention of one teacher is necessary; therefore, a second adult must be present to care for the other children.

By 8:15 ten of the twelve enrolled infants have arrived, and the third teacher is present in time to begin feeding the babies. The age span of this group is four months to seventeen months and their eating and self-feeding abilities reflect this diversity in age. Six of the children are learning to use a spoon and a cup, and they attempt to feed themselves. One of the teachers is assigned to this group. He puts bibs on them, helps them into small chairs at a low table, and serves them the same breakfast food that the older children in the center are served. Today they have oatmeal, toast and butter, banana slices, and milk. This teacher talks to the babies as they eat, encourages them in their efforts, gives them assistance when it is needed, wipes up spills without scolding but pleasantly gives instructions on how to prevent accidents. "Let's keep the cup up here, so it will not get knocked over." "Stevie, let me push your chair closer, so you can reach better." "Oh, Sally, you ate all of your oatmeal. Do you want more?" "Are you through, Erik? OK. Let's wipe your hands and face and take off your bib." While this teacher is creating a pleasant eating experience for these six children, the other two teachers are feeding the younger infants who cannot feed themselves. These babies sit in high chairs, and each teacher feeds two at a time. Two of these babies can eat the regular meal if it is mashed well. Lisa still eats in a high chair and needs to be fed by an adult. However, she is attempting to use her hands to feed herself, and this morning she holds her own toast and manages it pretty well. She is allowed to do as much for herself as she can and is gently assisted when she needs help. In this way she will gradually develop the necessary skills to join the older children at the table. The two youngest infants still need strained baby food. As in all other areas, whatever is necessary to meet the developmental needs of each child is done. During mealtime the babies are talked to, praised and smiled at by the adults. All of the babies have the undivided attention of their teachers.

When breakfast is finished, the infants are washed and their diapers are checked. While two of the teachers play with the babies on the floor, in the corral, or in their cribs, the third teacher cleans up the tables, chairs, highchairs, and floor. As this task is completed it is 9:30, and the staff and babies are ready to continue with the morning routine.

This morning the infant staff has scheduled a period of about thirty to forty-five minutes to encourage the motor development of all the children. Small scooters that develop leg muscles are brought out for the children who are walking or learning to walk. Several go zooming around in the riding area laughing gleefully. Large cubes with openings on several sides are arranged together, and the babies who are at the crawling stage occupy themselves crawling in and out of the openings and pulling up to the fascinating cubes. They play hide-and-seek with one of the teachers and each other. One teacher gathers three babies in a small circle with her and rolls a small cloth ball of unusual texture to each baby. As they practice sitting up, pushing the balls, and reaching and grasping to retrieve them, they are also developing their sense of touch with these balls of unusual texture. The small babies who cannot yet propel themselves are placed on soft quilts on the floor, given toys, and encouraged to kick or roll over or reach depending on each one's level of development.

This morning Lisa is with the group who is rolling the balls. She enjoys pushing the ball away from herself and eagerly waits for the teacher to roll it back. When it comes back, she grabs it and chuckles. She especially seems to enjoy the feel of the yellow corduroy ball. After a while she is satisfied with herself and her ball-rolling ability, and crawls off in the direction of the cubes. The teacher at the cubes greets the new arrival with a gay "Here is Lisa. Do you want to get in the cube?" and in Lisa goes.

Meanwhile, sixteen-month-old Timmy who has been on the scooter all this time goes a little too fast and topples over. He cries but is quickly retrieved by one of the teachers who checks him over, comforts him, and takes him to another less vigorous activity. The babies move freely from one activity to another. Occasionally, an activity is planned that interests no one, so it is put away in favor of something else. Tomorrow this same block of time will again be spent on motor activities, but the activities will be different. Perhaps the small slide will be brought out. Maybe Lisa will get to bounce in the swing. The selection of activities will be based on the physical needs and interests of each child. Although there is a considerable span in the ages and physical development of the babies, each one is provided with an activity that is challenging and interesting.

It is apparent that even though enhancing physical development is the primary goal of this period, many other goals are being met at the same time. The children were hearing a lot of speech as their teacher interacted with them. Through the speech and the activities, the infants gain important cognitive tools. They hear objects named as well as directions given that refer to location of self and objects. They are using concrete objects and all of their senses to experience the world.

During the motor development period, the infants are given attention, praise, love, and a feeling of success all of which lead to sound emotional growth. It is apparent that even though motor development was the major emphasis of this activity, it was not isolated and treated as something apart from the child's other needs. The total organism is considered at all time.

The interest in the balls, cubes, scooters, etc. begins to wane and by 10:00 it is time for a change. It is snack time and everyone has developed a thirst. The young babies are changed, fed a bottle, and put in their cribs for a morning nap or rest. The older toddlers are returned to the chairs and table and given cold juice and graham crackers. They drink heartily but eat slowly as they chatter and listen to the music that has been put on the phonograph. The record is one of nursery rhymes. The music is enjoyed by the toddlers, and it creates a mood to help the babies nap. While the younger babies sleep, the toddlers finish snacks, are washed and diapered, and are ready for more fun.

The next half hour, until 11:00 is devoted to activities that concentrate on sensory experiences or on manipulation of objects. These relatively quiet activities are chosen because the younger babies are sleeping and this staff has learned that the children seem to function best if quiet or restful periods are alternated with active periods of play. Today the toddlers are given simple puzzles with two to four pieces. They delight in taking the pieces out and putting them back. Jeff plays with a stack of three nesting blocks, each one slightly larger than the other. He tries several times to put the blocks together but does not succeed. One of the teachers comes to his assistance and helps him complete the stack. With assistance, Jeff has succeeded and is eager to try again. He takes the stack of blocks apart and seems to have an understanding of how the task is to be completed. He is not immediately successful, but after several trials and some apparent frustration, he accomplishes the task. He appears to be satisfied and he leaves the blocks for the puzzles. Jeff is just now beginning to develop the ability to reason. Initially, he could not complete the task of the nesting blocks, but once he was shown the way he seemed to understand how it was to be done even though he still had to work hard to accomplish it. He is beginning to develop cognition. Emily spends the entire time putting wooden rings on sticks. She puts them on and takes them off over and over again as if she wants to be sure she understands what it is she has mastered.

During the activities the children are exercising and developing the intellectual abilities discussed by Guilford. They are using their reasoning powers to determine how to put a puzzle piece back into the board. They are using their memory to remember how to put the puzzle together the second time. They are becoming capable of forming images of concrete objects in their minds. Todd was offered a puzzle by the teacher, but he pushed it away and said, "Pi-ee, pi-ee." This was interpreted as a request for the puzzle of the piggy that he had played with earlier in the week. When he was offered the pig puzzle, he smiled, took it, and went right to work. If Todd had not been able to form the image of the pig puzzle in his mind, he could not have requested it. This is also the beginning of what Guilford calls cognition.

Children's intellectual abilities develop rapidly at this age, but for maximum growth they need numerous and varied experiences to assist them. We have learned from Piaget that all children, but especially the youngest, must have many experiences to see; touch; taste; hear; crawl over, under, and through; pick up; put down; stretch on; hug; climb; drop; throw; and put in and take out if they are to have a rich basis upon which their future intellectual development will take place. The teachers at the West Side Day Care Center are aware of Guilford's structure-of-intellect model, and they recognize the numerous intellectual aspects that infants from birth to eighteen months of age are capable of developing. They are also aware of Piaget's theory of intellectual development, and they recognize the need for experiences using the senses and the body. It is these theories that guide the activities during this and other times during the day in the infant area.

By 11:00 most of the napping infants have awakened and have been diapered. The toddlers are ready to leave the manipulative toys for a playtime outside. All of the infants are eager to get out the door except Jeff. This is his first day back after a short illness, and he appears tired. He balks at the suggestion to leave his puzzle and go outside. The teachers do not insist that Jeff join the others. He is allowed to remain inside to play with his puzzle with one of the teachers who is keeping a watchful eye on the one remaining sleeping baby. This teacher takes advantage of the time inside to prepare tables, bibs, washcloths, and high chairs for lunch.

The babies share the playground with the group of children eighteen months to three years of age. The play area is equipped with a sand pile, small enclosed swings, a small climber, large open sided cubes, riding toys, wagons, and push and pull toys. Today the teachers have added bean bags and a low tub into which they can be thrown. This new activity delights Emily and Timmy. Lisa, who cannot yet stand alone, is not ready for this game. When she is offered one of the enclosed swings she giggles in delight. She enjoys spending a large part of her time outside being pushed in the swing by one of the teachers. This may appear to be a somewhat passive activity for a seven-month-old baby, but on the contrary it is really rather exciting. Lisa is in a sitting position, and this gives her practice sitting up and holding herself upright. She also enjoys the sensory experience of feeling her body propelled through space. In addition, when Lisa is sitting in the swing, she can see the rest of the play area and through her eyes and ears she is learning about life by observing others. When she sees an activity that has more appeal than swinging, she squirms and fusses and the teacher knows that she is ready to be taken from the swing to something that looks more interesting.

Lunchtime is approaching, and the teacher who is inside gives the signal that it is time to return and get cleaned up for lunch. The infants' hands and faces are washed, their diapers are checked, their bibs are put on, and they are seated at the table or in their high chair. The same eating procedure that was used at breakfast is used at lunch. Two of the teachers feed the babies who cannot feed themselves, and the third teacher sits with the toddlers at the table. At West Side the teachers join the children at the tables for mealtime and snack time. They are aware of the work by Bandura and Walters that has shown that one of the most effective ways children learn social behaviors is by modeling others who are loved or respected. The teacher eats slowly, talks softly, uses the proper eating utensils, does not spill or throw, and remains seated throughout the meal. The children slowly learn that this is appropriate mealtime behavior. Today lunchtime is a pleasant experience with a minimum of spills or disruptions. The children are not forced to eat all of their food, nor are they denied food. Today Emily ate all of her green beans but very little of her mashed potatoes. When she indicated that she wanted more green beans, she was given more. The teacher encouraged her to try more potatoes. She ate two more bites and wanted no more. This is typical behavior. The next time mashed potatoes are served Emily might very well eat a full serving. Today she simply wanted green beans.

After lunch the babies are washed and then allowed to play with balls and blocks for a short time. The care givers clean up from lunch, put on lullabies for nap time, and begin to diaper all the babies. After diapering, the infants' shoes are removed and they are put in their cribs. If they have a favorite doll or soft animal, they are allowed to have it. Many of the older infants prefer to have small books in their crib to look at before sleeping. Barbara seems restless today, so one of the teachers pats her on the back until she gets drowsy. Another teacher is patting Timmy and Jeff simultaneously. They are napping for the third day out of their cribs on low cots. Timmy and Jeff will be going into the next area with older toddlers within the next two months. There is not a firm birthdate that determines when children are changed from one group to the next. The decision is based on the child's level of development and ability to adjust to the new situation. In the next group, the children all nap on low cots. The teachers are slowly preparing Jeff and Timmy for the transition by giving them plenty of time to adjust to napping on cots in a familiar setting. The two boys do not object to sleeping on the cots, but they have not yet learned to stay on their cots long enough to go to sleep unless one of the teachers sits nearby and reads to them or pats their backs. The teacher praises them when they stay on their cots and rewards them with a story. Soon staying on the cot will become usual nap time behavior. By 1:00 all of the babies are resting quietly. They usually nap until 3:00. Some awaken earlier and some sleep longer, but the staff can generally expect a two-hour nap period.

In many day care centers nap time becomes a free time for the staff. They are often seen reading, doing handiwork, or writing letters. In other centers teachers gather and socialize in the hall, the office, or the staff room. At West Side this is not the case. Each teacher is given a twenty-minute break to be spent in the center. The teachers alternate their breaks so that there are still two adults in each group at all times. While the babies are sleeping, the teachers use their time to keep the room and equipment in order. Classroom equipment is expensive and most day care centers are not financially prepared for large outlays of money to replace equipment that is not properly cared for. The infant teachers know that they are allowed only a small amount of money each month for new equipment, so they are careful to keep what they have in good repair. During nap time they check for lost puzzle pieces and misplaced rings, replace records in covers, tape torn pages of books, tighten a screw in the scooter, and disinfect all of the toys used by the infants during the morning. One teacher washes a load of bibs and clothes in the laundry room, while another empties the garbage pails. This entire procedure takes only a short time because it is done every day.

After breaks are taken and the room is clean and orderly, the teachers fill out the daily sheets on each infant and make plans for the next day and the next week. With their goals firmly before them and their schedule as a guide for the day, they are ready to plan specific activities based on the observations. "Emily seems to have mastered putting the rings on the stick. I think she is ready to try the graduated rings." "Jeff and Timmy are both ready to be challenged by puzzles with more than four pieces. Next time let's get out the ones with six pieces for them." "I'm concerned about Jerry's motor development. Most babies can roll over by the time they are six months old. Each day I'm going to exercise his arms and legs and hold toys slightly out of reach to encourage him to roll over." The teachers also plan new and interesting activities that are beneficial to the children as a group. "Why don't we bring in the rhythm instruments and all make music next Tuesday? The older toddlers could use the drums and tambourines, and the little ones could shake maracas and rattles. What a listening experience that will be." "I'm collecting bits of paper, cloth, ribbon, and wood to make a feely board for a sensory experience. If you have anything, bring it tomorrow. I thought we could hang it low on the wall near the mirror." And so the planning conversation continues with each child, the group, and the limited budget being considered, as well as the very nature of what day care is and must be always being realized.

At 3:00 it is time for the first two teachers to leave. They have been at the center since 7:00 A.M. They are replaced by two other teachers who work only half a day. The director and the parents know that it would be preferable if the same adults could care for the infants all through the day, but this center is open for twelve hours each day and this is not possible. The two replacement teachers arrive at 2:30 so that they have a part in the planning and time to read the daily sheets and be briefed on anything of importance.

As nap time comes to an end, the babies are changed as they wake up, their shoes are replaced, and they are held and talked to. By 3:00 most of the babies are wide awake and ready for snacks. The snack routine is the same as in the morning. Today the babies get seedless grapes or strained baby food and milk.

At 4:00 the small babies are put in the corral and are provided with numerous toys such as squeeky animals, chiming bells, rattles, dolls, blocks, small boxes, etc. From the work of Maslow and others, the teachers know that all but the most unfortunately handicapped infants are born with a wonderful characteristic we call curiosity. Curiosity does not have to be developed in the infant; it is already present. But curiosity can be given opportunities to be satisfied and rewarded. All too often in and out of day care settings infants are confined, stopped, or stymied, and the wonderful desire to know, investigate, wonder, and find out is destroyed. At West Side the staff has a tremendous respect for the curiosity of each child. Every minute is not regulated with dictated activities, but neither are the babies left to their own devices without direction from their teachers. This afternoon the small infants are allowed to explore the toys in the corral, to taste them, to push and pull, to bang and to shake, to drop and to retrieve. The teacher does not say, "Don't throw the dolly, Lisa, you might hurt it." Rather, the doll is retrieved from the floor and given back to Lisa with a smile and a simple comment, "Here's the dolly, Lisa." While the younger babies explore in the corral, one of the teachers produces a large grocery bag filled with surprises for the older infants. They all gather around and wait with great anticipation. One toy is taken from the bag at a time and the teacher clearly says, "This is a telephone," and gives it to one of the babies. The next toy is shown. "This is a tractor." A second baby gets the tractor. This procedure is repeated until each infant has a toy; the teacher places several others on the floor so that exchanges can be made. The purpose of this short exercise is to give the infants labels that they can begin to attach to concrete objects. Now the babies are busy satisfying their curiosity about all the uses of these objects. These toys are not new. This staff rotates the toys, limiting the number that are available at any given time. When the toys that have been put up are brought out again, the infants are always glad to see them and respond to them as if they were new.

By 4:45 most of the babies seem to have temporarily satisfied their interests in all of the toys, so the toys are put away and large cardboard building blocks are brought out. While the toddlers and one of the teachers are busy stacking blocks and building towers and roads, the other two teachers hold the small infants in their laps and rock them and talk to them. Lisa enjoys being held, but some of the others prefer to be on their own. Shortly after 5:00 several parents arrive to pick up their babies after a full day for both parent and child. The parents are greeted warmly by the teacher and infants. They are made to feel welcome and are encouraged to spend a few minutes observing their babies. There is a spirit of cooperativeness and joint concern between the parents and the teachers. The parents are given a brief report on the events of the day, notified of any supplies needed, and baby and parent are bid farewell until tomorrow.

The teacher who has been present since morning leaves at 5:30, now that fewer babies remain. Lisa's mother arrives at 5:45. She is happy to see her baby and delighted to see that Lisa is playing contentedly on the floor with two other infants and one of the teachers. When Lisa is lifted up by her mother, she giggles and pats her hands. Her mother is informed of how well Lisa ate and slept and of her daily progress. Lisa's mother leaves the center satisfied that Lisa is receiving the kind of care that will ensure optimum development.

At 6:00 there are only three babies left. One of the teachers plays follow the leader with the children crawling on the floor with them. The other teacher takes this time to check the equipment that was used in the afternoon, empty the garbage pails, etc. At 6:15 only Timmy is left. His father drives a long distance to and from work, so he is usually the last parent to arrive. Being the only one left can give a child a feeling of loneliness and a sense of being abandoned if precautions are not taken. One of the teachers puts on a record and holds Timmy. They sing songs and play simple hand and finger games. Timmy enjoys the music and the attention. The time until 6:45 passes quickly and then Timmy's dad opens the door, claps his hands, holds out his arms for Timmy, and says, "Hi, Tim. Did you have a good day?" After Timmy and his father leave, the teachers check the room, check their supplies and leave, confident they are providing good day care for these infants.

Summary

Day care for infants is an extremely challenging matter for professionals. The quality of the early months and years of an infant's life has been shown to be particularly critical for future development. Thoughtfully planned and carefully controlled routine care and activities can help children develop optimally. Day care for infants can supplement and enhance the families' efforts at providing the best possible care for their children.

The goals for infant programs as well as the objectives and activities described in this chapter are illustrative of the possibilities available to day care personnel.

The description of a typical day in an infant center was provided to further illustrate how goals are integrated with routine care and daily schedules.

Suggested Readings

Gessell, Arnold; Ilg, Frances; and Ames, Louise Bates. *Infant and Child in the Culture of Today.* New York: Harper & Row, Publishers, 1974. A presentation of behavioral norms for children from birth to five years of age, based on the premise that children's behaviors change with age in a patterned and predictable manner.

Gordon, Ira J. *Baby Learning through Baby Play.* New York: St. Martin's Press, 1970. A collection of activities designed to help infants learn and develop.

Honig, Alice F. and J. Lally, Ronald, eds. *Infant Caregiving: A Design for Training.* New York: Media Projects, 1972. A guide for training infant care givers to provide for optimum development of infants in the areas of personality, nutrition, language, motor skills, sensory experiences, and intellectual development.

Huntington, Dorothy S.; Provence, Sally; and Parker, Ronald K. *Serving Infants.* Washington, D.C.: U.S. Dept. of Health, Education and Welfare, Office of Child Development, DHEW Pub. No. OCD73-14, n.d. An overview of infant development and suggested activities to assist in meeting the needs of the infant. Guiding principles for quality infant day care programs are also given.

Suggested Activities

1. Select a goal from Appendix B that would be appropriate for infants. Select at least three objectives from Appendix C or elsewhere that relate to the goal. Describe one activity for each objective.
2. Observe one or two infants in a day care setting. What kinds of goals did teachers appear to be fostering at the time of your observation?
3. Make a list of free or inexpensive materials that could be used by teachers and infants to help accomplish various goals.

Chapter Ten

Toddlers

The one year old is generally an agreeable child, as are most three year olds, but sometime during the second year of life, our subjects begin asserting themselves, rejecting suggestions, ignoring commands, testing limits, and generally flexing their muscles.

Burton L. White, "Evolving a Strategy," in Experience and Environment, *ed. White and Watts (Englewood Cliffs, N.J.: Prentice-Hall, 1973), pp. 10-16, Reprinted by permission.*

Children from eighteen months to three years of age are commonly referred to as toddlers in day care settings. In many ways this is a period of transition from infancy to childhood. Many of the skills that are to be acquired during these years had their roots in infancy and will become more refined during the years from three to five. This is the period when physical growth begins to slow down and language and intellectual development occur rapidly. For day care programs to serve toddlers successfully, the complexity of development during these years must be understood.

Goals for a Toddler Program

Day care programs for toddlers have many of the same characteristics as infant programs, primarily because much of the day is consumed by routine care. The children are awake more, however, and they are much more capable of moving around the environment. Therefore, a classroom of toddlers takes on a much more active appearance than that of a group of infants. The period of toddlerhood has often been characterized as a "difficult" time for both toddlers and adults who care for them. They have been labelled stubborn, contrary, uncooperative, and frustrated. These labels have probably been applied by people who did not understand children's development. Admittedly, this is a period where children want and demand independence and want to express themselves but frequently lack the language skills to do so. It is also the period where society is usually demanding some efforts at toilet training. However, teachers who are aware of these influences on children can create an environment and adopt attitudes that help children overcome these crises rather than stumble over them again and again. The goals offered in this chapter are not the only possible goals for toddlers. Indeed, additional ones should be selected to ensure that the total child is being considered. The goals offered relate to the areas of development that seem to characterize toddlers.

149

The Children Acquire and Refine Language Skills

Language skills develop at an exponential rate during this period of life. At eighteen months the baby might have a vocabulary of 6 to 10 words or maybe a few more. It is not unusual for a three-year-old child to have a vocabulary of 750 to 1,000 words. This phenomenal growth in language skill is not an automatic maturational process. It is dependent on many factors, the most important of which is adults who are willing to listen, elicit responses, talk to the child, ask questions, wait patiently for answers, and patiently answer the thousands of questions asked of them. Language development is very important at this age because it helps the child express feelings and needs related to other areas of development. Understanding the words *me* and *mine* helps toddlers express an awareness of their own individuality. The words *yes* and *no* enable toddlers to express independence. Other words that describe or show relationships such as *soft, little,* or *fat* help toddlers verbally express concepts that they comprehend. Language also enables toddlers to make their wishes known and helps prevent frustration. Examples are: "More milk." "No more beans." "I want the ball." The focus of language development at this age is on communication skills. Children have a real need to express themselves. Equally important is being able to respond appropriately to the speech of someone else. The objectives that will be offered as examples are based on these needs.

Since mealtime is such a time-consuming activity in day care, an appropriate objective is that the toddler "asks for things that are needed or wanted at the table." When toddlers are first learning to talk, the teacher will probably say, "Butch, do you want more peas?" Butch can respond with "yes" or "no" or a nod of the head. When Butch is capable of more speech and knows the names of some of the foods, the teacher can then ask, "Butch, do you want something else?" Butch nods yes. "What do you want?" Butch might say, "peas" or he might point to the peas. If he points, the teacher can say, "Oh, you want more peas. Can you say peas?" Butch responds with "Pea." One shrewd group of toddlers developed the habit of banging their cups on the table to request more juice at snack time. When one child started banging, several others would quickly join in. The skillful teacher gently held their hands to prevent the banging and asked Tony, the most verbal child, if he wanted more juice. Tony nodded yes and the teacher instructed him to ask for more juice. "Mo jui," said Tony. The other children listened to the teacher and Tony and also asked for more juice.

Another activity that is useful to assist toddlers to learn to ask for what they want at the table is to look at pictures of food and pretend that it is mealtime. The teacher can show a picture of eggs, sausage, toast, and milk and say, "I'm going to eat some eggs," and pretend to be eating eggs. "What do you want to eat Diana? Good, you eat the toast. Tell me when you want something else." This pretend behavior can continue until everyone is satisfied and "full."

Another objective that is appropriate for language development is that toddlers "can name or point to at least six body parts." Knowing the names for parts of the body helps toddlers understand more about themselves and also gives them more labels for things in their environment. Children enjoy playing games where they follow instructions that relate to body parts. "Touch your nose. Pat your hands. Stomp your feet. Touch your hair. Close your eyes."

Toddlers enjoy singing, and music and songs are often an effective vehicle to develop language skills. There are many children's songs that refer to body parts. "Put your finger on your nose." "I have two hands, one, two." Children can also be encouraged to name parts of the body that are touched by the teacher or label body parts that are seen in books.

According to Maslow, children are naturally curious and language ability is a new skill that toddlers can use to satisfy their curiosity. They can ask questions to obtain answers about the world. Therefore, an objective that is most appropriate is that the children "can ask questions about the environment using words like *why* and *how*." This is an objective that can be met easily by providing an interesting environment and interesting experiences that cause children to wonder. Adults can stimulate children to wonder and question by modeling this behavior. The work by Bandura and Walters indicates that children will imitate the behavior of adults whom they admire, and if this new behavior is rewarded, it soon becomes part of their behavioral repertoire. The teacher can simply say to a group who is building with blocks, "Why did that fall down?" or "How high can we build it?" and then help the children find answers to these questions. The teacher can reinforce questioning by showing an interest in the children's questions and answering the questions or helping the children find answers to their questions. If

Puzzles are a valuable tool to help toddlers develop intellectual skills.

children's questions are not taken seriously and given the respect of being answered, children might stop asking, and many opportunities for language development as well as intellectual growth will have been missed.

The Children Develop to Their Maximum Intellectual Ability

The language skills being gained during the toddler years give the child a new vehicle for thinking and expressing thought. In many instances it is difficult to distinguish between language development and intellectual development because they are so closely interwoven. Many objectives that are selected in the area of intellectual development require language skills. Children are requested to name, identify, ask, and describe. Language becomes a new mechanism for learning. In addition to language, toddlers continue to rely on their senses to experience the environment and develop intellectually.

One intellectual objective for toddlers that requires both language and the senses is that the children "can identify size relationships when given two or more objects." Younger children may not be able to give labels to the size of objects, but they can often indicate which object is being talked about by touching or pointing. For instance, "Carl, which truck is the biggest one? That is right, you touched the big one. Which one do you want to play with?" Carl may touch the one he wants or he may say, "Bigun." As toddlers develop a clearer understanding of size relationships, they can be challenged to use these concepts in their play. Jamie was building an elaborate block structure, and he began to cry. The teacher approached and asked, "What is it Jamie?"

"This one is too little."

"You tried that block and it was too little?"

"Yes."

"Could you try a larger one?"

"I did. It is too big."

"Is there another size that is in between these two—not so big and not so little?"

"I'll see. Here's one. It fits. In between did it!"

Jamie was assisted to compare the size of all the blocks to find the size that was needed. Initially, children compare most objects with the words *big* and *little,* then more descriptive words such as *huge* and *tiny* are added. Slowly after hearing the words many times and experiencing actual objects, words such as *long, short, tall, wide,* and *narrow* take on more meaning.

Bruner indicates that children represent the world in increasingly complex ways. During the first years of life the only thing that will confer reality on an object is direct action with the object. Manipulation and sensory experience with objects remains an important way to learn about the world throughout life, but during the toddler years children acquire a new ability to represent the world through images. Images can take the form of photographs, pictures, television shows, wooden or ceramic representations of real objects, or mental images contained in the child's memory. Bruner calls this method "knowing from imagery." When children can use imagery as a means of representation, they are no longer limited to direct sensory experiences for meaning and understanding of the world. An appropriate objective for toddlers might be "The child can identify pictures of common objects." Of course, children can identify pictures much more readily if they have had previous experience with the actual objects. The first activity that can help the toddler see the relationship between actual objects and pictures is to present the two simultaneously. The teacher can show a group of blocks and encourage the children to identify them. Then a picture of similar blocks can be shown and identified. "Here is a picture of some blocks. We have real blocks and a picture of blocks." After the toddlers see the relationship, the pictures can be shown without the actual objects. Children who can represent the world in images can be encouraged to look at picture books and identify the pictures they see. Colorful pictures can also be placed low on the walls and bulletin boards in the classroom to be enjoyed and identified.

The idea that development occurs sequentially is apparent in the preceding objective. Children first experience the world through actions and then progress to experience the world through images. Sequential development is also evident in the way information occurs or is conceived by the child. Slowly, toddlers come to recognize similarities and differences in objects and form classes. "Toddlers can classify objects on the basis of a simple attribute" is a reasonable objective for older toddlers. The size, shape, or name of an object can serve as the defining characteristic. Two groups of objects can be combined, and the child can be instructed to put all the blocks on one table and all the books on another table. On the basis of the familiar names, the child is able to classify each object as a block or a book. At pick-up time children can use their classifying abilities to put the blocks on the shelf, the balls in the box, the dolls in the bed, and the trucks in the cabinet. Next, children can be encouraged to classify on the basis of an abstract concept such as size. "All the big blocks go on the bottom shelf and all the small blocks go on the top shelf." The shape of objects is also a characteristic that toddlers use in classifying. There are a number of commercially available toys that provide opportunities for classifying on the basis of geometric shapes, animal shapes, and the shapes of common objects such as a tree, a heart, and a shamrock.

The Children Grow in Independence

The demand for independence is one of the characteristics that distinguishes toddlers from infants. The infant's peaceful acceptance of help is suddenly replaced by an insistence on doing things for oneself. The casual willingness to follow directions from adults is supplanted by an insistence to "do it my way." The process of developing independence involves gaining personal control over one's body and one's actions. The accomplishment of several of the developmental tasks given by Havighurst—learning to walk, to eat solid foods, to talk, and to control elimination—all provide enormous control of the body and the environment. According to Erikson, the crisis between autonomy and shame is triggered by the physical control that the child has just gained over most body parts. The child should be encouraged to use these new abilities to grow in independence.

An objective that is very important for helping children develop independence is to "create an environment that provides children with maximum control." Tables, chairs, cots, and toilets should all be child sized, so the children can take care of their personal needs rather than depending on an adult to lift them onto the toilet, push in their chairs, and help them onto their cots. Shelves should be low so that children can select and replace toys without assistance. Lockers and coat hooks should be low enough so that children can hang their own wraps and store their own treasures without waiting for the teacher's help. Water fountains and sinks at the child's level make drinking and washing easier tasks.

In addition to a well-planned physical plant, an orderly room and a regular daily routine assist the child to gain independence and personal control. If the organization of the room is orderly and consistent, Janet can get the blocks she wants from the same shelf they were on yesterday and not have to depend on the teacher to locate the blocks for her. Likewise, Richard can wash his hands after snacks and put his jacket on because he knows that outside play follows snack time. He does not have to wait for the teacher's instructions. The thoughtful planning of the environment gives children a head start on becoming independent.

Another objective that relates to the teacher's behavior that is especially fitting is "Give the children a minimum of help when they are trying to master tasks on their own." Overzealous teachers are often eager to be useful and helpful to the children, but they provide few opportunities for children to do things for themselves. Likewise, impatient teachers are often unwilling to take the time for children to do something for themselves that could be done in less time by an adult. Both types of teachers are damaging to the child's sense of independence. An effective teacher allows children to do as much as they can for themselves in hundreds of situations throughout the day. This will include such things as turning the door knob, eating, washing, turning on the faucet, pulling on sweaters, flushing the toilet, getting toys from the shelf, and putting up the toys. Giving a minimum of help might mean allowing children to assist in a task that they could not accomplish alone. It might also mean helping a child solve a problem, such as fitting all the blocks in the box, rather than doing it for the child, or it can simply mean waiting patiently for a child to accomplish a task that can be done without help. This objective clearly implies that the child's efforts must be respected and not criticized and corrected by an adult. Children will put their socks on inside out and will miss buttons on their sweaters and still proudly exclaim, "I did it by myself!" It is the effort, not the final product, that is important. Children should be praised for their efforts and encouraged to take responsibility for themselves.

Giving a minimum of help to children when they are striving for independence does not mean to deny help when they ask for it. Some tasks that children attempt are too difficult, and they seek help. It should be given. At other times a child will ask for help on a task that has long since been mastered. Help should also be given at this time to provide reassurance to the child that he is valued and the teacher is willing to take time to assist him. Assistance should be given when it is requested but withheld if it is not wanted or needed.

A third objective that relates to the teacher's behavior is "The children should be given choices throughout the day." Toddlers are insistent on deciding things for themselves. If they are given a choice where the alternatives are yes or no, the answer will probably be no. *No* becomes a favorite word even when it is not the intention. When two-year-old Andy is asked if he wants more pudding, he shakes his head no but at the same time takes more pudding and eats it. The choices given to a child should be legitimate ones. Karen should not be asked, "Won't you come and sit at the table with us?" if she is expected to join the others at the table. Her answer will probably be "No." The teacher could simply state, "Karen, now it is time to come to the table." In this instance, Karen was not given a choice because a choice did not exist. At the table Karen could be given legitimate choices: "Do you want the blue paint or the red? Do you want to use your fingers or a brush?" After the activity, she should not be asked if she wants to wash her hands unless it is really her option. Rather, "We are all finished. Now we must wash our hands." Throughout the day many choices must be provided so the children can begin to make decisions for themsleves. Legitimate choices must be provided to give the children a sense of self-control and self-will. Children may develop a sense of worthlessness if they are not allowed to act independently and make choices.

The Children Develop a Positive Self-concept

Self-concept is a global term that includes all the ways a child views himself. Self-concept encompasses the feelings, beliefs, expectations, perceptions, and attitudes one holds about oneself. The views that children hold of themselves are usually a reflection of the behaviors and attitudes of others toward them. When children are treated with respect and love, encouraged to participate in life, and rewarded for their efforts, they learn to think of themselves as competent, worthwhile people. On the other hand, children who are shamed and treated harshly, who are not made to feel loved and welcomed, and who are given no opportunities to experience achievement soon learn to think of themselves as useless, unwanted, and incompetent. One of the most basic rights of all children is the right to self-esteem and a sense of personal worth. The adults in a day care setting assume a major role to help the children develop positive feelings about themselves.

Being successful in daily tasks leads to a sense of accomplishment and a sense of pride. An objective could be "the children can perform daily tasks successfully." It is the responsibility of the teachers to plan success experiences for each child each day. Children can experience success playing with puzzles, doing art work, building with blocks, singing a song, or looking at a book. It is often the teacher's responses to the children's activities that give the children a feeling of competence. For instance: "Did you put all these pieces in the puzzle?" "The colors on your picture look like the rainbow." "My, what a big farm you have built." "The song you were singing is one of my favorites." In these examples, the teacher was not judgmental. The children were not told that they were good or wonderful or that their products were beautiful. The judgment of the child's efforts is a personal decision made by the child. The teacher has simply recognized the children's accomplishments and acknowledged them with a positive statement. Maslow maintains that a sense of accomplishment is crucial for children as young as three years old in order for them to develop a healthy self-esteem.

A sense of competence and worth is encouraged if the children "can explore the environment and make personal discoveries." Throughout life making personal discoveries creates feelings of excitement and accomplishment that are commonly shared by a toddler who says, "Oh, I see," a school child who says, "I found out," and an adult scientist who exclaims, "I discovered." An active curiosity is a characteristic common to most toddlers. They must be provided with opportunities to develop and satisfy their sense of questioning and wonder. When a safe, stimulating environment is provided and the inquiries of a toddler lead to an expanded meaning of the world, a sense of pride and ability are created. These feelings contribute to a positive view of oneself.

Teachers can assist children to accomplish this objective by providing times during the day when the activities are not planned but a stimulating environment is created in which children are allowed to follow their own interests. Teachers can also allow children to explore new toys and discover how they are to be used without immediately being shown the "right" way. Adults can also pose problems for children that invite investigations and discovery. For instance, "Our doll cradle is broken. What can we use for a cradle today?"

The areas of body awareness and personal identity are important concerns for the development of a healthy self-concept in a toddler. Piaget maintains that infants are not aware of their own image and do not associate parts of their bodies with themselves. An appropriate objective for younger toddlers would be "Each child can recognize himself in a mirror and respond." A full-length mirror should be available in the room for the toddlers to view their own reflections throughout the day. Toddlers enjoy patting the baby in the mirror, but they often do not realize that it is their own image that is being patted. The teacher can play games with the toddler in front of the mirror. "Look, Helen, this is a picture of you, and this is a picture of me! I am going to touch your head. See, I'm touching your head in the picture, too. Can you touch your head? You are touching it in the mirror, too," Opportunities should be taken to show toddlers their image when something is unusual. For instance, "Priscilla, let's look at your hands in the mirror, so you can see the paint on them. Your hands are all red," or "Donald do you want to look in the mirror and see the bandage on your knee? Look, this is your leg, this is your knee, and this is the bandage."

In Maslow's hierarchy of needs, the belongingness and love needs emerge when the physiological and safety needs have been met. As children feel safe and secure in their environment, they need to feel accepted and loved. Another objective in developing a good self-concept is "Each child feels like an important member of the group." This can be accomplished by providing each child with special places in the room such as a locker, a special chair, and a personal cot. Children soon recognize that this is Janna's chair and this is Leroy's locker. Children should be greeted warmly every day and welcomed into the activities. Activities should be planned with all the children's interests in mind. When children have been away for a few days, special efforts must be taken to make them feel secure and loved. They should be told that they were missed. As children are leaving for the day, a good-bye that says, "I will see you again tomorrow," makes the children feel that they belong and are a part of the group.

Children can be assisted to feel like contributing members of the group by being assured of a role in group activities. Building a mountain in the sandbox, constructing a collage at activity time, and decorating the class valentine box are projects that can involve each child and create a sense of togetherness and belongingness. Displaying the children's creative efforts on the walls and shelves helps each child feel important and worthwhile. Mounting photographs of the group and the individual children around the room helps each child feel that "this is my room; these are my friends. This is where I belong."

The Children Acquire Skills That Require Motor Development

The area of motor development will be divided into gross motor development and fine motor development for the purpose of discussion and planning objectives and activities. Fine motor development involves control of the small muscles. Two terms that are often associated with fine motor control are *manipulation* and *eye-hand coordination*. An objective that is appropriate at this age is "The child can hold a crayon in the palm of the hand with all of the fingers wrapped around it. This technique will slowly be refined as the child develops more control and has experiences in marking. Young toddlers who are first experiencing pencils and crayons will use their entire body and arm to guide the instrument to make marks on the paper. For this reason, they may be given large sheets of paper spread out on the floor so that they have sufficient room to make their marks and have a successful experience. As children develop more hand and finger control over the crayon, their drawing surfaces can become smaller. A large sheet of paper on the table or an easel covered with paper make good marking surfaces for the toddler. Varied experiences with crayons and pencils will help develop the skill that is desired.

Many activities that children enjoy when they are older are built on skills learned in the early years. For instance, the ability to build complex structures from blocks at the age of five is only possible if the child develops eye-hand coordination as a toddler and learns how to stack one block on top of another. "The children can build with blocks, stacking up to four or five" is a realistic objective for toddlers. Children this age enjoy many kinds of block activities such as building and stacking small colored blocks at the table with their friends. During this activity the teacher can challenge the children by saying, "How high can we stack these?" or "Can you put one more block on your tower?" Toddlers also enjoy large wooden blocks that require more strength and skill to stack. A group building project is appropriate for toddlers to learn to manipulate these heavier blocks. Sturdy hollow blocks also give the toddler additional experience in stacking and constructing with large blocks that are easier to handle. Another type of block enjoyed by toddlers are those that snap or fit together in some way. These blocks may require some adult assistance at first, but the children learn to use them very quickly. When the blocks have been snapped together, they are secure and not prone to falling over. Children are thrilled to be able to build a stack as high as their heads. Small stable objects such as dominos or match boxes require more precise control than the larger blocks and are appropriate stacking and building equipment for a child who has gained experience and expertise from the other types of blocks.

The objectives that the child "can properly replace the pieces of a four-piece puzzle," "can insert geometric shaped objects into a box through geometric-shaped openings," and "can place five pegs in a pegboard" all require similar skills.

Children must be able to coordinate their hand movements with what they see and must be able to manipulate objects by turning and twisting them in order to accomplish any of the objectives successfully. Eye-hand coordination and manipulative abilities can only be developed through actions and experiences that require these skills. Children will learn to manipulate puzzles, pegs, and geometric shapes only by having actual experience with these objects.

Gross motor skills are developed through actions and experiences that require the large muscles. Once a child learns to walk, many adults take large muscle development for granted. It is assumed that children will learn to run, skip, hop, and climb. Indeed, most children will develop these abilities with very little instruction from adults if they are provided with encouragement, appropriate equipment, space, and opportunities. In other words, the successful achievement of these skills, like most others, is dependent on an environment that is conducive to their development. Both inside and outside settings should be safely designed to promote gross motor development. For instance, safe climbing structures such as inside or outside jungle gyms, climbing ladders, or a stack of sturdy boxes should be available to encourage children to climb. If suitable equipment is not available, some children simply will not learn to climb. Others will learn in spite of the lack of equipment. They will learn to climb on tables, chairs, shelves, stacks of cots, and window sills. Equipment does not have to be elaborate and expensive. Simple toys such as tricycles, balls, bean bags, stick horses, planks, crates, cardboard boxes, and a sand pile are all relatively inexpensive and all can contribute to sound motor development. For instance, the objective "The children can remain balanced while walking a five-foot line" might be selected. The children can practice this skill by walking on a balance beam if one is available or by walking a four inch wide plank placed on the floor. Colored tape on the floor can also be used as a balancing line on which the children can walk. This example illustrates the point that the same motor skills can be learned with or without expensive equipment.

Teachers can also plan games that encourage motor development. If the objective is "The child can hop on one foot," the teacher could play follow the leader and part of the action could be hopping on one foot. The teacher could also head a small group in a mirror game. The teacher sits or stands in front of the children, and they serve as the mirror doing everything the teacher does. One of the movements that could be performed is hopping on one foot. There are also numerous records available that instruct the children to perform actions to music. These records can be played, or the following instructions could be given by the teacher: "wiggle like a worm," "crawl like a snail," "rock like a rocking chair," "pedal a bicycle," "tiptoe through the tulips." Adults can encourage all kinds of motor development in toddlers by creating a safe, stimulating physical environment, offering suggestions, and interacting with the children in physical activities.

Typical Day for Toddlers

The day in the toddler group begins early every morning as Melanie, Holly, Amy, and Quincey all arrive together at 6:45 A.M. The mothers of these four children share a car pool to the day care center and then go on to work. The mothers work the early shift at the local factory. Amy has been attending the Children's Center since she was six months old. She is now two and one-half. Her mother has been so pleased with the program available for young children at this center that she has encouraged her co-workers to enroll their children in this facility. The other three children who arrive with Amy are two years old and have been attending the center for six months. The four children are good friends, and in spite of the early hour, they usually arrive in a happy mood and are ready to tackle the world.

Today, however, as the mothers and their toddlers enter the building, Amy can be heard crying. The sight of the colorful toys and decorated walls does little to relieve her unhappiness. The four toddlers are greeted by their teachers, and one teacher immediately focuses on Amy, while the other one helps the other three children put up their clothes and find an interesting book. Amy's mother reports that Amy probably needs to rest because she had been up late the night before and had been awakened during the night by a siren. Amy is gently taken by the teacher even though she clings to her mother, and the four mothers kiss their children good-bye for the day. The teacher's efforts to cheer Amy are not successful, and she continues to whimper and scowl.

Breakfast at Children's Center is served at 8:30 A.M., and the wait for food is too long for these four who arrive so early in the day. The teachers realize this and provide them with fruit juice and a slice of toast or crackers soon after they arrive. Today when Amy is offered the juice, she stops crying and drinks it. Then she asks the teacher to rock her. The teacher holds Amy in her lap and gently rocks her until she falls asleep. She is placed on her cot and isolated from the rest of the children where she sleeps peacefully until breakfast.

The toddler class has eighteen children enrolled. As the children arrive throughout the early morning, information from parents is recorded on the information sheet that is referred to by all the staff. The information might pertain to medicine that is to be given to Denise, a message that Grandmother Lopes will pick up Alfonso today, or an observation that Crystal was constipated last night and might have difficulty having a bowel movement today. One key to a successful day care program is open communication between the staff and the parents and a sense of joint concern for the children's well-being. At Children's Center the parents play an active role in policy making and program development, and there is a spirit of cooperation between most of the parents and the staff.

At 7:50 ten of the eighteen children have arrived. Two are sleeping, one teacher is reading to a small group, and the others are playing with trucks and balls. Suddenly a child can be heard coming down the hall crying loudly. The teachers know immediately that this is Armando, the new child in the class. Yesterday was Armando's first day at Children's Center. He is almost three years old and until yesterday he had never been separated from his mother. Because of financial reasons, his mother has started to work and she is as apprehensive about leaving Armando as he is of being left. The teachers have encouraged Armando's mother to stay with him at the center for a time each day until he feels secure enough to be left. Yesterday Armando's mother stayed with him most of the morning and then she left before lunch. Armando enjoyed the morning, but he cried for his mother off and on during the rest of the day. When he was not crying, he seemed to enjoy the other children and the teacher. Today his mother will again stay with Armando, but only until 10:30 when the children go outside. As Armando enters the room, his crying disturbs Teresa and Audrey and they, too, begin to cry. One teacher quickly goes to the girls, comforts them, and reassures them that everything is all right and that Armando will be fine. The other teacher greets Armando and his mother and tries to make them feel comfortable. When Armando sees his mother hang up her handbag, he stops crying and becomes interested in the trucks and plays with one very near his mother. By 8:30 the third teacher has joined the group, all of the children have arrived, and it is time for breakfast.

From Erikson the teachers know that children of this age are striving to become autonomous and to do things for themselves, so the teachers allow the children as much responsibility as they can handle. Breakfast time is announced to the children by a simple statement: "It is time for breakfast. You need to get your chairs and wash your hands." The children proceed to push chairs up to the table and file into the washroom to wash their hands and faces. The sinks are low enough for the children to reach the faucets easily, so they are allowed to turn on the water and wash and dry their own hands unless they ask for help. One teacher is stationed in the washroom to give needed help and to supervise the activity to ensure that most of the water goes down the drain and not on the floor or the children.

Another teacher is stationed at the tables to assist the children to get settled in their chairs, and the third teacher ties a bib on each one. In a short time there are six children at each table ready to eat breakfast. Two of the teachers begin to recite finger plays and sing simple songs with the children, while the third leaves the room to get breakfast. These teachers have learned from experience that mealtime proceeds more smoothly if the children are all seated at the table before the food is brought into the room. Other teachers will find a different routine that works best for them.

When the teacher arrives with the food, she asks Armando's mother to assist her in serving the children. The teachers are trying to help Armando become a member of the group gradually without depending on his mother's presence for security. Armando allows his mother to leave him, and he listens intently to the songs being sung. When all the children have been served, the teachers join the children at the tables and they all eat breakfast together.

During the course of breakfast the children engage in conversations about the spring flowers and the kites in the sky. The teachers take this and many opportunities throughout the day to encourage the children to talk and listen to others.

During the course of the meal the group runs out of toast, and more is needed from the kitchen. The teacher requests that Armando's mother leave the room to get it. The teacher assures Armando that his mother will return shortly. He does not cry, but he does watch the door anxiously. The teachers reason that Armando must have several experiences of having his mother leave and then return again before he can be confident that she will come back to him at the end of the day. Short separations like this one reassure Armando that his mother is not going to abandon him. When his mother returns to the room he smiles and begins to eat again.

Breakfast at the Children's Center is a leisurely affair. The children are allowed to eat slowly and enjoy one another's company. As the children finish, they are again given responsibility. They are encouraged to scrape their plates and stack them on the serving cart; then they remove their bibs and wash their hands and faces. Any child who needs help receives it. Today Nancy refuses to take her plate to the cart. She says, "I don't want to do it." The teacher does not become angry and insist, "Oh, yes you are because I said so," rather the teacher says, "I will do it for you today, Nancy, and then you can take mine for me another day," and the teacher cheerfully removes Nancy's plate. The teachers avoid power struggles with the children. Erikson says that the personality of the child is formed by what the child can will. In this case Nancy was determined not to take her plate. Since her decision was honored, she probably will not assert herself in this area. If her resistance to cooperate persists, the teachers may have to insist that Nancy cooperate, but children are usually cooperative if they think the choice is theirs.

By 9:15 the children are finished with breakfast, they are washed, and the tables are cleaned. The toddlers who have bowel and bladder control are encouraged to use the toilet if they need to. Others who are being trained are set on the small toilets for a short time and they are encouraged to urinate or have a bowel movement. When the children are successful, the teachers praise them and occasionally reward them with a treat. The children are not punished if they do not use the toilet or if they soil their pants. Skinner's principles of operant conditioning are applied to the toilet-training process. The invitation to use the toilet is made many times throughout the day until the children gain control and can remember to use the toilet without being reminded. There are a few toddlers in this class who are not physically ready to be toilet trained. No pressure is put on these children. They wear diapers and are changed regularly. While one teacher helps the children in the bathroom, the other two teachers have activities available for the children in the classroom.

The teachers have formulated a general schedule that guides the daily activities. The schedule allows time for selected goals to be worked toward each day. Specific activities are planned well in advance, so each teacher knows exactly what must be done. The first block of time following breakfast today is devoted to fine motor development and/or concept formation. The teachers have discovered that objectives in these areas can often be worked toward simultaneously because much of the equipment that they have available for fine motor development also involves using concepts.

From Piaget the teachers know that by the time children are two years old, they have usually advanced into the preoperational stage and are capable of forming concepts. This morning the teachers have placed puzzles at one table, beads and string for rug work, pegs and pegboards, geometric form boxes, and graduated cylinders on other rugs, and small table blocks on another table. The children are allowed to select the activity that appeals to them and move from one activity to the next as they like. The teachers rotate from area to area and from child to child, giving assistance where it is needed and responding to the children's efforts and accomplishments.

Today Amy has decided to string beads. She enjoys this activity and her ability to get the beads on the string has greatly improved over the last six months. When she first began to use the beads, getting a bead on the string was a real challenge. Now she is skilled at it and interests herself in patterns and designs with the various-colored and shaped beads. This morning she intently strings only the beads shaped like a cube. She carefully looks through all the beads picking out only the cubes. The teacher watches Amy and offers her a few cube-shaped beads. Amy takes them and puts them on the string. Then the teacher offers her a cylinder-shaped bead. Amy takes the bead, looks at it, then looks at the teacher and laughs. She says, "Not that one, this one," as she picks up another cube-shaped bead. The teacher says, "You are right, I'm a silly," and they both laugh.

Then the teacher moves on to Quincey who is playing with the puzzles and experiencing some difficulty. The teacher asks, "Quincey, do you want some help?" He nods yes so the teacher suggests that he turn the piece around to see if it will fit. Quincey does not seem to understand the word around, so the teacher demonstrates how to turn the piece as the instructions are given. Quincey then slides the piece into its space in the puzzle board. When he tries the next piece, the teacher says, "Turn it around." With only a little help, Quincey turns the piece and fits it in. Quincey picks up the third piece and tries without success to put it in. He looks at the teacher who smiles and says, "Turn it around." He turns the piece around and slips it into place. Then he claps his hands because he knows that he did it without help. The teacher praises Quincey and says, "You did that one all by yourself. Do you want to try it again?" Quincey eagerly turns the puzzle over to empty the pieces and try again. The teacher moves on to another child confident that Quincey can complete the puzzle by himself. If he should have difficulty, he is nearby and can be given assistance. The competent teacher is the one who can take advantage of a situation that arises to help a child learn and gain confidence. This teacher seized this small opportunity to help Quincey comprehend the meaning of the phrase "turn it around" and at the same time allowed him to do as much as he could by himself to feel successful and more competent.

The teachers maintain a flexible schedule that allows the children's interests in specific activities to influence how long each activity lasts. By 9:45 the children appear to be ready for another activity. The teachers have planned a short music session. Children's songs are an excellent medium for language development, and musical instruments give children a sensory experience that requires them to listen closely to the sounds that are made. The music period is announced, and the children are assisted to complete the toy with which they have been working and join the group on the rug in the middle of the room. The teachers sit on the rug with the children, and today Amy chooses to sit next to the teacher who is leading the group. When the teacher asks for requests, Amy quickly shouts "Old McDonald's Farm." The song begins and different children are called on to name a barnyard animal that will be included in the song. Other children request favorite songs and the singing continues.

Godfrey, who is only eighteen months old, has just moved into this group from the infant group. He is not accustomed to sitting in a large group, so he gets up and goes to the block area. He is retrieved by one of the teachers and brought back to the group to sit by a teacher. Today he agrees to be brought back, and he enjoys being next to the teacher. If Godfrey had not wanted to be with the group, he would not have been forced to participate. He would have been allowed to pursue another interest as long as it did not disturb the group.

Today after the first ten minutes of singing, rhythm instruments are introduced. The children are encouraged to listen to each instrument individually as it is presented by the teacher and then each child is given an instrument to play. Amy eagerly waits for the triangle and enjoys hearing the sharp, clear sound it makes. The children accompany their singing with the instruments and are excited to be able to create their own music. Then the teacher leads the children in a march around the room, down the hall, and onto the playground. After marching around the playground several times, the teacher leads the children into a circle and everyone sits on the grass. The children play one more song; then they are instructed to place the instruments in a box that has been provided.

Now that they are on the playground, they are free to play. Armando's mother tells him that she must leave now, but that she will return after naps. Armando begins to cry as she leaves, and he struggles after her. He refuses to be comforted by any of the teachers, but Amy approaches him and seeing his discomfort, she offers to let him ride the tricycle she is on. He accepts the offer and rides off weeping. Children often sense the moods and needs of one another even at this early age.

The primary focus of the time on the playground is on motor development, but many other objectives can also be worked toward while the children are outside. Objectives that relate to self-concept, language development, and sensory acuity are especially appropriate. The permanent pieces of playground equipment are a sandbox, a small jungle gym, a low slide, swings, several tricycles, two wagons, and several large boxes and barrels to be crawled through or over. The equipment was chosen to provide opportunities for muscles to be developed and strengthened. The children can pedal, climb, crawl, run, and dig. As objectives dictate, other pieces of equipment are provided such as balls, balloons, bean bags, tires, and wading pools. One of the objectives that has been selected to be worked toward today is "The children can ascend and descend stairs." The teachers have provided two low sets of steps on two sides of a platform. The children can go up one set, rest on the platform, and then descend on the other side. The children are in varying stages of proficiency at this task. The youngest children crawl up the steps using hands and knees, other children can walk up the steps if their hands are held to help keep them steady, and more skillful children can walk up alone using a handrail. Only a few of the children can descend without assistance. All of the children are encouraged to go up and come down the steps several times while they are outside. One teacher stays near the steps to assist the children and to praise them for their efforts.

Another objective for today is "Give the children a sensory experience in the sand." The teachers have provided shovels and pails, sieves and funnels, and bottles and cups. The children are encouraged to dig, mold, and pour the sand. A portion of the sand is sprinkled with water, so the children can feel the contrast between dry and wet sand.

Today is a beautiful, warm spring day and the toddlers are enjoying their time outside. Because of the weather the teachers make arrangements with the kitchen staff to serve morning snacks outside. Tubs of warm water and disposable towels are brought outside to wash the toddlers' hands and faces before they are given their snacks. After the toddlers are cleaned, they find a space on the grass and wait for their juice and carrot sticks. Snack time provides an opportunity for the children to rest and relax for a few minutes and to take a break from their busy play. They have been active and are quite thirsty. Armando has joined in a little of the outside play, and he, too, is ready for juice. Snack time passes quickly, and the children are ready for more play.

The next fifteen minutes are spent outside in vigorous rough-and-tumble play with both male and female teachers rolling in the grass with the children and playing tag and keep-away. The teachers entice the children to use their entire bodies to reach, stretch, climb, run, and hop.

At 11:00 the group returns to the building for some quiet play before lunch. As the children return to the room, they again are given an opportunity to use the toilet. Those in diapers are checked and changed. One teacher offers a story for the children, while the other teachers prepare art activities. The story is a familiar one to the children, and the teacher tells it with the aid of felt figures on the flannel board. The language objective of today's story is "The children will be able to identify five of the felt objects used in the story." The teachers are aware of Bruner's theory that children begin to represent the world through images during the second year, so they make a special effort to present representations of familiar objects that the children have personally experienced. The flannel figures in the story are a dog, a pair of shoes, an umbrella, a bowl, a girl, a fork, and a spoon. When each of these figures is presented, the teacher pauses and waits for the children to make the identification. The attention span of children this age is short, especially when they are in a large group. Activities in large groups are limited to ten or fifteen minutes. Today's story takes about ten minutes, then the children are ready for their art activity.

There are several options available for the children. Easels with tempera paints have been put up; paper, paste, and miscellaneous collage materials are on one table; and soft clay with rolling pins, cookie cutters, and assorted instruments are on another table. The objectives of these activities are to give the children sensory experiences with the various media, small muscle development through manipulation of the objects, and most importantly, a success experience for each child that helps form a positive self-concept. The teachers are aware of Maslow's findings that children need to have a sense of accomplishment by the age of three for a healthy self-esteem to develop.

Amy chooses the easel and eagerly begins to paint. She works intently for awhile and then announces to the teacher, "I'm through. I will make another one." The teacher tells Amy that the colors she chose are bright and pretty as she hangs the painting up to dry. Then she gives Amy a fresh sheet of paper. Amy feels proud of her work, and she returns to the easel to do another painting. Armando is feeling a little more secure and much more interested. He only resists a little and then timidly begins to manipulate the clay. Slowly he gains enough confidence to pound and roll it. Denise is at the collage table. She works meticulously for twenty minutes pasting pieces of macaroni and bits of cloth in a special design. When she finishes, she sits back and sighs and looks at the creation. The teacher says, "Denise, you certainly have been working hard. You pasted that macaroni very well. Where shall we hang it?" Denise goes with the teacher and selects a space on the bulletin board to hang her work. Then she selects a book and sits down near her collage. She glances at the collage every time she turns the page and then smiles and returns to the book. She has gained a sense of personal satisfaction from her work this morning.

As the children complete their projects, they select toys or books from the low, open shelves and play until lunchtime. The teachers attempt to keep the play during this time happy and quiet to prevent the children from becoming too excited just before lunch. Quiet music is put on the record player, and the children are encouraged to play with balls, the jack-in-the-box, the play telephone, and other toys that do not require the children to be too active. The children are allowed to play with toys they select until it is time to get ready for lunch.

Suzanne's father serves as a parent volunteer who comes to the center three days each week to help serve lunch to the toddlers. He is responsible for setting the tables and bringing the food, while the teachers pick up the room and get the toddlers ready for lunch. At 11:40 he arrives, and the children know that it is time to put the toys away. The children are diapered or given a reminder and an opportunity to use the toilet. They all wash up for lunch.

Six children sit at each table, and one teacher sits with each group. Suzanne's father rotates among the groups. The children can feed themselves quite well but spills are frequent. Lunchtime today is no exception. Godfrey tips over his milk, Amy knocks her bowl of pudding onto the floor, and at least three others drop their spoons. The children are not scolded. Rather, the spills are wiped up, and the teacher gives instructions on how to prevent future accidents. "Your pudding bowl needs to be back from the edge, so it will not fall off." When the children follow the teacher's instructions, they are praised and this behavior is reinforced. "Yes, Amy, that is where the bowl belongs. It will not fall from there. Thank you." Aside from the spills, lunchtime is a pleasant experience. The teachers consciously encourage the children to talk, and they take the opportunity to talk to each child. Every child is made to feel like an important member of the group. The children are allowed enough time to eat slowly and enjoy the mealtime experience.

After lunch the familiar routine of washing and toileting is followed. One of the teachers supervises the bathroom activity, while Suzanne's father and the second teacher clear away the food and clean the eating area. The third teacher sets up the cots and prepares for naptime. Toys that might distract a child are put away, soft music is put on the record player, and the room is darkened. Each child sleeps on the same cot every day, and the cots are located in the same places. Every child has a personal blanket brought from home and a favorite doll, animal, or other cuddly object.

Naptime can be a difficult time with a group of toddlers who are eager to be independent and occasionally defiant. A set routine helps the children know what is expected of them. When the time comes for the children to get on their cots, the teachers play a quiet whispering game. One teacher says "Sh-sh-sh-sh,-" and a hush falls over the room. Then each teacher whispers to a child that it is time for a nap and helps this child onto his or her cot. Each child receives a whisper and the help of a teacher to get on the cot and settle down for a nap. Today, however, at the sight of the others getting on their cots and lying down, Armando begins to scream and cry. The teachers understand his anxiety. He has not been with the group long enough to be sure he is safe and that his mother will return for him. He may be feeling somewhat abandoned. He has managed to survive the morning with several signs of real enjoyment, but sleep is a state that can leave a person vulnerable to unknown factors and Armando is frightened. One of the teachers goes to Armando's assistance and tries to comfort him. The teacher talks to Armando in Spanish, his first language, reassuring him that he is among friends and that he is safe. The teacher offers to sit next to him while he rests on the cot. No mention is made of sleep. He is asked only to rest, so he will be ready to play this afternoon. As Armando lies down on his cot, he focuses his attention on another teacher who is telling a favorite fairy tale to the resting children. When the story is over, soft music is played on the record player and the teachers go from child to child making sure that each one is covered and resting comfortably. Any child who needs a few minutes of the teacher's time is given attention. After the long morning and the vigorous outside play, most of the children are sleeping or resting comfortably by 1:30. The children usually nap from one and one-half to two hours.

The two teachers who have been at the center since 6:30 end their day at 2:30. All the teachers spend the hour from 1:30 until 2:30 in planning and preparation. The plans for the next week were finalized yesterday, so today they make a list of the supplies they need, make finger paint for tomorrow, straighten the room, check to make sure all the equipment is in order, and prepare the bulletin board that will be put up next week. At 2:30 the first two teachers leave, and the director of the center joins the remaining teacher in the classroom for the next half hour until the two afternoon teachers arrive.

Amy and Silas awaken early and begin to giggle and chatter. They are ready to get up and play. Armando did not sleep today, but he did rest and now he, too, wants to get up. The teacher takes these three children down the hall to a large playroom that is used for active play on rainy or snowy days and for nappers who awaken early and threaten to disturb the rest of the class. This teacher is asked to supervise the play of two older children who have also risen early. These older children were in the toddler class last year, and they feel comfortable being left with this teacher. As other toddlers wake up, they are allowed to join the group in the playroom.

At 3:00 the two afternoon teachers arrive. Many of the children are waking up. Cots are put away and preparations are made for afternoon snacks. Amy asks if she can help put the napkins on the tables, and she is given this responsibility. By 3:15 the children are sitting at their tables, eating crackers with peanut butter and drinking chocolate milk. This is a favorite treat.

The day that began so early for Amy and her friends also ends early. Their mothers arrive at 3:30 and are greeted by four happy children. The mothers are given a report of the day's activities and good-byes are given until tomorrow. Armando's mother also arrives shortly after 3:30, and she is eager to hear how the day was for Armando. She is delighted as she enters the room to see Armando sitting at the table eating snacks with the other children. As he sees his mother, an expression of relief crosses his face but he does not cry. He runs to his mother and hugs her. The teacher tells Armando's mother of his progress during the day and asks her to stay for a shorter time tomorrow morning. Armando is given a big good-bye from the teachers and the children, and he is told that everyone will be happy to see him again tomorrow.

At 3:45 the children are given the option of playing outside again or staying in and building with blocks or playing at the water table. Block play is selected by a small group, and one teacher joins them. One of the objectives during block play is "The children learn to play together cooperatively." Toddlers usually do not join together to build one common structure; instead, they play in the same area and each builds a personal structure. However, they do gain experience in sharing the blocks. The floor space for building is shared also, and the teacher encourages them to respect one another's work by moving carefully so that nothing is knocked over.

A sensory experience is one of the purposes of water play. It also helps children comprehend the concepts of floating and sinking. One of the teachers supervises this activity and provides the five children with plastic bottles, bowls, funnels, corks, wood chips, and sponges. The children are provided with plastic aprons to keep their clothes dry, and they are allowed to experiment with the water and the objects. After fifteen minutes of play, soap flakes are added to create bubbles. This is exciting and Suzanne fetches a rubber doll to bathe in the bubble bath.

At 4:30 the teacher brings in the children who have been outside and this teacher leaves for the day. There are only ten children left in the class now and all but three are picked up by 5:00. The parents of the remaining three children never arrive before 5:45 because they do not finish work until 5:30. These three children are allowed to continue with block building and water play, or they select other toys or books off the shelf. While one teacher interacts with the children, the other teacher puts the room in order for tomorrow. At 5:45 Jill and Godfrey's parents arrive. At 6:00 Suzanne waves hello to her dad as she watches him drive into the parking lot. She runs to greet him, and the day has ended at Children's Center for this group of toddlers.

Summary

From eighteen months to three years of age children become more assertive and autonomous. Many goals and objectives can be achieved through routine care as well as special activities. The goals discussed in this chapter are representative of both routine care and special activities, and like the goals discussed for infants, are illustrative of some of the possibilities. The description of the typical day provides another look at how the goals and objectives are treated within an actual context.

Suggested Readings

Furfey, Paul H., ed. *Education of Children Aged One to Three: A Curriculum Manual.* Washington, D.C.: Catholic University of America, 1972. A guide for classroom activities, techniques, and equipment designed to promote intellectual development in toddlers.

Gordon, Ira J.; Guinagh, Barry; and Jester, R. Emile. *Child Learning through Child Play.* New York: St. Martin's Press, 1972. A collection of activities designed for two and three year olds that promote intellectual and physical development and stimulate imaginative play and creative expression.

Keister, Mary Elizabeth. *The Good Life for Infants and Toddlers.* Washington, D.C.: National Association for the Education of Young Children, 1970. A report of a research demonstration project offering care for infants and toddlers and a description of a model designed to provide quality care for young children.

Suggested Activities

1. Select one or more goals from Appendix B and indicate several objectives and activities appropriate for toddlers.
2. Visit a day care setting and observe toddlers at play. How would you describe their social behavior? Are they cooperative and sharing with one another or do they play independently? Compare your findings with other's observations.
3. Toddlers are more assertive than infants. Describe an activity that accommodates this natural assertiveness and helps toddlers become more autonomous.

Chapter Eleven

Three to Five Year Olds

There is an eccentric passage in an early work of Piaget where he says that children in the playground seem to be using intellectual concepts, e.g., causality, a couple of years earlier than they are "developed" in the classroom, but he sticks to the classroom situation because it allows for his "scientific" observation.

Paul Goodman, Summerhill: For and Against
(New York: Hart Publishing Co., 1970), p. 212.

Children are complex creatures whose complexity increases with age. Between the ages of three and five, children develop rapidly. Their vocabularies multiply at an amazing rate, and their physical skills become smooth and coordinated. Many of these children suddenly become very social. All of their intellectual abilities become increasingly complex. Children of this age cannot be typified because of the variability among them.

Goals for Three to Five Year Olds

If a day care setting is intended to be comprehensive in terms of the children's total development, the goals and objectives selected for these ages must reflect the variety of areas in which children develop. The goals and objectives discussed in this chapter are examples of the goals and objectives appropriate to this age range. The list of goals is illustrative, not exhaustive. It is the reader's responsibility to consider the goals offered, formulate other ones, and try out a set of goals that best fits the particular setting in which they will be used.

Create an Environment That Encourages Motor Development

The same division of fine and gross motor development will be maintained that was introduced in Chapter Ten to ensure that objectives and activities are planned in both areas. As children leave the toddler years, their gross motor skills are becoming more coordinated, and their movements are more certain and graceful. During these next years they extend and refine the many skills learned during toddlerhood. Whereas a two and one-half year old must work hard to hop on one foot, an agile four year old can hop on one foot successfully enough to play hopscotch. Likewise, the strained effort to jump up and land on two feet has been replaced by the ability to jump rope casually for long periods of time. With adequate space, equipment, and encouragement, the years from three to five can be a time when motor activities become movements performed with skill and ease rather than effort and concentration. Many objectives that are selected for gross motor development relate to specific pieces of play equipment. For instance, the child "can ride a tricycle using pedals correctly," "can climb up and come down a slide," and "can propel himself in a swing" are all dependent on the child having numerous experiences with the equipment and receiving directions and encouragement from a caring teacher.

Other objectives such as "can throw a ball with reasonable accuracy" or "can catch a ball" will require practice with playmates and the teacher. A large, flexible ball such as a beach ball can be used at first to assist in catching. The size of the ball can be decreased until the children are skilled with a firmer, smaller playground ball. Children below school age seldom have the control to catch a ball as small as a baseball. Most children respond with glee to an invitation from the teacher to play ball. A small group of children can form a circle and play a game in which the object is to toss the ball to a friend and eagerly wait to catch it again. In this and all other areas of gross motor development, there is a great deal of variation in the ages when children gain proficiency. The effective teacher recognizes the differences between children and plans objectives and activities accordingly. By arranging the environment and organizing materials prudently, the teacher can assure that each child will be provided with interesting, challenging activities that promote optimum physical development.

A day care setting provides numerous opportunities for the development of fine motor skills. The ability to manipulate all the fasteners on clothes leads not only to independence for the child but also to small muscle control. The objectives that the child "can tie shoes or sashes," "can zip with help," "can button," and "can snap" are all excellent for fine motor development. Oftentimes children cannot perform these tasks on their own clothes until they have perfected the technique elsewhere. There are several ways to give children experience with these tasks before they use them to dress themselves. Dressing and undressing dolls can help children develop control of buttons and zippers. The dolls and clothes should be large enough so that the fasteners can be handled easily. A small doll with minute buttons would only serve as a source of frustration to a child inexperienced in buttoning. Dressing frames or boards can be purchased or made that provide experience using fasteners. These boards might have large snaps, different-sized buttons, shoelaces and hair ribbons to tie, a separating zipper and a nonseparating zipper, the top of a canvas shoe for lacing, and a belt for buckling. Practicing on an impersonal board that can be held at arms length simplifies the task of learning to fasten. Other pieces of equipment such as lacing cards, snapping blocks, and zipping tote bags can be used to help the children develop these skills.

Applying these new abilities to one's own clothes can sometimes be difficult because of the awkward location of many fasteners on children's clothes, but the children should be encouraged to try and to help each other. Hubert, can you help Ralph tie his shoes before you go outside? Patricia is having difficulty with her zipper. Jeanette, can you help her?" Before long the children will be proclaiming, "I tied my own shoes and buckled my own overalls." When this day comes, the children will have gained new fine motor abilities and will have gained a new sense of ability to care for themselves. This is a clear example of the same activities assisting the children to meet more than one objective.

The housekeeping corner is another ideal location for developing fine motor skills. The children "can sift with a sifter," "can use an egg beater," and "can pour from one container to another" are objectives that concentrate on fine motor control. Most children enjoy using real kitchen utensils and real food products in their pretend play. A sifter filled with flour, corn meal, or sand will give children wonderful practice in squeezing to force the substance through the holes. Children are often fascinated by their ability to move the flour through the sifter and will repeat the process again and again. The use of an egg beater requires finger, hand, and arm control. Children enjoy whipping up soap suds, colored water, or finger paint. Pouring, often a frustrating experience for children, can become a fun activity if it is introduced in a sequence of progressively complex steps. Each step should be mastered before moving to the next step. The first attempt in pouring should be to pour a light substance such as rice or dried split peas from a small container to a larger one. Then liquids can be attempted from a small container to a large one. Then the dry ingredients should be poured from a large container such as a small pitcher to a small container such as a glass. Last a liquid can be poured from a large container to a smaller one. Teachers might easily add other steps to this sequence.

Other kitchen tools such as jars with lids, measuring cups, wire whisks, and basting tubes are useful to help children develop small muscle control. When the children have had some experience using kitchen utensils in pretend play, they are ready to use their skills in cooking projects. There are many simple recipes available that require only basic utensils. Food preparation should be planned for a small group of children so that each one has an opportunity to sift, stir, beat, and scrape.

Another objective appropriate for fine motor development for three to five year olds is that the children "can cut with scissors." This traditional early childhood tool has been elevated in status as an ideal mechanism to develop control of the finger and hand muscles. And, indeed, scissors can serve just this purpose. However, children can easily become frustrated with the task of cutting if they have not learned to use scissors properly. Steps in cutting should be presented sequentially. The first step in using scissors is to show the child how to hold the scissors properly and then, using the proper action of the scissors, cut into a soft substance like clay, bread dough, or sand. Next children can be given cotton balls, pieces of thread, blades of grass, or paper drinking straws that can be cut with one snip of the scissors. After the children master this, they are ready to be introduced to cutting paper. Their first experience with paper should be narrow strips of sturdy paper that can be cut into pieces with one snip of the scissors. Then they can be allowed to cut at random on larger pieces of paper. Children should not be asked to cut on a line until they have had many experiences with scissors and paper. The first line that a child cuts on should be straight. Then the child can progress to simple shapes like a large circle or square. Children under six seldom have enough control of scissors to cut out intricate designs or pictures.

*Create an Environment That Provides
for Maximum Intellectual Development*

According to Havighurst and Muller, the primary intellectual task of early childhood is forming simple concepts of social and physical reality. Basic concepts that relate to chemistry, biology, history, math, language, sociology, physics, music, general science, and many other fields can be acquired by young children. These concepts help the children organize and understand the world in which they live. The number of concepts that children can and should acquire during these years is phenomenal.

The child "can establish a one-to-one correspondence up to five" is a concept that must be acquired before other more complex math concepts are learned. Children can gain an understanding of one-to-one correspondence by assisting the teacher in routine organization of the environment. "Sylvia, the cots are ready for nap time. Will you put one book on each cot, so everyone will have a book to read?" If Sylvia skips a cot or puts more than one book on a cot, the teacher can

*Questions such as how many? how much? and what happens?
are asked and answered as the child investigates.*

assist her and say, "One book on Lisa's cot, one on Jim Bob's cot," and so forth. Another daily routine that requires one-to-one correspondence is setting the table. "Abel, five people will be at your table today. I have placed five chairs around the table. Will you please set one plate, one fork, and one glass for each person at the table?" Other chores that are usually performed by the teacher can be assigned to the children to help them gain independence and at the same time develop this concept. "Rachel, we have notes for our parents today. Will you put one note in each cubby? One note in this cubby, one note in this one. Fine." "Jack, I have put out one sheet of paper for each person. It would be a big help if you would put a paint brush on each paper."

During activity time a one-to-one correspondence can be established by the numbers of children in each area being limited by the number of pieces of equipment. For instance, "Today we have three bean bags, so three people can play with them. One for Daria, one for Michelle, and one for Robert. We have two typewriters. One for Lance and one for Kimberly." Puzzles and pegboards with pegs, which are usually available in day care settings, are especially good for demonstrating a one-to-one correspondence. Each puzzle piece fits in one space, and each hole in the board requires only one peg. Children using pegboards often talk aloud saying, "One in this hole, one in this one, and one over here."

Another objective that can be applied to both the physical and social environment is that the children "can perform simple if-then deductions." Initially, children must hear if-then statements to learn about the environment. "If you turn the water on fast, then it will splash all over the floor." "If we are all finished with snacks, then it is time for a story." "If you turn the puzzle piece around, then it will fit." Children slowly come to see that what happens now has a relationship to what happens later. After they are familiar with if-then statements, the teacher can supply the "if" part of the statement and let the children supply the result. This can be done in real or fantasy situations. The teacher can present a small group of children with a statement such as "If a wonderful fairy flew into our room right now, then . . ." The children can each offer a possible outcome. Children can be encouraged to seek answers to questions such as "If you put the sand in the sieve, what will happen?" or "If you put one more block over here, would it make a difference?" The children experiment to gain answers.

In social situations, questions using "if" help the children reflect on their behaviors. "If you take so long to put the blocks away, what will happen?" The children can think of the logical consequences. "Then we will miss snacks," or "We won't have much time outside." "Roland and John, if you can't play cooperatively with the wagon, then what will happen?" The boys think of the possible results and then decide whether or not to play cooperatively. Using if-then statements in social situations helps children realize that they can foresee the consequences of their behaviors and decide on the basis of the consequences how to behave.

If children have been encouraged to make if-then deductions, by the time they are five they are usually capable of forming the complete deduction without help. "If you will let me play, then I will give you a cookie." "If you don't let me play, I won't be your friend." Once children master this ability, teachers are often bombarded with requests such as "If we are quiet at nap time, can we serve snacks?" and "If it stops snowing, can we go outside?"

Seriation is the graduated ordering of objects in ascending or descending order on the basis of size, length, diameter, amount, or some other attribute. According to Piaget, this is one of the concepts of the physical world that begins to be acquired during early childhood. A reasonable objective is that children "can place five objects in correct order using one attribute as a guide." Children need many experiences with objects that demonstrate the concept "seriation." Blocks or cylinders that nest inside one another and are different only in diameter or size provide a good example. In the block area seriation can be demonstrated with blocks that vary only in length. The housekeeping area provides numerous opportunities to use inexpensive kitchen utensils such as measuring spoons, measuring cups, and mixing bowls that are graduated in size. Empty cans of various diameters can be put on the shelves for make-believe play and nested according to size. Seriation is a concept that requires little explanation if the environment is rich in objects that demonstrate the idea. Children can be encouraged to manipulate felt objects that are graduated in size on a felt board or play with representations of the three bears in three different sizes. Picture books such as *The Three Billy Goat's Gruff* that demonstrate seriation help the children grasp the concept. The number of objects available in the environment to demonstrate seriation is only limited by the teacher's imagination. One innovative center set up a beauty parlor and provided the children with two sets of plastic hair rollers. One set was graduated in height and the other in diameter. As the children removed and replaced the rollers in the containers, they were practicing seriation.

As was seen in the last chapter, toddlers can usually classify on the basis of shape and the name of an object. By the time children are five, they can classify on the basis of more complex attributes and can often use more than one attribute at a time to group objects. A realistic objective is that the children "can classify objects using one or more criteria." For instance, the children can be given an assortment of blue and red buttons to sort in any way they wish. Three-year-old Jennifer will probably sort the buttons into two groups; one group of large buttons and one of small buttons. Four-year-old Pedro might sort the buttons into four groups. The groups could be small red buttons, small blue, large red, and large blue ones, whereas the four groups made by five-year-old Kathleen could be red buttons with four holes, red buttons with two holes, and the same categories with the blue buttons.

Many other classifications are possible, and the children should be encouraged and invited to try many different ones. Children can use their abilities to classify to help organize the room. Alfred can be asked to arrange the books on two shelves. The small books go on the top shelf, and the large books go on the bottom shelf. Children are fascinated with classification as a scheme for organizing the environment. They are quick to place all the square puzzles together and then all the rectangular ones together. All the red pencils can go in one box and all the blue ones in another. All the broken crayons are put in one container and all the unbroken ones in another.

Functional classification can be encouraged by playing the game, "Which one does not belong?" Children are shown several pictures that are related, such as articles of clothing, and a picture of something that does not relate, such as a tractor. They are asked to identify which picture does not belong to the group. If children can think in terms of the function of the object, they can select the odd member of the group. This game can be altered, and one child can be given eight to ten pictures and asked to sort them into groups. The number of the groups may vary depending on the functional area selected by the child. For instance, a tractor, a cow, and a straw hat might be placed in three different groups or they might be placed in the same group if things found on a farm is used as the criterion for inclusion in the group.

Another appropriate objective for three- to five-year-old children is that they "know the function of parts of the body." This objective can be met by talking and reading about parts of the body and how they function. Children who usually depend heavily on sight often do not realize the importance of their other senses. After reading a story about the importance of hearing, the children can close their eyes and have experiences in hearing without seeing an object. They might raise their hands when they hear a sound or try to identify the sound or try to match two identical sounds. This same technique can be used to give children experiences in smelling and feeling. Children might also be encouraged to think of ways their hands help them and how many things they do that require their feet. They can also be made aware of some of the internal organs of the body such as the heart and lungs. Books and pictures help chilren grasp these concepts. And children can be shown how to use a stethescope to listen to their breathing and heart beat.

Create an Environment That Stimulates Language Development

An important concern regarding language for young children is to develop skills that are needed to communicate with others. This remains an important aspect of language throughout life. In addition to serving a communicative function, language for the three to five year old takes on a new role as a medium for self-expression. Children of these ages enjoy playing with words and sounds and are capable of using words to express their thoughts, ideas, and feelings. The two broad areas from which sample objectives will be chosen are communication and self-expression.

Communication is a complex process that involves talking, gesturing, listening, following directions, and understanding the written word, codes, and many kinds of sign language. One of the objectives important to developing communication skills is that children "realize that written language stands for spoken language." This objective can be accomplished by providing varied experiences in which the written word is associated with the spoken word. For instance, each time a child does art work, the teacher should offer to print the child's name on the picture and say, "I have just written your name on your picture. This says Jake." Recognizing the relationship between the sound of one's own name and the printed letters of one's name is often the first step in understanding the relationship between spoken and written language. Children's names can be put on their cots, chairs, cubbies, and clothes to help reinforce this relationship. Labels all over the room help the child grasp the concept of the written word. The teacher can casually say, "This sign says blocks," or "This one says records." When the children leave the day care setting to go on field trips, they can read traffic signs and billboards. At story time the relationship between the print in the book and the verbal story can be made each time a story is read. Story time can even be reversed occasionally. The children can tell the teacher a story that is recorded on a chart and read back to the class. In this activity, the children hear their own words, see them written, and then hear them repeated.

The ability to listen when others speak is a crucial skill that is necessary for effective communication. An objective in this area could be that the child "can listen for up to five minutes when someone else is talking or reading." Listening does not mean simply avoiding talking when someone else is talking; rather it implies hearing and comprehending what is being said. Reading aloud or telling a story to children can provide a good time for meaningful listening if the stories are chosen with the children's interests in mind. Flannel figures or picture book illustrations help focus and hold the children's attention on the story. Some day care settings have listening centers equipped with tape recorders or phonographs with stories that have been recorded on tapes or records. The children insert the tape or put on the record to hear their selected story as they follow along in the book. They are instructed by a signal on the record when it is time to turn the page. The children gain experience in listening to the story and must remain alert to hear the signal.

Other activities that help develop listening skills are group games that require listening and following directions such as "Jack in the box, Jack out of the box" and "Simon Says." These are action games where the children perform bodily movements in response to the directions. Other games can be made up that require the child to listen and follow directions. Children should also be encouraged to listen to each other. Mealtime provides a fine opportunity for children to sit comfortably and talk to each other. The teacher at the table can model good listening skills for the children by being attentive, responding, and asking questions. Each child at the table should be encouraged to listen and contribute to the conversation.

Children enjoy words and find pleasure in using words even when communication is not the purpose of their speech. One only needs to visit a playground and listen for a short time to hear speech being used solely as a means of self-expression. "I'm in the swing, swing, swing that goes faster and faster and then so slow." "Hi, bird. Hi, tree. Hi, sun." "I'm scared of this big slide. I'm getting down." Children's expressive speech often takes on a rhythmic, chanting quality. It is often repetitious and nonsensical. Upon seeing a kitten one child said, "Fat, fat, fat, cat, cat, cat, fat, fat, cat, cat, fat cat, fat cat." Even though he might have been, he was not talking to anyone. He was simply expressing his thoughts about the cat. Teachers can encourage creative expression by capitalizing on a silly mood of the group and encouraging the children to talk nonsense. If the teacher participates, the children will probably be most eager. "Good morning, Mrs. Goddlegee Gum. Where are you going the Feedledee Fun?" will encourage many eager. and equally ridiculous responses. Talking is fun and even the shyest child has nothing to fear because everything is nonsense. Making up stories, jokes, and riddles is an effective way to help children express their ideas and feelings. Stories, jokes, and riddles can be told to the teacher, to a friend, to the class, or spoken into a tape recorder and then played back.

Children are aided in their expressive abilities when they have a vocabulary rich in descriptive words. "Adjectives and adverbs are frequently used in speech" is a reasonable objective. The teacher can bring in new and familiar items and ask the children to describe the articles with as many words as possible. Teachers can introduce new descriptive words to the children through their own use of the words. "My, the little boy in that story was a rascal." "The rainbow is breathtaking." "Our long trip was exciting to me." Soon the same words will appear in the children's speech.

Create an Environment That Allows the
Children to be Imaginative and Creative

According to Erikson, the personality of children at this stage crystalizes around what they can imagine. This is the age where offers of "Let's pretend," "Let's play like," and "Let's make-believe" are frequently heard. Children can easily leave reality and assume the role of an admired adult, a fierce monster, or the family pet. Children act out their dreams and their problems. Imaginative play allows children to express feelings and actions that they cannot express in reality.

The imagination is a useful vehicle for pretending and fantasizing. It is closely related to creativity. Children's creations might be a product made of wood, clay, or paint. They might be an unusual combination of words or movements, or they might simply be unique uses of common objects. Children are naturally creative, and their creativity can either be encouraged or destroyed by the environment. Maslow contends that remaining creative throughout life assists one to become a self-actualizing adult. At a young age children are often told to follow instructions exactly, accept given answers, and not to seek further explanations. They are told to accept security and not to take risks in any areas of their lives. Children who experience this kind of environment usually color the grass green and the sky blue. Coloring books are all they know about coloring, and they are careful to stay inside the lines of the pictures. These children dance the way the teacher does and believe a chair is only for sitting. Children whose creative abilities have been encouraged may color the grass brown and the sky pink because grass and sky are often that way. A blank sheet of paper invites their efforts. These lucky children dance the way the music moves them and know a chair can be part of a train, a tunnel, or a cage for a lion.

Imagination and creativity are two of the wonderous qualities of humans that appear early in life. It is important that these abilities be guided and strengthened, so they can serve the child and the adult the child is to become. The following objectives are specific examples that teachers and children can work toward. Many others will need to be developed to ensure an environment that supports children's creative and imaginative efforts.

The objective that children "engage in creative and imaginative play" is a good starting place. Most children will naturally engage in make-believe play. An environment that stimulates and adults who encourage this kind of play give the children an assurance that make-believe is acceptable and worthwhile. The props that are available to children often dictate the theme that will be chosen by them. A dress-up area that contains only high-heeled shoes, flowered hats, handbags, and jewelry is appealing but has limited appeal. Men's shoes, hats, and topcoats will encourage more boys to participate. Hats and accessories such as a sailor's hat, a fireman's hat, a doctor's bag, and an executive's briefcase that represent professions give a wider selection of roles that can be portrayed by all children. A pretend corner equipped with a kitchen, pots, pans, dishes, dolls, cradles, and utensils can stimulate play that is related to the home. Including boy dolls will encourage boys to adopt the role of a nuturing parent in make-believe play. The pretend corner can easily be modified to be a grocery store by adding empty cans and boxes, a shopper's cart, and a cash register; or it can become an Italian restaurant by adding pizza pans, candles, a chef's hat, and menus. A beauty shop, barber shop, fire station, department store, office, or library can all become the setting for pretend play by adding new props. Children will be encouraged in their imaginative play if an understanding teacher adopts the role of clerk, big sister or pizza chef.

The block area can serve as a stimulus for imaginative play. In this area, children can express their feelings through the accessory pieces that are available. The tiger at the zoo becomes angry at being caged or the farmer is stubborn and refuses to drive the tractor.

Outside time is also valuable as a time for pretending. Space ships can be constructed to take a group to Mars, mountains can be conquered, and a jungle island can be tamed. There are many opportunities throughout the day for teachers to assist children in imaginative play by rearranging the environment and supporting the children's efforts.

Another objective that relates to creativity and imagination is that children "can freely express their feelings and personalities through various media." There are many opportunities in the course of a day during which children should be free to express themselves creatively—dancing to music, singing, modeling clay, sculpting, building with blocks, shaping sand, talking at story time, and making pictures or designs. For children to express themselves creatively, they must have frequent experiences to become familiar with these and other media. When children are given opportunities for self-expression, it is crucial that they not be limited by being told how to build or being shown what to mold. Children can be shown techniques for using each of the media. For instance, they can be shown how to wipe a paint brush to prevent the paint from dripping, how to work clay to make it more pliable, and how to stand a block on end to achieve a different result. But teachers should refrain from modeling a product that the children will be tempted to imitate. If the teacher gives each child a lump of clay and then proceeds to show the children how to make a basket, how to make a dog, and how to make a bird nest many of the children will limit their expression to these same objects even though the teacher did not ask them to limit themselves. Similarly, an activity that requires all children to follow the same instructions to produce an identical product such as a Halloween pumpkin or a May basket can have some merit, but it cannot be considered an activity that allows for creative expression.

Mimeographed or dittoed pictures that are colored by the children leave much to be desired in inspiring creativity. A coloring activity that allows for self-expression would allow each child to draw a personal picture and then color it.

Research studies have shown that intelligence and creativity are not highly correlated traits. In other words, highly creative children are not necessarily highly creative. However, Guilford has identified one distinct intellectual capability called divergent production that is also closely related to creativity. He maintains that to a large degree creative abilities represent a collection of learned behaviors that can be extended or limited by the environment. Divergent production is the formation of new information from existing information. This is in itself a reasonable objective for children: "Children can form new information from existing information." Children can be encouraged to think divergently by being presented with problems that can have many solutions. The children can be asked to think of different uses for a paint brush or a piece of lumber. Children often think of uses that would never occur to an adult. Teachers can allow children to use equipment for purposes other than the original intent. A blanket used at nap time can be used as a tablecloth, a superman cape, a tent, or a tumbling mat. Likewise, a table can become a cage, a house, a mountain, a bus, and a stage. Of course children will not always be able to use classroom furnishings and equipment as they would like, but they should be encouraged to use what is available in reasonable alternative ways. Children should be supported when they offer alternative ways to carry out the daily routine. Kate is showing divergent thinking and creativity when she suggests that the class have music outside and make music with what is found on the playground rather then using rhythm instruments on the rug inside. A teacher who is aware and concerned with children's divergent thinking and creativity would happily follow Kate's suggestion.

Create an Environment That Is Free
from Sex-Role Stereotyping

This is a goal that is being selected in many day care settings across the nation as parents and educators realize the importance of the early years in forming personal identities and social attitudes. This goal is being discussed in this chapter as an appropriate goal for three- to five-year-old children because this is the age when many social attitudes and behaviors become apparent. Ideally, this goal should be adopted for children of all ages.

One objective to help reach this goal is "to present both boys and girls in active and quiet play." The image of young children that is commonly portrayed in children's books, toys, and television programs is rigidly defined according to the sex of the child. Boys are usually involved in sports and outside activity. They are adventurous and daring but seldom quiet and thoughtful. On the other hand, girls are most frequently portrayed as inactive and incapable of physical activities. They are usually inside playing quietly and passively. Children's storybooks are one of the primary sources of portraying these limited images of children. The story content of many books directly prescribes behaviors that are appropriate for each sex. The illustrations in many books subtly reinforce these same prescriptions.

*Both boys and girls should be encouraged to engage in vigorous
outside play.*

Teachers in day care settings must carfully screen books used with the children to ensure that both boys and girls are portrayed enjoying active and quiet play.

The work of Bandura and Walters indicates that children model the behavior of a same-sexed model more readily than a model of the opposite sex. For this reason, it is desirable to have teachers of both sexes working with young children, and it is crucial that teachers of both sexes engage in both active and quiet play with the children. Both male and female teachers should run on the playground, climb the jungle gym, and play tag just as they should both play the puzzles and water the plants.

Another aspect of children's personalities that is stereotyped by books, toys, television, and adults in the environment are the emotions that are appropriate for each sex to express. Boys are taught very early to be brave, fierce, tough, aggressive, and mischievous. They are told not to cry or to be tender. Girls are clearly expected to be passive, dependent, easily frightened, courteous, and pretty. They can cry and show love, but they must not be brave or assertive. Another appropriate objective to help meet the goal is "to encourage boys and girls to develop and express a full range of emotions."

Again, children's books are a culprit in promoting and reinforcing this false image of children. Young boys aged three to five are not brave enough to fight alligators and trap burglars, nor are three- to five-year-old girls. When children are presented with literary heros who perform such outstanding deeds of bravery, feelings of inferiority can develop because the children know they cannot live up to the actions of the models. However, children of both sexes are capable of bravery when more realistic situations such as sleeping in the dark, attending a new school, moving to a new neighborhood, and being separated from mother or father in a department store are discussed. Children of both sexes are also capable of fear, sadness, and happiness, and they should be allowed to express these emotions by crying, laughing, and showing love. Children's books that allow all children a full range of emotions must be selected. Fortunately, many children's books are now appearing that show both boys and girls involved in all kinds of play and expressing many different emotions.

The emotions that children learn to express are often the ones that they are allowed to express. Either directly or subtly, adults let children know what behaviors are acceptable and what emotions they may openly express. How many times have teachers of young children told little boys, "Don't cry. Big boys don't cry. Wipe your eyes. You're all right now"? These same teachers will usually respond to a crying girl with a hug and a pat and no direction to stop crying. However, if this same girl becomes angry and stomps and hits, she is quickly stopped and told to be a lady and not to act "ugly." She is to tell the teacher or accept an injustice. Boys, on the other hand, are allowed to express anger and defend themselves against unfairness. Teachers of young children in day care and other group settings must carefully examine their own attitudes, actions, and expectations that might be limiting the emotional expression of the children in their charge.

Another objective for presenting an environment free from sex-role stereotyping is "to present men and women performing a variety of jobs outside the home." It is no wonder that 90 percent of preschool girls say they want to be a teacher, a nurse, or a mommy when they grow up. These are the only roles they see women performing! Girls and boys should be exposed to adults of both sexes performing many different kinds of work. In day care settings and kindergartens all over America, a unit on community helpers is commonplace to introduce the children to the community and the world of work. When this unit is planned, both men and women can be shown working in roles of service to the community. Perhaps a male and female letter carrier can be invited to the classroom, or maybe the children could visit a female doctor in her office, or a female police officer could take the children on a tour of the police station. Men and women telephone operators could be discussed as well as men and women telephone installers. Books should be selected that show adults selecting their occupations on the basis of interest rather than gender. One delightful book titled *The Sheep Book* (Carmen Goodyear) tells the story of a farmer who feeds the sheep, shears the wool, and makes the wool into yarn. The story is unique because the farmer is a woman. Sometime in the future such stories may be less unique.

A Typical Day for Three to Five Year Olds

Children's Land Day Care Center is a small facility that provides care for twenty-one children from three to five years of age. The center is located in a remodeled three-bedroom house in a residential area. Most of the children who are enrolled live in the area, and the majority of the parents work nearby.

The day begins in a lively way every morning at 7:00 A.M. This is when the center opens, and Bryan always arrives promptly at seven. Bryan is an active four year old who is full of energy and mischief. This morning is no exception, and he bursts through the door ready to start the day. The teachers welcome him and invite him to talk or play. This morning Bryan chooses to talk, and he has the undivided attention of the teachers. He tells them every detail of the television programs that he viewed the evening before. Soon Bryan is joined by Erin and Lisa. These girls are neighbors and very good friends. They ask to play on the playground and invite Bryan to join them. One of the teachers accompanies the children outside, and the other remains inside to greet the rest of the children. During the next half hour, children arrive and are allowed to play inside or out. This time in the early morning is not scheduled with specific activities, but the children are allowed to choose toys off the shelves, play in the learning centers, or play outside. At 7:45 Shane and his mother enter the center. Shane hangs his sweater in his cubbie and asks the teacher where Bryan is. These two boys spend a lot of their time together.

As these three to five year olds arrive this morning, one can readily see how different they are from infants and toddlers. They are self-sufficient and relatively capable of taking care of themselves. Their movements are definite and come easily. The children are social and talkative and happy to see their friends.

By 8:00 the house is buzzing with conversation and busy with children building, working, drawing, and looking at books. The playground is also an active place where the children are running, climbing, and riding. At 8:15 the children are given notice that it is time to pick up, put the room in order, and get ready for breakfast. Sabre, Frank, and Dianna are reminded that it is their day to set the tables. Throughout the day the children are encouraged to assume responsibility for the routine of the center. By 8:30 the toys have been put away, hands are clean, and the tables are set. Dianna announces to the group that it is time to come to the tables for breakfast.

All the meals here are served family style and the children fix their own plates. A teacher sits at each table to give assistance and talk with the children. Breakfast is a casual time during which the children retell favorite events and make plans for the day. During breakfast the door opens and Adrienne enters with her mother. One of the teachers goes to the door to say good morning and to invite Adrienne to join the group for breakfast. As she nears the tables, Lara shouts, "Adrienne, come sit by me." Adrienne smiles and joins the table for breakfast.

When the children have finished eating, they stack their plates on a tray, push in their chairs, and leave to wash their hands. Tony is leaving the table, and the teacher reminds him, "Tony, you forgot your plate." "Oh, yea," says Tony as he returns to place his plate on the stack. Even though the activities change, the daily routine remains the same at Children's Land because the teachers are familiar with Maslow's findings that young children need and like routine. A set routine helps children know what is expected of them and gives them control of themselves and their environment. The children know that they are to find a place to sit on the red rug when they have washed up after breakfast.

It is only 8:50 and all but four of the children have finished breakfast and are on the rug. One teacher stays with the children at the tables, and the other two join the children on the rug. The teacher on the rug tells the children who are still eating, "Take your time and finish breakfast. We will sing songs until you are through." The teachers and the children form a circle on the rug and sing several songs suggested by the children. Today they enjoy songs with many motions and a lot of action. Then Chris suggests that they sing a song in rounds. Everyone agrees. The group divides in half and they sing. "Row, Row, Row Your Boat" as a round. On the first try the group finishes together, but on the second try they are successful and everyone is delighted. The four children from the table join the group, and the teacher says, "Everyone has finished and we are all together. Now we can have our story." Again, from Maslow the teachers know that children need to feel that they are loved and belong to a group. The teachers take many opportunities throughout the day, such as this one, to let the children know that each one is loved and valued as a member of the class.

"Do you remember yesterday when we walked through the park to see the signs of spring? Can you each remember something that you saw? Frank, what sign of spring did you see?" "The mushrooms," Frank replies. "What did the mushrooms look like? What other signs of spring did you see, Erin? Oh, yes, the new green leaves on the trees!" The teacher continues talking and posing questions to encourage the children to use their memories to recall the sights seen on yesterday's trip and to use their language abilities to describe the sights. From Guilford's structure of intellect, the teachers know that the memory is one component of intelligence, and therefore provide opportunities for the children to exercise their memories by recalling past events and verbalizing about them. After each child has had an opportunity to share a personal observation with the group, the teacher reads a story about spring that includes many of the things the children saw yesterday.

Then the teacher offers to teach the children a new song about spring. The children respond in a positive way and are eager to hear it. One teacher plays the piano, while the others sing the song for the children. One phrase is sung and the children repeat it. In just a short time the children can sing the verse and the chorus. Songs help increase children's vocabularies and group singing enables even the shyest child to use language as a means of expression. When the song is finished, the children know that it is now activity time.

Activity time lasts about an hour. It is an exciting part of the day. The teachers have organized this facility into separate learning centers. Each center was planned with the specific needs of three- to five-year-old children in mind. There is a block area, a library, a listening center, an art area, a dress-up and pretend corner, a woodworking area, a science table, and a water and sand area. Other areas are set up from time to time to provide new experiences for the children. The children are allowed to select an area to play in and they are dismissed from the rug. The children can move from area to area during the hour, and the teachers are actively involved with them during this time. They help direct the children so that no area becomes overcrowded, and they assist the children in their play. Today Bryan and Shane begin the activity period at the science table. They help one of the teachers clean out Susie's cage. Susie is a golden guinea pig that lives in the classroom. She is gentle and chatters constantly. Bryan goes to the kitchen to get vegetable scraps for her and Shane fills her water bottle. The boys enjoy the responsibility of caring for Susie. They wash their hands after this chore and then they experiment with magnets at the science table. They discover that not all objects are attracted to a magnet. The boys form two classes of objects: those that are magnetic and those that are not. The teacher assists the boys to use the available evidence and information to determine that only objects that contain iron are attracted to a magnet. The process of arriving at a unique answer from existing information is called "convergent production" by Guilford. Even though the rule of magnetic substances is known to many adults, it is a novel discovery to these two boys. The teachers provide many opportunities every day for the children to form logical deductions about their environment.

When the boys feel satisfied that they understand magnets, they leave the science table and go to the pretend corner. Erin and Lisa have been in this area setting up a grocery store since the period began. They have organized the shelves with all the cereal boxes on one shelf, the spice jars together next to the boxes, and the cans of vegetables on another shelf. They are exhibiting an understanding of the principle of classification discussed by Piaget when they group the objects in this way. Lisa is now the cashier and Erin is the manager who is busy stocking the shelves. They welcome their first two customers of the day, but Shane and Bryan object. They state flatly that women shop at grocery stores and men are the stockers and checkers. They want to trade places with the girls. The girls insist that men do shop and that the boys must be the shoppers if they want to play. An argument ensues that frustrates all of the children. The teacher listens and waits to see if the children can resolve their dilemma without teacher intervention, but it appears that they need help. A male teacher intervenes and asks the children to present the problem. Bryan quickly protests that grocery shopping is a woman's job and that Erin and Lisa should be the shoppers. The teacher offers that he frequently does his own grocery shopping because that way he gets to buy the kind of food he wants and that at his store both women and men shop for groceries and both men and women work in grocery stores. The children consider this explanation and agree to take turns being shoppers and workers. Soon the children are engaged in a pretend game of shopping with grocery carts being wheeled about and extravagant purchases being made. Expressions such as "The price of food today is awful," "This bread is stale," and "Mmm, what nice big tomatoes" can be heard. The teachers encourage frequent use of the pretend corner because from Erikson they know that children grow and develop from assuming the role of others and that the personality crystallizes around what children imagine they can be. During activity time, the pretend corner is never empty. Here the children experience the world through their imaginitive play.

At 10:20 the children are informed that they have only ten minutes left in the activity period. This is a cue for them to begin to finish their play. At 10:25 another notice is given and the children begin to put away their equipment and get ready for morning snacks. Snack time passes quickly with the children assuming most of the responsibility. One child at each table passes out the crackers and another child pours the juice from a small pitcher.

Within fifteen minutes the children are outside for active play. Their outside area contains an adventure playground designed and built by a group of parents. They used common materials such as boxes, telephone poles, rope, tires, barrels, sand, and railroad ties to create an exciting environment out-of-doors. The equipment encourages climbing, sliding, swinging, balancing, and jumping. In addition, tricycles, wagons, and balls are always available. Other pieces of equipment are also added for special activities. The children enjoy the familiar equipment and they run, pedal, dig, and have many experiences to use their large muscles. Today Shane, Bryan, Dianna, Tony, and Lexy form a wagon train comprised of tricycles and wagons that heads for the West. The wagons break down, the train is attacked by bad guys, and they must take many detours because mountain passes are snowed in, but somehow they arrive in the West before time to go inside. While two teachers supervise the children on the playground, the third stays inside and prepares for the upcoming activity.

The next thirty minutes are devoted to individual intellectual and manipulative tasks. This period of time is called work time by the children and the teachers. The children select from many pieces of equipment that are designed to promote intellectual development. The teachers know from Havighurst and Muller that the major intellectual task of early childhood is forming concepts. The equipment is selected to foster an understanding of math concepts, spatial relations, science concepts, seriation, classification, temporal relationships, and other abstract concepts. The equipment includes puzzles, geometric form boards, number sorters, beads for stringing, shape sorting boxes, nesting barrels, dominoes, toys that show likenesses and differences, graduated cylinders, rhyming pictures, felt letters, attribute blocks, counting boxes, sequence pictures, and other aids.

The children select pieces of equipment and take them to their spaces on the rug to work with them. The equipment challenges them, and they are eager to master each piece. For example, Bryan selects a set of sequence pictures, but he is not sure what to do with them. The teacher assists Bryan to think about what happened first and what happened next. "Bryan, what was the frog before he was a frog?" "He was a tadpole." "Right, so which picture comes first? "Oh, sure. The tadpole, I get it." This activity helps Bryan think about temporal relationships. Each child works with one piece of equipment at a time. When this piece is returned to the shelf, another piece is selected. The teachers go from child to child giving assistance and encouragement and praising the children for their efforts. "Lexy, you have almost finished with the cylinders, and it did not take you long at all."

Today Frank is not interested in the work. He refuses an offer to go to the library and look at books or to the listening center to listen to a record and he persists in disturbing the children around him. The teacher remembers from Bandura and Walters' studies of imitation that children's behaviors can be affected by the consequences received by a model, so the teacher looks around Frank for a child admired by him who is behaving in a cooperative manner. The teacher approaches Tony and says, "Tony, I like the way you are working today. Since you have been so cooperative, I will let you choose the story for story time." The teacher does not direct any attention to Frank but makes the comment loudly enough for Frank to hear it. Then the teacher gives Tony a pat on the back and goes on with the activities. Frank listens to the teacher, sits quietly for a moment, then begins to work. The teacher makes a mental note to let Frank choose the story tomorrow if his behavior at the work period is acceptable. The children work intently during this half hour; then the equipment is put away. Now it is story time. Tony selects a story about a wagon train and the Wild West.

While one teacher reads to the group, the other two teachers prepare the tables for lunch and ready the cots for nap time. This story is a familiar one to the children, and they assist the teacher in presenting it. The teacher pauses at the key words and the children eagerly fill in the blanks. The teacher also tests the children's listening skills by substituting inappropriate words for words in the story. The teacher solemnly reads, "The mountains were covered with ice cream." The surprised children shout in unison, "No, covered with snow!" "Well, you all are becoming such good listeners I cannot trick you anymore." At the end of the story, the children wash their hands and come to the tables for lunch.

Lunchtime at Children's Land is usually a happy time. The food is excellent and plentiful. The children are not forced to clean their plates but are encouraged to eat a balanced diet. The children serve their own plates, and they are reminded to take only as much as they can eat. The children are encouraged to talk and share their experiences with each other, and they often make plans for the afternoon during the lunch period.

After lunch the children divide into three small groups for their "circle." This is the only time during the day when the children are divided into age groups. Each teacher makes a presentation to one group that is informative and interesting. When these lessons are planned, the children's levels of intellectual development are considered. From Bruner and Piaget the teachers know that children this age are capable of representing the world symbolically. That is, codes, sounds, or signs that have no meaning in and of themselves come to have meaning because of their attachment to an object or an idea. Today, as part of a unit on travel and transportation, Bryan's group is introduced to traffic signs and the meanings that these symbols represent. Most of the children can recognize and explain the meaning of the stop sign; the red, yellow, and green traffic light; and the railroad crossing sign. However, the yield sign, one-way sign, and pedestrian crossing sign are unfamiliar to them. The children are intrigued with the important function that a group of symbols can serve, and they request traffic signs for the playground. The teacher agrees that this would be a good idea and suggests that they make them during activity time the day after tomorrow. The children agree and decide they will need four signs. Now it is 1:15 and time for naps.

The children are allowed to select a book and a puzzle to take to their cots. Working with puzzles helps them get quiet and relax. They recline and look at their book or work their puzzle. The teachers trade the books periodically, so the children can have a variety. Most of the children in this group still take a one- to two-hour nap. Records are put on the record player for those who do not sleep. There are several children who no longer require naps. They must rest until 2:00, then they are allowed to go outside until the other children awaken.

The activity that follows naps each day is creative art, so the teachers take advantage of the nap period today to get all the materials ready. At 2:00 two of the teachers leave and two others arrive in time to supervise Lisa, Erin, Bryan, Shane, and Lara on the playground. By 3:00 all of the children are awake and ready to get up. Those outside come in.

Books, puzzles, and cots are put away and hands are washed in preparation for snacks. Today snack time is a special occasion. The afternoon snack consists of large, pig-shaped cookies. The children made pigs as an art activity yesterday. The teachers mixed the dough, and each child rolled out a ball of dough and pressed out the pig shape with a cookie cutter and then decorated the cookie. The cookies were baked and cooled; and the children agreed to save them for today's snack, so now the time has arrived and the children chant, "Little pig, little pig, I'm going to eat you up," and indeed they do. The children request another cooking activity, and the teachers promise one for next week.

After the cookies have been eaten, it is time for art and the children are given several choices. Wood scraps, glue, nails, and hammers are available in the woodworking area for wood sculpture. Easels are set up. Paper, tempera paint, sponges, and string are on one table for sponge painting and blow painting. Another table offers the makings for uncooked clay that the children can help make and then use for modeling. The children also have the option of selecting markers, crayons, pencils, paste, scissors, and paper off the art shelves and planning their own activity. With such a wide variety of choices, all the children easily find an activity that interests them.

Today Adrienne is encouraged to do a wood sculpture because she has had little experience with the hammer. She agrees but has difficulty managing the wood, the nail, and the hammer all at the same time. She decides to leave this area. The teacher helps her select another activity and makes a note on the lesson plans for next week to help Adrienne gain experience with the hammer by allowing her to drive nails into an old tree stump that has been brought into the area for this purpose. The stump is heavy and sturdy, so Adrienne will be able to concentrate on driving the nail.

This afternoon Bryan chooses to help make the clay. He measures the flour and helps stir until the clay is smooth. Then he begins to form a pond filled with worms, fish, and alligators from the clay. The principal objective during art period is "to provide the children with opportunities for creative expression," but many other goals are also being served such as manipulation, social development, and a healthy self-concept. The children are allowed to use as many media as they like and stay in the art center for as long as they like.

At 4:30 the children are given two other options in addition to art work. They may go outside or play in the learning centers. Bryan decides to put up the clay and go to the block center. He enjoys spending some time each day playing with the blocks. In the block center, the wagon train theme is taken up again and Bryan builds trails and mountains that must be crossed on the journey west. His imagination converts cars and trucks to covered wagons and modern space explorers to pioneers. His mother arrives at 5:15 just before the train arrives in the West, so she agrees to give him five more minutes to get the travelers to their destination. This is easily accomplished. Bryan and his mother put the blocks away and say good-bye to friends until tomorrow. Several other parents are arriving as Bryan and his mother leave, and by 6:00 everyone has gone home for the night. They will be back in the morning to begin again.

Summary

By definition, comprehensive programs for three to five year olds require attention to all areas of development. Goals should be selected that foster development in all the areas discussed in Section Three. As is the case with the other chapters in Section Four, the goals discussed are merely samples of some of the possibilities. The typical day provides a view of an actual program that attempts to implement the purposes and goals of a curriculum.

Suggested Readings

Cherry, Clare. *Creative Art for the Developing Child.* Belmont, Calif.: Fearon Publishers, 1972. A collection of art techniques and activities that use a variety of media that provide opportunities for creative expression.

Hymes, James L., Jr. *Teaching the Child Under Six,* 2d. ed. Columbus, Oh.: Charles E. Merrill Publishing Co., 1974. A discussion of critical issues related to the education of young children with the needs of children given primary consideration.

Seefeldt, Carol. *A Curriculum Guide for Child Care Centers.* Columbus, Oh.: Charles E. Merrill Publishing Co., 1973. A guide for planning a child care program that considers the diverse needs of children and a discussion of the influences of teachers, parents, community, and nation.

Sprung, Barbara and George, Felecia. *A Model for Non-Sexist Child Development.* New York: Women's Action Alliance, 1975. A report of a project designed to develop a nonsexist curriculum guide for early childhood education. Goals, objectives, and activities are included.

———— *Non-Sexist Education for Young Children: A Practical Guide.* New York: Citation Press, 1975. A description of goals and activities of a nonsexist nature that are appropriate for young children.

Suggested Activities

1. Select one or more goals from Appendix B and indicate several objectives and activities appropriate for three- to five-year-old children.
2. Observe some three to five year olds in a group setting. Do the children seem to differentiate between play and work? If so, how? If not, speculate why not.
3. Can you find three year olds as large and/or as proficient at some skills as some five year olds? What are some implications of your findings for planning activities for three to five year olds?

Chapter Twelve

School-Age Children

> . . . the business of a school is not, or should not be, mere instruction, but the life of the child.
>
> *George Dennison,* The Lives of Children
> *(New York: Vintage Books, 1969), p. 6.*

School-age children who spend their out-of-school hours at home without adult supervision have been termed "latchkey" children. This term was coined because these children frequently wore the key to their homes on a string around their necks to let themselves in and out of the empty house until the parents arrived later in the day. As more mothers began to work, the number of latchkey children in America rose sharply because there were few day care facilities that offered care for the school-age child. This problem has not been rectified by any means, but there has been a realization of the day care needs of school-age children both before and after school and on days when they are not in school.

Day care settings for school-age children must be equipped with toys, games, and supplies that are appropriate for six to twelve year olds. Elementary school children are amused for a short time by simple wooden puzzles and rocking boats, but the novelty soon wears off and more challenging equipment is needed.

Another area where day care centers must make an adjustment when school-age children are enrolled is in the rules that govern the children's behavior. The same rules that apply to young children are often foolish and inhibiting to a school child. For instance, most day care centers require that an adult accompany the child into the center and leave the child in the charge of a staff member. This is a reasonable rule that ensures the safety of each child. However, eight-year-old Ben has been walking four blocks to and from school for three years. In the summer he attends a day care center. Is it necessary that an adult accompany him from the parking lot into the classroom? Of course not! Expecting this is insulting to the child and to the parents.

The day care setting for older children should include more varied experiences than day care settings for younger children. School-age children need a home base to check into every day and much time will be spent in this place. But field trips, a hike to the neighborhood park, visits to the library and museum, swimming lessons at the city pool, and other activities will occupy a great deal of time and frequently take the children out of the immediate day care facility. These excursions should be expected and well planned. Parents should be made aware of them in advance by signing a blanket permission slip for short trips and giving special permission for longer jaunts.

In a word, day care programs for school-age children must be designed to meet the developmental level of these children rather than expecting them to adapt to a setting they have long since outgrown.

Goals for School-Age Children

The process of selecting goals for a day care program serving school-age children will differ somewhat from the process of selecting goals for younger children. This difference is caused by the increasing number of institutions having an influence on older children. In addition to the family, the school, the church, and youth organizations are all attempting to guide children's development in one or more areas. The role of the day care center should be to supplement and support the family and these other institutions. The resources of the community should provide a foundation for the day care program with the program taking advantage of existing services to help meet the children's needs. The emphasis of the day care setting will be on goals from areas of development that may not be met by the other institutions. The goals that are selected will vary from child to child and from setting to setting based on the children's needs and the parents expectations. Some parents expect a day care setting for older children to provide tutorial experiences to assist children in schoolwork; others view day care as a recreational arts and crafts program; while others consider it as a substitute home-neighborhood setting that assists in social development by providing friends and a place to play. Day care for school-age children can meet one or a combination of these and other expectations. It is conceivable that when the day care curriculum is being developed or evaluated, the older children should be represented on the committee and be allowed to contribute information on their interests, dislikes, levels of development, how much independence they would like, and how much responsibility they can assume. The curriculum should remain flexible and be subject to change depending on the needs and interests of the children currently being served.

In essense, the parts of the day care curriculum designed for school-age children should provide for positive relationships among the children and between the children and the staff. Guidance and activities that help children develop optimally should be considered also. All of this should be offered as a supplementary service to the other institutions that affect the child.

Provide Opportunities for the Children to Develop Socially

There are numerous external factors that affect the social development of a school-age child. Family, home setting, teachers, friends, youth organizations, television, books, and the school are only a few of the direct and indirect influences on the children's social development. During early childhood children primarily look to the family and other adults for guidance, support, and an identity. As the children progress into middle childhood, the attitudes and behaviors of peers begins to exert more influence on their social behaviors. The older the children become, the more powerful peer influence becomes. Children at this age enjoy one another's company and attention.

They enjoy talking, laughing, and sharing ideas with each other. Children need opportunities to develop and cultivate friendships. This need, often overlooked in school settings, can easily be met in day care where the environment is flexible and large portions of the time can be spent with friends in mutually satisfying activities.

Havighurst offers that the social task of middle childhood that consumes a great deal of the children's energies is learning to get along with age-mates. This task implies that children develop social skills of taking turns, sharing, working cooperatively, and being considerate of others. The acquisition of each of these skills can be an objective that is actively worked toward. Children can be assisted to learn to take turns by playing group games that require playing in a given sequence. Board or table games such as Checkers and Monopoly help children to learn to wait for their turn. Class guidelines can be set up that limit the use of favorite pieces of equipment. For instance, the typewriter can only be used for fifteen minutes, then it must be given up if another child is waiting for it. This practice helps children learn to share and to wait for a turn. Group projects that require planning and a joint effort such as making a valentine box provide children with experiences to work together in a cooperative way. The acquisition of these and other social skills takes place in all activities during the time spent at the center under the guidance of a conscientious teacher.

The third level in Maslow's hierarchy of needs is the belongingness and love needs. At this level children feel a need for close friends and a membership in an accepting group. They can feel loneliness and rejection if they are not accepted by their chosen group. The social unit that comes to have meaning for the school-age child is the club or the gang. Children formulate clubs on the basis of interests and needs, oftentimes without adult assistance. The children write the rules that specify criteria for membership, activities, and the grounds for expulsion. Clubs give children a sense of belonging and a feeling of rejection and unworthiness if they are not included. Teachers in day care settings should assist children to use their clubs for positive social interaction rather than for discrimination. These clubs are typically short-lived but with adult guidance they can become a more stable organization that provides a sense of unity among the children and an avenue to meet objectives pertaining to positive social growth. Through clubs children can be helped to plan goals and then work to meet the goals, thus developing a sense of social responsibility. For instance, a Christmas club formed during the holiday season to decorate the room and the tree could be guided into other activities such as singing Christmas songs for the younger children and making cookies for the Christmas party. A tennis club formed in the summer might seek adults to teach the children the game and then plan a weekly outing to the tennis courts for practice. A monster club could share stories and books about monsters. An understanding teacher could show an appreciation for this unusual interest by assisting the children in planning and producing a horror show for the Halloween party. Teachers should take advantage of children's natural tendencies to band together around common interests to help the children develop social skills and learn to live by rules agreed on by the group.

The shift in the way children perceive the world also has an influence on their social development. The early childhood orientation toward fantasy and play is slowly replaced by reality and a need for competence. Erikson calls this the age of industry in which children are concerned with mastery of the technology and skills of society.

School-age children are intrigued with the work and hobbies of adults and seek instruction on how to do things. One objective that relates to a sense of industry is that the children "actively seek competence in skills and techniques that provide control of the environment." This objective is broad enough to include many areas of interest. Children may want to help with yard work, or they may want to be responsible for bringing in the mail, feeding the hamster, stacking the chairs, decorating the bulletin board, putting the records on the record player, or setting the table. There are literally hundreds of adult-related activities that are performed in a day care setting that older children can assume. One day care center analyzed the requests for participation by the after-school youngsters and designed different jobs for which the children could volunteer. One job was an office helper who answered the telephone and took messages for the director, filed pictures, and checked books in and out. Another was a kitchen helper who helped prepare and serve afternoon snacks and assisted in food shopping. Still another was a baby helper who assisted in feeding, dressing, supervising, and entertaining the babies. The children were made to feel like responsible contributing members of the group and indeed they were.

Gaining a sense of industry does not need to be limited to routine activities performed by staff members. Special projects such as gardening, cooking, and building a model railroad help children acquire skills and a feeling of competence. Projects that involve equipment such as microscopes, tape recorders, and looms used by adults are also very appealing to children. When children have been given opportunities to expand their abilities and master new skills, they have been assisted toward becoming responsible, competent people

Provide Opportunities for the Children to Develop Motor Skills

During middle childhood the children's motor abilities continue to develop and become more refined. Specifically, children develop more coordination and more precise control over their movements. They become faster and stronger. Children this age the world over are characterized by their abilities that involve the use of these new physical skills. Perhaps these children are most noted for the games they play. The fondest memories of many adults revolve around childhood games. The traditional games played by children such as leap frog, tag, chase, jump rope, and kick-the-can require physical action, practice, and more than one participant. Many children today are being deprived of the physical development, social interaction, and pleasure that games provide. Children's free time is frequently occupied by television, electric football sets, and dolls. An after-school or summer day care program is an ideal setting for children to experience the physical stimulation and mental satisfaction that can be gained from playing games. An objective could be "The children play and enjoy simple games." Group games that require the children to be active but do not require specific complex skills such as Red Rover, Statues, Musical Chairs, Mother May I, Drop the Handkerchief, and Crack the Whip are fun and a good introduction to the world of games. Older children are generally ready to practice and gain skills that are necessary for other games such as baseball, soccer, football, volleyball, shuffleboard, and horseshoes. Games that require the control of small muscles can also make an important contribution to motor development in middle childhood. Jacks, marbles, pick-up-sticks and tiddleywinks are traditional favorites. Games for children develop physical skills and at the same time help children learn to follow rules and play cooperatively.

Middle childhood is the period when children develop the physical abilities and interests necessary to pursue individual efforts in sports and the physical arts. An objective that states "The children be introduced to and encouraged to participate in many activities that require individual effort" is worthwhile. For instance, a dance instructor could be invited to give a six-week course in introductory ballet or a judo expert could be called in to instruct the children in this Oriental technique of self-discipline. Swimming lessons, as well as opportunities for tumbling and gymnastics should be available for interested children. Other activities that are frequently sought out are twirling, archery, skating, bowling, and wrestling. It would be unrealistic to expect one day care setting to provide children with experiences in all of these areas,

The school-age child works hard to become proficient on equipment requiring physical skill.

but an occasional trip to the bowling alley or the skating rink should be possible. Frequently, however, many of these activities are available in the community through youth centers, community centers, and park and recreation departments. Coordination of services between the day care setting and these other agencies leads to the activities being available to the school-age child enrolled in day care.

Erikson characterizes the child at this age as industrious and interested in learning the technology of the society. The motor abilities slowly being acquired throughout middle childhood enable children to become proficient in using the tools commonly used by adults. An objective that the children "can use tools effectively" is a broad one that allows for many specific interests of children. Children of both sexes should be allowed and encouraged to participate and gain skills with a variety of tools. Frequently the tools chosen by children are those that help the child create a finished product.

The area of woodworking and construction is one that interests many children and can provide many success experiences. Children must be shown the proper way to use a hand saw, a hammer, nails, and clamps. After these basic tools have been mastered, the children can be introduced to wood chisels, hand drills, and planes. Mastery of each tool requires coordination and precision of movements and a lot of practice, but with mastery comes a strong sense of pride and competence.

Needlework is another area that has increasing appeal for the young. Knitting needles, crochet hooks, embroidery needles, and the variety of yarns and threads available is fascinating to children, and the products that children can produce with these tools is often amazing. Eye-hand coordination and the precise control of the hand and finger muscles are developed by needlework.

Gardening is a task that offers new tools to the child and an opportunity to use large muscles. The muscles of the arms, back, and legs are all used in chopping, digging, and raking. Gardening is a task that requires hard work and regular attention over a period of time, but the fruit, vegetables, and flowers that grow as a result of the efforts give the children a sense of pride and achievement.

The number of tools used by adults that children can master is endless. Typing provides an excellent opportunity to strenthen finger muscles as do many musical instruments. Mechanical activities that require wrenches, nuts and bolts, screwdrivers, and screws provide opportunities for eye-hand coordination and precision of movements. Sewing machines, kitchen utensils, hedge trimmers, calculators, and many other tools provide valuable experience for children to master motor control over the environment and at the same time develop feelings of accomplishment and competence.

Provide Opportunities for the Children to be Creative

If American schools can be universally criticized for one shortcoming, it would probably be that children are not allowed to develop individuality and that few opportunities are given for self-expression. In a word, children are not encouraged (in some instances, not allowed) to be creative. A day care setting can provide an environment that both allows and encourages children to be creative. The first advantage that a day care setting has for encouraging creative expression is that large blocks of time are available that do not have to be broken up into periods or classes.

*School-age children enjoy being creative with clay and a variety
of other media.*

Children who want to paint for three hours can be allowed this freedom, and those who
choose to spend every day for two weeks constructing a fort can also be allowed this
option. Therefore, "the creative use of time" can be one objective for older children.
They do not have to follow a predetermined schedule guided by bells and buzzers
mechanistically. They may plan their own activities or choose from others that have
been prepared by the teacher and personally decide how long to stay with their choices.
Wise teachers do not tell children how to spend their time; they simply assist the
children to make wise decisions.

The children in day care can also be creative in the arrangement and decoration of
their room. Unlike many other educational settings, day care centers are not limited by
rows of desks bolted together or to the floor and chalkboards that cover the walls. Day
care settings offer a more flexible environment in which children can freely revamp,
rearrange, and organize in ways that suit their immediate needs. The decorating of the
day care classroom is an ongoing creative endeavor as children make murals for the
walls, designs for the bulletin boards, mobiles to hang from the light fixtures, and
sculptures for the shelves.

The day care setting can also "offer children opportunities for creative expression in
music, drama, dance, and art." In music children can be given opportunities to sing in
groups or individually, and to use simple instruments. With a little encouragement

children can compose simple melodies on the instruments, and they can be guided to use objects in the environment for producing music.

Creative dramatics is an avenue of expression that appeals to many children if they are reassured that this type of behavior is acceptable and respected. Puppets that are available or made by the children can serve as a source of security for initial efforts at creative expression through drama. Gradually, children will gain confidence and respond eagerly to an invitation from the teacher or other children to put on a play. The plays that are presented are often "written" as they are acted out. A great deal of planning goes on during the production, and many scenes are repeated numerous times until they are satisfactory. Children are enormously encouraged by an audience (usually the teacher and one or two other children) that responds favorably. After children have gained experience and confidence in dramatic expression, they will frequently request small audiences. The approval of adults and other children serves as a positive reinforcer for their creative efforts. While spontaneous productions allow for self-expression, formal presentations before large audiences can be inhibiting and frightening. More-organized, rehearsed plays should occur only at the request of the children involved.

Opportunities for creative expression using many art media should be abundant in day care settings. Finger paints, water colors, tempera, and acrylic paints should be available for painting. Pencils, chalk, charcoal, crayons, and felt-tipped markers offer a variety of instruments for drawing. These supplies should be available to the children so that the choice of the media is their choice. Many kinds of clay should be offered for modeling, and materials such as wood, soap, and soft stone can be used for sculpting. Construction activities that use wood, paper, boxes, and assorted odd items enable the children to create something of beauty out of scrap throwaway materials. There are many other art and craft forms, such as sand candles, weaving, pottery, block printing, and batiking that call on the child's creative abilities. An innovative teacher with creative children will think of many others.

Another appropriate objective to help achieve this goal is that children "have opportunities for creative writing." Some children will be eager to combine creative writing and creative dramatics to write plays that they present. Often a small group of children will collaborate to write and present a play. Other children will want to write their own stories or dictate them to the teacher or into a tape recorder. Still others will enjoy writing poems or making up jokes. All of these techniques can be combined in a class newsletter or newspaper with original stories, poems, jokes, and interviews being included. Reports of past events and future projects also can be added. Each child should have an opportunity to make a contribution. As children become older, they frequently want to keep their creative products to themselves and are reluctant to share them with others. This need for privacy should be honored, but the opportunities for creative expression should still be available.

Typical Day for School-Age Children

The enrollment of the Citizen's Committee Day Care Center increases greatly in the summer because a program for school-age children is offered for thirty children six to twelve years of age. Because of the demand for school-age day care, the class is always filled early in the spring and remains full all summer. One of the first children to be enrolled is ten-year-old Dana. This is her fourth summer to attend Citizen's Center. Her parents have come to depend on the center to provide a safe environment and good supervision for their daughter. Dana enjoys coming because the program is designed around the interests of school-age children and it is fun and stimulating. She has also become close friends with several other children who attend in the summer, and renewing friendships each year is exciting and special to her.

The summer program begins at 6:30 A.M. because this center is located in a suburb of a large city, and many of the parents commute a long distance to work. There are four staff members who work staggered eight-hour shifts in order to cover the long day adequately. One arrives at 6:30, one at 7:30, one at 9:00, and one at 10:30.

Social learning theory indicates children identify with and model the behavior of a person of the same sex more than the behavior of a person of the opposite sex. There are two male and two female teachers at the center. All four teachers equally share the responsibilities of the center.

The first child to arrive this morning is nine-year-old Kristen. When she sees that no other children are in the class, she asks permission to go to the room for four year olds and play with her younger sister. The teacher goes along with her and asks the teacher in the class for four year olds if Kristen may join the group for a while. The teachers of the younger children enjoy having the older children visit their classes, so Kristen is invited to stay and she is soon reading a book to a group of four year olds. Many of the school-age children have younger siblings who attend the center, and all of the teachers cooperate to enable the siblings to spend time together throughout the day.

Soon other children begin to arrive. Some are dropped off by parents, others are accompanied into the class by an adult, and still others walk the short distance from their homes to the center. A child is allowed to walk to and from the center only if the child's parents and the center staff have jointly agreed that the child is ready to accept this responsibility. As the children arrive, they are given many choices of activities. They may play outside, play table games, listen to records, use the art supplies, or read. Dana is one of the children who walks to the center, and she arrives at 7:45 this morning in time to play several games of checkers with her friend Bronwyn before breakfast.

At 8:30 breakfast is served. The children are responsible for setting the tables, serving the food, and cleaning up the tables after the meal. Many children are hearty eaters, and the amount of food consumed is sometimes staggering. Breakfast is a time for sharing ideas and talking. The room is alive with chatter from many directions.

The breakfast period lasts from thirty to forty-five minutes, and afterward the children gather in the middle of the room for a committee meeting. During the meeting, the children make decisions about the day's events and make plans for the next day and the next week. This is also the time during which they are encouraged to voice grievances about the program, the teachers, or one another. The children are not expected to design activities or think of interesting field trips without the teachers' assistance. The planning usually consists of the teachers offering numerous suggestions that the children can add to and then select from. Some decisions, such as going to the zoo, are made that involve the entire group. Other activities are selected only by a small number and this activity is then scheduled for a small group. Many activities that are planned require an extended period of time to complete successfully.

Today eight children decide to learn to do macramé next week, seven choose puppetry ten select sand candles, and five choose papier-mache trays. The children will work on these projects each day until they are completed. They also decide on a trip to the airport next Friday. The children are given many opportunities throughout the day to make decisions that affect them and the program at the center. Another choice for today involves switching the regular activity period and the outside period to take advantage of the cool early morning for outside play. The late mornings have been extremely hot this week. The children agree to this switch, and they are dismissed to the playground.

It is now 9:30 and the children gather up playground equipment to take outside. It appears that soccer is a favorite choice this morning. One of the female and one of the male teachers head to the soccer field, and both boys and girls join in the game. Another group has chosen jump rope and they are already chanting, "Down by the meadow where the green grass grows, there sits Beth as sweet as a rose. . . ." Dana, Brownwyn, and Steve settle on the sidewalk to play jacks. They have become very proficient at the game this summer and they can often play three or four hands without a miss. Several others have gathered on one side of the yard to run relay races. The outside period is designed to give the children physical exercise and opportunities to develop their large and small muscles. Today running and jumping are the two main activities. Coordination of movements is also accomplished by playing jacks and jumping rope.

When the period is half over, several of the children have not yet engaged in any active play. Rhonda and Donna have been standing, turning the rope; and Dana, Bronwyn, and Steve have been sitting playing jacks. One of the teachers approaches these children and asks them to join together in a game of leap frog. They are challenged to leap all the way around the building. The children eye the teacher suspiciously and gingerly accept the challenge. It takes them twenty minutes, but they return to the starting place and flop down. Dana says to the teacher, "You didn't think we could do it did you? But we did! We can do almost anything we put our minds to." Then they lie in the grass and laugh at one another and talk about the leaping journey around the building. The soccer players join them for a short rest in the grass before going inside.

When the children return inside, snacks are served, and the cool juice refreshes them. The cheese and cucumbers help restore their energy. The children eat slowly and take this opportunity to relax and think about what they are going to do during the activity period. It is 10:30 and the children are allowed to spend their time in any of the learning centers using the equipment provided.

These centers have been designed specifically with the school-age child in mind. From Erikson the teachers know that children this age are developing a sense of industry. They want to become familiar with the tools and technology of their society, so the centers are designed to provide the children with this opportunity. One of the favorite centers is the typing center. Two regular-sized typewriters are available for the children to use. The woodworking center houses hammers, nails, saws, screwdrivers, and screws. The listening center contains a record player, a tape recorder, microphones, and headphones. A cash register, kitchen utensils, clothes, play money, and store merchandise can be found in the dramatic play area. Needles, thread, cloth, a loom, and yarn are available in the sewing center. All kinds of board games, cards, and dominos are in the game center. Books and pillows comprise the library, and the science center contains a microscope, a scale, magnets, animals, and plants. Special projects are frequently introduced that require special tools and techniques.

During activity time, the children mingle and visit with their friends and select an activity that interests them. Beth says, "I'm going to find Dana to come and sew with me." She finds her friend and offers, "Dana let's go sew. We can make bookmarkers to leave in the library." Dana answers that she cannot come just now because she has just started to work a jigsaw puzzle, but if Beth wants to help work the puzzle, they can sew together the last half of the period. This arrangement suits both girls, and they settle down to work on the puzzle, agreeing that one will find all the pieces with a straight edge and the other will find the pieces for the sky. Their work is progressing successfully when Greg suddenly backs into their table and knocks the puzzle onto the floor, destroying most of their work. He had just completed a large block structure and was backing up to admire it when he inadvertently knocked the girls' puzzle to the floor. Dana is usually a gentle cooperative child, but she is taken aback by the mishap and she is suddenly angry and vindictive. She demands, "Greg why did you do that? You did it on purpose! We were almost finished, and you ruined our work. Now we have the right to knock down your tower. You messed up our work, so now we are going to mess up yours." The accident and the outburst from Dana startle Greg, and he looks frightened and says, "Dana, I didn't mean to. Don't knock down my tower." "Oh, yes we are. We have a right to," replies Dana.

One of the teachers was in the block area and saw the unfortunate accident and heard the angry statement made by Dana. It is clear to the teacher that Dana is operating at Kohlberg's stage two of moral reasoning in this situation. She is thinking in terms of an eye for an eye. Her idea of justice is one of reciprocity even if the act is one that will cause another to suffer. What is right is seen from the viewpoint of satisfying herself. The teacher knows that children's moral reasoning progresses through the stages one step at a time and that no stage can be skipped, so the teacher uses stage-three logic to help Dana consider another solution to the problem. In stage three, the intention behind an act is considered, so the teacher approaches Dana and asks her to tell what happened. Dana retells the story. The teacher then asks her to consider that Greg had not intended to knock off the puzzle but that it happened accidentally when he backed up to look at his own work. Dana is asked to think about how she would feel if she had backed up to view her completed puzzle and accidentally knocked over Greg's tower. Would that give him the right to mess up her puzzle? By using reasoning one stage above the moral reasoning Dana was using, the teacher assists Dana in accepting the incident as an accident. Then Greg and the teacher offer to help Dana and Beth get the puzzle back to the way it was before the accident. The girls accept the help and resume their work. There is still enough time in the period for Beth and Dana to complete the puzzle and begin sewing on their bookmarkers.

The activity period lasts until 11:30. Then the children have ten minutes to put the room in order before the story time and lunch. One of the objectives that is being worked on all summer is "to help the children gain an appreciation of good children's literature and an awareness of how reading can bring personal satisfaction." Since there is such a wide range of reading abilities in the group, the thirty minutes before lunch are spent in oral reading by one of the teachers. The children lounge on pillows or lie on the rug and relax and listen to a story they have chosen. Today the teacher finished the last three chapters of *Harriet the Spy* (Louise Fitzhugh), and the children applaud as it is finished. There is time before lunch to select a new book to begin tomorrow. The teacher presents brief annotations of three books, and the group votes to hear *James and the Giant Peach* (Roald Dahl) next. The story period is also a language exercise to help the children increase their vocabularies and gain an appreciation of the beauty and usefulness of language as a means of expression. The story period also helps calm the group so that lunch can be a relatively peaceful experience.

At lunch the children serve their own plates, and requets to "please pass the beans" are heard frequently. A homey atmosphere is created because the children eat in small groups with an adult at each table. Conversation flows freely at the lunch tables. The teachers have learned that most school-age children are eager to talk and only need an interested listener. Children who are reluctant to talk are encouraged to join in the conversation. The teacher poses questions such as, "Sheila, will you tell us what you did in activity period," or "Scott, what did you use to make that picture?" to quiet children. After lunch the children again stack their plates and help clean the table.

All of the children in this group have been in elementary school for at least one year, so they have grown accustomed to not taking a nap. Indeed, that is one of the distinctions that separates them from the "little kids." From the time lunch is over until about 1:15, the children are asked to rest by playing quiet games, listening to quiet music, or reading. From 1:30 until 3:00 or 3:30, they frequently take field trips to nearby locations. This community offers many interesting activities for children in the summer, and the day care staff takes advantage of the community services to provide a wide range of experiences for the children. Today, from 1:45 until 3:00, they will attend a children's film at the local library.

Early in the summer the teachers and the children developed very specific guidelines that govern the children's behavior during field trips. They are expected to follow the guidelines while on the bus and at the location of the trip and to behave in a responsible manner at all times. To ensure that the children realize the importance of their behavior while they are away from the center, the staff has implemented a token economy using Skinner's principles of operant conditioning. At the end of each field trip, the children who have behaved responsibly and followed the guidelines are given a sticker that they adhere to a card with their name on it. Children who do not behave responsibly are not given a sticker, but they are given an explanation on how they can improve their behavior. Every other Friday an all-day trip with a picnic lunch is taken to an interesting place like the airport, the zoo, or a farm. Tickets to the all-day trips are "purchased" with the earned stickers. The ticket to the airport next Friday will cost six stickers because six short field trips will be taken during these two weeks before the trip to the airport. Any child who has not earned six stickers will not be allowed to go. However, tokens not spent for the airport trip can be saved and applied to the next big trip. The teachers are firm in their application of the system. If a child's behavior does not earn a token, one is not given. If children do not have enough tokens to go on a big trip, they stay at the center. The effect that the token economy has had on the children's out-of-center behavior is obvious to everyone, especially the children.

At 1:30 all the children board the bus and ride the eight blocks to the library. Then they leave the bus and enter the film room of the library in a courteous manner. Dana, Carol, Susan, and Rhonda find seats on the front row and view the film with interest. They laugh and applaud and enjoy the afternoon and still behave in an acceptable manner. When they return to the center, each is given a sticker for following the guidelines for good behavior.

Upon returning to the center at 3:15, the children eat afternoon snacks and prepare to work on their projects. This week Dana's group is learning basic embroidery stitches. The teachers know from Bandura and Walters that new skills or novel behaviors can often be quickly learned by observing a model perform the new behavior. Today the teacher instructs this group to "watch as I show you how to make a French knot." The children watch closely. Then the teacher demonstrates for each child individually and assists each child in making the knot. After the teacher shows Dana how to make the stich, Dana says, "Show me one more time and I think I'll have it." She watches intently and then performs the stitch perfectly. The children have learned three stitches, and they are now ready to incorporate them into a design. Each child sketches a simple design on a cloth and uses the three stitches to embroider the design.

Another group is actively involved in making stage props for a skit that they will perform for the summer festival held annually at the center. These children wrote the script for the skit, and now they are designing and constructing the props. Next week they begin on the paper costumes. According to Maslow, one event can serve to satisfy several levels of needs simultaneously. This activity helps each child feel like an important member of the group because the children are working together to accomplish the task and the contributions of each child are needed for success. This helps fulfill the need for belonging. At the same time, the personal contribution to the project made by each child helps the child gain a sense of accomplishment and pride that helps satisfy the esteem needs. The objectives being served during project time are numerous: small muscle control, social interaction, a sense of industry, creative expression, and many others. Each project is designed to help the children develop in many areas.

At 4:30 the projects are put away, and several of the children prepare to go home. Those remaining are given an option of playing on the playground, playing in the learning center, or going to the music room to receive a lesson on square dancing from a member of the community. Dana opts for the square dance lesson and enjoys the complex movements and unique calls. The children learn enough to do one simple dance before the hour is up. The teacher agrees to come back once a week if the children are interested. They assure him that they are and promise to practice until the next lesson. At 5:30 these children join their friends on the playground, and Dana and Carol take up a game of jacks. At 6:00 Dana's mother arrives and kisses her daughter hello. They gather up Dana's shoes and other belongings and chat with a few other parents and the teachers. As they leave Dana's mother asks, "How was your day?"

"O.K.," says Dana.

"What did you do all day?"

"Nothing, Oh, Mommy, do you know how to make a French knot and do a do-si-do?"

"I thought you didn't do anything today!"

"Oh, Mom, you know."

And her mother does know. She knows that the program is meeting the developmental needs of her daughter, that she is busy with many fun activities, and, most importantly, that Dana is happy to spend her summer here.

Summary

School-age children who are too young to stay at home unsupervised need day care accommodations. Day care settings that serve school-age children should consider the special needs of this age group when planning goals, objectives, and activities. Services and facilities offered by other community and private agencies can be coordinated with day care to better serve school-age children. The sample goals discussed as well as the typical day describing a summer program for school-age children are illustrative of the many possibilities of which day care personnel can avail themselves.

Suggested Readings

Cohen, Donald J.; Parker, Ronald K.; Host, Malcom S.; and Richards, Catharine. *Serving School Age Children*. Washington, D.C.: Office of Child Development, 1972. An overview of the development of school-age children and a discussion of their unique day care needs.

Gessell, Arnold and Ilg, Frances. *The Child From Five to Ten*. New York: Harper & Row, Publishers, 1946. A discussion of the behavioral characteristics of children at the ages of five to ten.

Hoffman, Gertrude L. *School Age Child Care*. Washington, D.C.: U. S. Department of Health, Education and Welfare No. (SRS) 73-23006, n.d. An excellent description of the state of the art regarding child care for school-age children.

Ichper Book of Worldwide Games and Dances. Washington, D.C.: International Council of Health, Physical Education, and Recreation, 1967. A collection of group games and dances from all over the world that are appropriate for school-age children.

Suggested Activities

1. What after-school arrangements are available for school-age children in your community or neighborhood?
2. Make an inventory of activities or projects school-age children might enjoy in an after-school program.
3. What community, church, or other organizationally sponsored activities are available for school-age children? Are any day care settings availing themselves of these resources?

Section Five

Overview

This final section contains two important discussions. One is about research, and the other is about the future. Research in the behavioral and social sciences provides the foundation for making decisions about policies and programs. A look ahead at the future and the possibilities existing therein provides the direction for guiding research and discussing the present.

The first chapter in this section includes an overview of research and the role it should play in helping people make decisions about day care settings and their curricula. Selections from the research in three areas of concern to day care personnel are described to acquaint the reader with some of the methods and techniques of research as well as the tentative contributions they yield to knowledge about these areas. The three areas are the effects of maternal employment on children, the effects of day care on children, and the effects of different curricula on children.

The last chapter is a combination of speculation about trends in day care and recommendations about the needs that should be met now and in the future.

Chapter Thirteen

Research

Research is a method through which knowledge is tested as being valid. Research is a systematic investigation of a problem. There are four kinds of researchable problems:

1. Conflicting evidence—this is a problem based on previous research efforts over the same topics that have produced conflicting findings. An example of a conflicting evidence problem is the question of whether or not a child's IQ will be affected by attending a day care setting.

2. Unconfirmed fact—This problem relates to any actual practice that is not based on research findings. An example would be the common practice of requiring all the children to take naps or rest at a specified time of the day.

3. Anomaly—This problem pertains to an occurrence that is quite unexpected. An example would be boys outperforming girls in language facility.

4. Uncharted area—This problem includes any investigation that attempts to shed light on a phenomenon that has never before been studied. An example of this kind of problem would be the effects of day care on child-father relationships.

To the scientist research is used to confirm or disconfirm statements of relationships. The specific statements come from more general descriptions of phenomena. When the specific statements are confirmed, thereby making the more general ones more credible, the scientist will have increased confidence in the theory from which the general and specific statements emanated. A valid theory is one that has been tested and found to be a reliable description of certain phenomena.

Research is a relatively objective technique for determining whether or not generalizations or theories are accurate descriptions of phenomena. The physical scientists rely heavily on research as their primary source of testing whatever they purport to know about their particular field. Social or behavioral scientists have followed the lead of physical scientists in trying to confirm and make more reliable what is known about people and their behavior. Using the physical science model of research and experimentation has been and continues to be a source of controversy in the social and behavioral sciences.

There are obvious differences between the subjects for study in the physical and social sciences. Physical scientists are able to exercise a great deal of control over the objects they measure, and those same objects are very amenable to measurement. Social and behavioral scientists who deal with human subjects cannot exert as much control over their subjects, nor are the subjects—that is, their behaviors and attributes—as easily measured. Experimenting with mice, rats, and pigeons provides the control but does so at the expense of providing necessary relevance for humans. Many human attributes or competencies are not directly measurable. For example, language competence can only be inferred and estimated from language performance. Intelligence is also inferred from behavior. The leap necessary when making such inferences, in spite of all reasonable controls, is still a leap. Those working with mice, rats, and pigeons make the leap of inference plus the leap of applicability to humans.

Despite the controversy surrounding the appropriateness of using research as a tool for carving out new knowledge in the social and behavioral sciences, and despite the inherent difficulties in measuring human attributes and competencies, we consider research as potentially the most reliable source of information available to those interested in providing high-quality service to people. Other sources of information are available but their general application and long-term usefulness are questionable.

Personal experiences of working with children in the past is probably drawn upon most frequently in school, nursery, and day care settings when teachers face problems of planning and providing for the children in their charge. The specific nature of the personal experience utilized varies from individual to individual and is oftentimes not easily examined by the individuals or others for reliability. We would not deny that many effective and caring teachers draw primarily from their own experiences in deciding what is good for children. Our point is that although those teachers are doing fine jobs with their children, there is little generalization from what they do to what other teachers can do. The question of how important experience can be in providing insights for helping children is related to the old question of whether good teachers are born or made. We believe good teachers are born, like everyone else, and capable of being made better. Past experience with other children will always play a major role in helping people decide what is appropriate. Unfortunately, using past experience as a guide oftentimes degenerates into mindlessly doing something this year because that is the way it was done last year.

Inexperienced teachers may rely on what their colleagues do as a primary source for making decisions regarding children. Indeed, the socializing force of experienced teachers on the inexperienced is awesome. The neophytes usually "fit in" in terms of their behavior or are made so uncomfortable for being different that they leave. The real difficulty in learning from others this way, however, is trying to model behavior based on previous experience to which the modeler has not been privy.

The final source of information and knowledge to be discussed is the professional and scientific literature in psychology, education, and related fields. The professional and scientific literature has the most potential for providing valid and reliable information to those interested in helping children develop. The fact that the writing is in the public domain, accessible to anyone for examination, is in stark contrast to the experience-based source described. Because scientific and professional literature is public, it is open to trial and testing by others. The potential is there for verifying, denying, or modifying what is known about children and appropriate service to them. We have to say potential at this time because even the best of the scientific and professional literature in social and behavioral fields is in its infancy when compared to the physical sciences. Much remains to be discovered and known, tried and tested, but no other source of knowledge has the potential for helping so many.

Descriptions and Prescriptions

A recurring problem members of any helping profession must face is differentiating between descriptions and prescriptions found in the literature that pertains to the profession. Studies in child development may be carefully conducted to the extreme and produce reliable descriptions of certain aspects of development. These descriptions serve the purposes of research by making clearer to people interested in child development the exact nature of development. In Section Three several theories of development were described. The major characteristic of each was its descriptive nature. Our premise throughout has been that such descriptions can provide the bases from which prescriptions are made for developing a curriculum. There is nothing new in this approach, but some of the inherent weaknesses in it are often overlooked. The two most obvious weaknesses are motives of the researchers and confusing what is with what ought to be.

Researchers in child development and related fields share a common goal of describing human behavior. Their motive at this point in time is to describe, not to prescribe. Eloquent testimony to this is White and others' study, *Experience and Environment,* wherein 244 pages are devoted to describing the study and its conclusions whereas three pages are devoted to ramifications for society.[1] Prescriptions can best follow good descriptions, but the prescriptions themselves need to be tested and refined. Too often a leap is made from descriptions to prescriptions without acknowledgement to the source or openness about the tentative nature of such untested prescriptions.

Confusing what is with what ought to be is another error well-intending professionals commit. If white middle-class girls outperform white middle-class boys in certain verbal abilities and these differences can be traced to implementing current cultural values of sexist stereotyping, it may be satisfying to know the explanation; but it does not necessarily follow that we should accept that fact with scholarly smugness for discovering a plausible cause-effect relationship. The fact alone does not indicate any action of any kind. Certain values may indicate one action over another. Those values are related to the question of what ought to be. The confusion arises when the distinction between what is and what ought to be is blurred. The description of what is is cloaked in the relatively objective context of social or behavioral scientists. The prescription of what ought to be done may also sound objective, but it is a value-laden suggestion based on assumptions of equality and justice. The prescriptions can prove to be effective and have positive outcomes. We have no quarrel with any prescription except that we believe it should be clearly labelled as such and the values on which it is based be made as explicit as possible.

Professional educators, like others in the helping professions, are in the business of making prescriptions. Research is a tool that can be used to test those prescriptions for the kinds of effects they may have on children. Unfortunately, educational re-seachers do not enjoy a very favorable reputation for the quality of the research they conduct. A random sample of research reports appearing in educational journals in 1971 was compared to a random sample of research reports from journals in related professions.[2] The findings were in favor of related professions but, more importantly, only 39 percent of the education articles were rated as acceptable as is and/or with minor revisions. The percentage of reports acceptable "as is" was 9. A similar study was carried out on a representative sample of research articles appearing in 1962.[3] Both studies indicate a serious problem with the quality of educational research, but the more recent study indicates an improvement in procedures. Research reports in related professions, though reportedly of a higher quality than those found in educational journals, are by no means perfect. Presently, one must be critical when reading research reports. Educators and others interested in using research as a basis for developing curricula cannot afford to consume all research uncritically. Judgments must be made about the quality of research. Perhaps skills in the critical reading of research are just as important as skills in the methods and techniques of child care. Space does not permit an explication of the skills and understandings necessary for distinguishing between good and bad research, but the problem of making those distinctions remains.

Research Related to Day Care

Our purpose is to describe research that is related to day care. The descriptions will be limited to those studies we believe have a direct bearing on day care or on issues related to it. Because entire books have been devoted to similar tasks, we will look at reviews and summaries of studies and a few specific studies that especially pertain to maternal employment, effects of day care on children, and curriculum development activities. Discussion of these three topics will be followed by generalizations gleaned from the studies.

Effects of Maternal Employment

In 1960, 18.6 percent of the women with preschool children were employed; in 1971, the percentage rose to 29.6.[4] In 1973, the percentage was 32.7.[5] No other socioeconomic fact impinges on day care as much as these employment data.

The research into the effects of maternal employment on young children is of special importance to day care personnel for two reasons. First, many of the children of working mothers who are studied are enrolled in a day care setting. Knowing how the day care children fare when compared to children who receive care exclusively from their mothers at home can provide some insights about programs and practices. The second reason research into the effects of maternal employment is of special importance to day care personnel is that it may shed more light on the issue of maternal deprivation, which will be discussed later.

The effects of maternal employment on children have been discussed in a number of comprehensive reviews of the literature. The professional journals, *Child*

Development and *Merrill-Palmer Quarterly,* publish original research related to the effects of maternal employment on children as well as periodically review and summarize research reported on elsewhere.[6] Nye and Hoffman edited a collection of studies and research reviews of maternal employment in their book, *The Employed Mother in America.*[7] Studies of maternal deprivation and maternal employment have indicated quite clearly that the question of effects on children has more to do with the quality of the environments in which the children are left and the quality of the interaction between mother and child, respectively, than with separation or employment alone.

In general, the studies that compare children whose mothers are employed with children whose mothers are not employed report no differences between the children. As mentioned earlier, however, reliable measures of children's characteristics as well as reasonable control of other variables mitigate against definitive statements that can be applied to all situations. Furthermore, researchers interested in this area have begun to look beyond the simple employment versus unemployment of mothers. For example, full- or part-time working mothers may be different. The kind of work and the mother's attitudes toward it could have differing effects on children. Finally, examining and controlling for the mother's social class, the age and sex of the child, and how long the mother has been employed can be more revealing than simply lumping children into one of two groups, those with mothers who are employed or those with mothers who are not employed. There may well be effects on children, both positive and negative, stemming from their mother's employment, or the fact of employment may be of secondary importance to some other variable, such as an unstable father or a particular social class. Juvenile delinquency, for example, appears to be related to maternal employment in middle-class families but not lower-class families.[8]

Day care personnel need to be particularly interested in the effects of maternal employment on young children. Several studies have examined this age group in terms of dependence and independence, anxiety and anti-social behavior, and other personality characteristics. Children in these studies were carefully matched according to age, sex, and other variables to control for factors other than maternal employment that might explain any differences between them. A glaring omission in these studies was a description of the kind of substitute care the children received while the mother was employed. It might be assumed that all kinds of different accommodations were made, such as staying with relatives or neighbors, babysitters in the home, or some kind of family or center day care. The nature and quality of substitute child care must be more important than the fact of the mother's employment, but apparently the researchers assumed the substitute care, whatever its nature, was of comparable quality in all the cases of maternal employment.

Results of the dependence-independence study indicate no difference between children whose mothers were employed and children matched in terms of social class, class in school, family size, and birth order, but whose mothers were not employed. The study dealing with anxiety and anti-social behavior in young children likewise showed no differences between those of employed mothers and those of unemployed mothers. Finally, a study of seventh- and eleventh-grade children whose mothers were employed during the first three, second three, and first six years of the child's life revealed no differences in personality characteristics and academic achievement.

One study showed some difference in children's behavior, depending on whether or not their mothers enjoyed their work. Children of mothers who enjoyed their work were no different from children whose mothers were not employed, but children whose mothers reported negative attitudes toward work were rated by their teachers, classmates, and mothers as tending to be more assertive and hostile.

A study conducted by Moore compared children whose mothers were employed and who had received at least one year of day care before the age of five with children who had been exclusively with their mothers before entering school.[9] The nature of the day care—stable if it was provided by the same person or persons, and unstable if there were frequent changes of caretaker—was noted. The children from both groups were matched according to sex, socioeconomic status, birth order, maternal age, and amount of separation. Data were collected from interviews with mothers and teachers, and from tests and observations of the children. At age six few differences were found between children cared for exclusively by their mothers and those receiving stable substitute care. The latter were more self-assertive. It appeared from this study that children who receive stable substitute care were no more disturbed than children who stayed with their mothers.

Etaugh reviewed a number of maternal employment studies concerned with the effects on children's attachment to their mothers, and the children's mental and personality development. Her conclusions warrant repeating here:

> Young children can form as strong an attachment to a working parent as to a nonworking one, provided that the parent interacts frequently with the child during the times they are together; and stable stimulating substitute care arrangements are important for the normal personality and cognitive development of preschool children whose mothers work.[10]

Studies overlapping with maternal employment, but focusing more on the substitute care provided, will be discussed under the "Effects of Day Care."

Maternal attachment is related to maternal deprivation. It is important to note the devastating blow day care inadvertently received from a report to the World Health Organization in 1952. Bowlby was commissioned by the World Health Organization to report on the effects of institutionalization on young children. He suggested a maternal bond was established in normal mother-child relations. He claimed the bond was qualitatively different from other bonds children subsequently established with others and that institutionalization prevented the establishment of these bonds. Spitz had previously coined the term *hospitalism* to describe the infants who suffered from institutional neglect. The upshot of Spitz and Bowlby's work has been a relatively negative association in many people's minds with any institution that takes the place, even temporarily, of the mother. A recent review of studies on maternal deprivation sheds new light on the matter and corrects some inappropriate perspectives.

Rutter has reviewed the maternal deprivation studies as well as carried out his own, and challenges Bowlby's maternal bond theory.[11] Rutter suggests a child establishes a number of bonds, differing in intensity (quantity) but not quality. Furthermore, the primary bond may or may not be with the mother. A case is made that a child who establishes several bonds is more independent than a child who has just one bond. Rutter also reminds the reader that the institutions that have had such negative effects on children are not the kind any reasonable person would ever try to defend. He describes them thus:

. . . nonstimulating environment, where there is only low intensity of personal interaction, where infants tend to be left when they cry, where care is provided at routine times rather than in response to the infant's demands, and where there are multiple caretakers none of whom has regular interaction with the child over a period of many months or longer.[12]

The institutions that fall into this description are unequivocally bad. Nothing positive could ever possibly be associated with them.

The misplaced emphasis on maternal deprivation, according to Rutter, is that the investigations seldom if ever focus on the nature of the substitute care. He maintains "that it is not whether you are brought up at home or in an institution which matters for cognitive growth, but rather the type of care you receive.[13]

The Effects of Day Care

Compared to investigations of the effects of maternal employment, studies of day care have been fewer in number and involved smaller numbers of children. It is also important to note that the day care centers in which the children were enrolled were not a random selection of centers but were (and are) centers with carefully planned programs delivering, in several cases, a number of services to children and their families. The ideal conditions these centers try to provide include "gratification of basic needs, a relatively high frequency of adult contact, a positive emotional climate, varied and patterned sensory input of moderate intensity, an optimal level of need gratification, clear and consistent behavior on the part of others, a minimum of social restriction on exploratory and motor behavior, an organized physical and temporal environment, and appropriate play materials."[14]

The Children's Center in Syracuse, New York, was organized in 1964 as a research and development day care center. The aim of the center was the development of a day care program for children three years of age and under that would foster their subsequent educability. Between 1965 and 1968, 108 children who participated in the program were compared to 49 children from comparable backgrounds who did not participate in the program. Measures of cognitive development were made at entrance and near the end of the study period. Pre- and post-tests were also administered to the control group of 49 children. Those children participating in the day care program made statistically significant gains over time and greater gains than the control group. Indeed, the children who entered the program under three years of age showed an increase in IQ of seventeen points, while the comparable control group children showed a decrease of six points.[15]

Another study from an infant center funded as a Children's Bureau demonstration project in Greensboro, North Carolina, indicated no cognitive gains associated with day care experience. Caldwell speculated about the differences between the Syracuse and Greensboro studies.

The difference between the findings of these two studies can perhaps be explained by the fact that they served different types of populations. Approximately two-thirds of the children in the Syracuse project represented economically and socially disadvantaged families, whereas those in the Greensboro sample came from middle-class families.[16]

Another study from the Syracuse project involved thirty-two one-year-old black infants from lower-class families. Sixteen infants attended either a morning or an afternoon enrichment program for six months. The sixteen control group children received no intervention. The experimental infants performed significantly better on Piagetian Infancy Scales than the control children. The noteworthy contribution of this study was that it used an assessment technique that is part of a theoretical system of cognitive development.[17]

In Beller's review of the studies of infant development in enriched day care settings, he concluded:

> To date, all educational programs for infants which have evaluated the impact on cognitive development have found significant evidence for their effectiveness.[18]

There is always concern, however, that gains in cognitive development may be at the expense of some other aspect of development. There has been special interest in the emotional adjustment of children under three who participate in group care because many have overgeneralized from Spitz and Bowlby's reports of institutional rearing of infants. There has been a concern that any kind of group care for children under three, no matter how long the length of separation from family, has detrimental effects on the children. The following studies allay the fears that gains in cognitive development or attendance in a day care setting before the age of three have deleterious effects on children.

Caldwell and her associates were concerned about the possible negative effects associated with very young children participating in a group care setting. It is important to note again that these settings were ones in which careful safeguards were taken to ensure that each child received the attention of one caretaker for the major part of the day and week. The same person attended to basic needs, such as feeding and changing diapers, as well as putting the child to sleep and being there when he awoke. Each child maintained a continuing relationship with members of his family. The staff hoped to help the child maintain the identity of family members and not confuse the educational personnel with family. Each infant received a fifteen- to thirty-minute daily interaction with staff that involved holding, rocking, going for walks, or playing learning games. In addition, daily schedules included activities that were carefully planned by the teaching staff that combined free selection of activities by the children and more structured experiences such as reading stories, labelling objects, and playing group games. An attempt was made to match teaching activities to the child's level of development as indicated by tests and observations.

Braun and Caldwell had a child psychiatrist make intense and participatory observations of thirty children in the center that provided the kind of environment and routine described. Nineteen of the children had enrolled prior to age three, but the psychiatrist did not know which nineteen they were. All the children were rated on a five-point scale in regard to the following four areas:

1. Child's effect on materials, adults, and peers.
2. Child's ability to be reflective about feelings and actions.
3. Child's ability to elaborate ideas and activities.
4. Child's recognition and gratification of needs.

The results indicated no difference in socioemotional development between the children who entered the program prior to age three and those who entered after age three. Five-sixths of all the children were rated as making a reasonable socioemotional adjustment. This is significant in light of the fact that many of the children came from homes that suffered some kind of social problem with which the adults had to cope that had led to the enrollment of the child in the day care program.[19]

Another aspect of social and emotional development—children's attachments to their mothers—was also studied at the Syracuse project. Eighteen mother-child pairs in which the children were involved with day care from age one were compared to twenty-three mother-child pairs in which the children had remained in the exclusive care of their mothers. Assessments of the children were made when they were approximately thirty months of age. The children were observed with their mothers for a three-hour session. Mothers were interviewed at home about their child's behavior. In all, a cluster of ratings pertaining to maternal attachment was gathered for each child. There were no significant differences between the day care and home-reared infants in terms of the children's attachment to their mothers. Furthermore, the day care infants enjoyed interaction with other people more than the home-reared infants.[20]

In a summary of research related to maternal attachment and day care, Caldwell noted:

> Only one of four research studies (of maternal attachment) has shown any negative con-
> sequences associated with day care participation; in the other three, day care children
> appeared as attached to their mothers as were the control children. . . . As things now
> stand, proponents of day care tend to cite the study (Caldwell and her associates) which
> found no differences between the day care and the home-reared children, and opponents
> of day care tend to cite the study (Blehar[21]) which reported differences.[22]

Caldwell further noted that the two studies with differing results used a combined total of only eighty-one children—a number far too small to use as a basis for establishing social policy.

Farran and Ramey conducted a study involving twenty-three infants and toddlers who had attended a day care center for an average of seven hours a day.[23] The children began attendance between the ages of six and twelve weeks and at the time of the study ranged in age from nine to thirty-one months. The purpose of the study was to determine if the children preferred to be near and interact with their mothers rather than their teacher and to see if the children perceived their mothers as help givers when faced with a mildly difficult problem. Results indicated the children were attached more intensely to their mothers than to their teachers and that they perceived their mothers as help givers.

Kagan, Kearsley, and Zelazo conducted a longitudinal study to assess the psychological effects of a day care program on children during the first thirty months of life.[24] The children in the day care setting were compared with a control group consisting of children reared totally at home but matched in terms of ethnicity, social class, and sex. Assessments included evaluations of social behavior with peers, attachment behavior to the mother and caretaker, and tests of memory and linguistic knowledge. The day care children came from predominantly intact families, and the day care program was monitored closely by the investigators and implemented by mature, conscientious, and nurturant caretakers. The data revealed little difference between the day care and home control children with respect to cognitive functioning, language, and attachment to the mother. In all the comparisons between the day care and home-reared children, the authors note that the similarities are more salient than the differences. They conclude that all the data from their study support the view that day care, when responsibly and conscientiously implemented, does not seem to have hidden psychological dangers.

Effects of Curriculum

It was made clear in Chapter Two that children learn all the time, whether or not anything is planned for them to learn. The presence of a curriculum in any educational setting is evidence that those responsible for the setting are endeavoring to take some of the responsibility for what the children learn.

Sometimes a curriculum can be characterized as being primarily a teacher-centered one or another primarily as a child-centered curriculum. In most instances, there is a combination of high teacher involvement and high child involvement. The general orientation of a curriculum might be around some developmental theorist such as Piaget or a curriculum might be eclectic in orientation, drawing from a number of developmental theorists. A curriculum might emphasize language development far more than other aspects of development. In general, a curriculum can be any combination of the preceding, depending on the philosophy and concerns of those people—both parents and staff—who develop it.

Research in the area of curriculum has looked at many facets of educational settings. Generally, the majority of research in the area has been concerned with comparing certain combinations of content and method with other combinations of content and method. These comparisons have usually been conducted to see if one combination was better than another. Some examples of such studies are the comparisons of one method of teaching reading, science, or language with another method. The methods typically involve different content or emphases on subject matter and skills. Results of these studies have been mixed. Oftentimes no differences are found between children receiving one method and those receiving another.

Volumes could be devoted to reviewing and summarizing these research efforts. Several attempts have been made to glean some understandable generalizations from the many studies, but such attempts usually fail because of a serious lack of uniformity and agreement in definitions of words like *curriculum* and less than adequate controls of variables that get in the way of sound inferences and generalizations. So much research in the curriculum field has been atheoretical and, therefore, difficult to tie together with other research efforts.

When we examine the research in curriculum that relates to the definition of *curriculum* used in Chapter Two—that is, a plan or a point of departure for planning the educational experiences of children—we find nothing in terms of day care curriculum but a few studies dealing with preschool programs for disadvantaged children that have some relevance to our purpose.

The most ambitious study was one that compared different curricular orientations in Head Start settings. It was conducted by Bissell.[25] Over 1,500 children enrolled in Head Start classes that had preacademic, cognitive, or discovery orientations were compared to over 1,000 children enrolled in regular Head Start classes. The preacademic models purported to foster development of preacademic skills and placed heavy emphasis on systematic reinforcement and drills on individualized programmed instruction. The cognitive models were to promote the growth of basic cognitive processes by helping children develop appropriate verbal labels and concepts while they engaged in exploration. The discovery models embraced a view of learning as part of the humanistic growth of the whole child with emphasis on free exploration and self-expression.

The effects of the various programs on the children were assessed in terms of academic achievement, general cognitive development, and style of responding. All the children made intellectual gains beyond what could be explained by maturation alone as a result of their preschool education. The children enrolled in the three programs that had preacademic, cognitive, and discovery orientations made larger intellectual gains than those children enrolled in regular Head Start programs, but there were no differences in gains among the three models.[26] Response styles of children were less uniform. Children from all the programs became less impulsive in their responses, but those from the discovery program made greatest progress in being less impulsive. Significant gains on another measure of response style were found for children in the preacademic model. Of particular importance is the fact that the children in the three programs with special orientations were, with the exception of mixed findings in response-style assessments, generally equally affected by their respective programs, suggesting that a particular orientation of a curriculum program is less important than many of their proponents would have us believe. What is important in having an effect on children was best described by Weikart.[27]

Weikart started the Ypsilanti Preschool Curriculum Demonstration Project in the fall of 1967 in Ypsilanti, Michigan to compare the effectiveness of three curriculum types. One curriculum was the "cognitively oriented curriculum" that was based on principles of sociodramatic play and principles derived from Piaget's theory of intellectual development. Another curriculum was called the "language training curriculum." It was developed by Bereiter and Engelmann at the University of Illinois. It is a task-oriented curriculum that uses techniques from foreign language training and is carried out at an intensive, fast pace. Essentially, the curriculum consists of three twenty-minute periods during which language, reading, and arithmetic are taught. The third type of curriculum was called the "unit-based curriculum." This third type emphasized social-emotional goals and most closely represented the traditional nursery school curriculum.

Children in the study were retarded three and four year olds. They were randomly assigned to one of the three curriculum models. Two teachers were assigned to each model; over the three years of operation, this yielded about a one to four or five ratio of teacher to children. Weikart states:

> The teachers taught class for half a day and then conducted a teaching session in the home of each of their children for ninety minutes every other week. . . . Essential to the demonstration aspect of the project was that all three programs had clearly defined weekly goals. The curriculum implementation followed a carefully planned daily program designed independently by the three teams of teachers to achieve the goals of their own curricula. The provision for teacher involvement was a crucial aspect of the overall project.[28]

Data were collected for a three-year period and included Stanford-Binet IQ scores, classroom observations, observations in free-play settings, ratings of children by teachers and independent examiners, and evaluations by outside critics.

Results after one and two years indicated significant gains on virtually all the measures by all the children, irrespective of the curriculum model. After the third year, the children in the unit-based curriculum model began to taper off in IQ, but Weikart attributed the decline to problems of supervision, not the model itself. Weikart draws two conclusions from this study that bear repeating:

1. Broad curricula are equivalent. As far as various preschool curricula are concerned, children profit intellectually and socioemotionally from any curriculum that is based on a wide range of experiences.
2. The curriculum is for the teacher, not the child. The primary role of curriculum is (a) to focus the energy of the teacher on a systematic effort to help the individual child to learn; (b) to provide a rational and integrated base for deciding which activities to include and which to omit; and (c) to provide criteria for others to judge program effectiveness, so that the teacher may be adequately supervised.[29]

In effect, Weikart has suggested shifting concern from curriculum model to staff model. His staff model included the following elements: teacher satisfaction with curriculum, explicit planning, careful supervision, adequate staff training, plenty of help in the classroom, and contact with parents.

There remain many unanswered questions in the area of early education, but we believe the question, Which curriculum model is most effective? has been adequately treated by the two studies mentioned above. The data from both studies indicate that several different curriculum models can have similar effects on children. Weikart's three-year study begins to specify what some of the other variables are that appear to make a difference in impact. Teacher involvement with weekly and daily planning as well as supervision and evaluation vis-à-vis those plans appear to be essential parts of any effective program.

Discussion and Implications

More research is needed. That has become a commonplace statement, but nonetheless, it continues to be a true one. When we know more about the effects, if any, of maternal employment on children, we can better tailor the experiences of day care children whose mothers work. If maternal employment is less important than other factors in the child's life, identification and examination of these other factors should continue. The more that is known about what affects children outside of a day care setting, the more that setting can accommodate the children it serves. The studies of the effects of day care on children must look more closely at specific practices in a day care setting. There is wide variation in the kinds and quality of specific practices taking place in day care settings. We need to know more precisely what routines and activities have good effects on what kinds of children. Finally, the various methods of teaching, the degree to which teachers interact with children, the room environments, and use of materials need to be examined to provide more reliable information to guide practices. The curriculum studies indicate active planning on the part of teachers is more important than the kind of curriculum they use to guide their planning, as long as the curriculum provides a wide array of experiences for children. Essentially, then, the focus of curriculum studies might well be the curriculum system of a day care setting rather than the kind of curriculum document.

Summary

Research is the systematic investigation of a problem. Research in the social and behavioral sciences has many obstacles to overcome before it will yield information as reliable as that from the physical sciences. The potential benefits of research-based information outweigh the current difficulties in conducting carefully controlled investigations. Curriculum developers must distinguish between discription and prescription.

Studies of maternal employment produced mixed findings, but suggest more precise delineations of other variables associated with mothers and employment that might affect children's behavior. Day care studies need to be increased to include more children and other variables associated with specific day care practices that could affect children. Curriculum studies could provide more useful information if they focused on aspects of a curriculum system rather than the kind of curriculum document.

NOTES

1. Burton L. White and J.C. Watts, *Experience and Environment: Major Influences on the Development of the Young Child* (Englewood Cliffs, N.J.: Prentice-Hall, 1973).

2. Annie W. Ward, B. W. Hall, and C. F. Schraman, "Evaluation of Published Educational Research: A National Survey," *American Educational Research Journal 12* (Spring 1975): 109-28.

3. E. Wandt, chairman, "An Evaluation of Educational Research Published in Journals," mimeographed (Washington, D.C.: American Educational Research Association Committee on Evaluation of Research, 1967).

4. "Statistical Abstracts of the United States," 93d ed. (Washington, D.C.: U.S. Government Printing Office, 1972).

5. Committee of Finance United States Senate, Russell Long, chairman, *Child Care: Data and Materials* (Washington, D.C.: U.S. Government Printing Office, 1974).

6. See for example, L. M. Stolz, "Effects of Maternal Employment on Children: Evidence from Research," *Child Development 31* (1960): 749-82; A. E. Siegel and M. B. Haas, "The Working Mother: A Review of Research," *Child Development 34* (1963): 513-42; and C. Etaugh, "Effects of Maternal Employment on Children: A Review of Recent Research," *Merrill-Palmer Quarterly 20* (April 1974): 71-98.

7. F. J. Nye and L. W. Hoffman, eds., *The Employed Mother in America* (Chicago: Rand McNally Co., 1963).

8. Lois W. Hoffman, "Effects on Children: Summary and Discussion," in *The Employed Mother in America*, ed. F. J. Nye and L. W. Hoffman (Chicago: Rand McNally Co., 1963), p. 195.

9. T. W. Moore, "Effects on the Children," in *Working Mothers and Their Children*, ed. S. Yudkin and A. Holme (London: Michael Joseph, 1963), pp. 105-24. Reviewed by Etaugh, "Effects of Maternal Employment on Children": 74-75.

10. Etaugh, "Effects of Maternal Employment on Children," p. 75.

11. Michael Rutter, *Maternal Deprivation Reassessed* (Baltimore, Md.: Penguin Books, 1972).

12. Ibid., p. 100.

13. Ibid., pp. 83-84.

14. Bettye M. Caldwell, "On Designing Supplementary Environments for Early Child Development," *BAEYC Reports 10* (1968): 1-11, Quoted in Bettye M. Caldwell et al., "Early Stimulation," in *Mental Retardation and Developmental Disabilities, Vol. 7*, ed. Joseph Wortis (New York: Brunner/Mazel, 1975), p. 152.

15. Bettye M. Caldwell, "Impact of Interest in Early Cognitive Stimulation," in *Perspective in Child Psychopathology*, ed. H.E. Rie (Chicago: Aldine-Atherton, 1971), p. 308.

16. Bettye M. Caldwell, "What Does Research Teach Us About Day Care for Children under Three," *Children Today* (January-February 1972): 8.

17. A. S. Honig and S. A. Brill, "A Comparative Analysis of the Piagetian Development of Twelve-Month-Old Disadvantaged Infants in an Enrichment Center with Others Not in Such a Center" (paper presented at the annual meeting of the American Psychological Association, Miami, 1970). Reviewed by E. Kuno Beller, "Research on Organized Programs of Early Education," in *Second Handbook of Research on Teaching,* ed. Robert W. Travers (Chicago: Rand McNally and Co., 1973), p. 544.

18. Beller, "Research on Organized Programs of Early Education," p. 544.

19. Samuel J. Braun and Bettye M. Caldwell, "Emotional Adjustment of Children in Day Care Who Enrolled Prior to or After the Age of Three," *Early Child Development and Care 2* (1973): 13-21.

20. Caldwell, "What Does Research Teach Us About Day Care: for Children under Three," p. 9.

21. Mary C. Blehar, "Anxious Attachment and Defensive Reactions Associated with Day Care," *Child Development 45* (1974): 683-92.

22. Bettye M. Caldwell, "Statement Prepared for the Senate Subcommittees on Children and Youth, and on Employment, Poverty and Migratory Labor and the House Select Subcommittee on Education," mimeographed (presented in Washington, D.C., June 19, 1975).

23. Dale C. Farran and Craig T. Ramey, "Infant Day Care and Attachment Behaviors Toward Mothers and Teachers" (revision of a paper presented by Craig Ramey at the annual meeting of the American Psychological Association, Chicago, September 1975).

24. Jerome Kagan, Richard B. Kearsley, and Philip R. Zelazo, "The Effects of Infant Day Care on Psychological Development" (paper presented at a symposium of the American Association for the Advancement of Science, Boston, February 1976).

25. Joan S. Bissell, *Implementation of Planned Variation in Head Start* (Washington, D.C.: U.S. Department of Health, Education and Welfare, Office of Child Development, 1971). Reviewed in Beller, "Research on Organized Programs of Early Education," pp. 579-83.

26. Beller, "Research on Organized Programs of Early Education," p. 581.

27. David P. Weikart, "Relationship of Curriculum, Teaching and Learning in Preschool Education," in *Preschool Programs for the Disadvantaged,* ed. Julian C. Stanley, (Baltimore, Md.: The Johns Hopkins University Press, 1972), pp. 22-66.

28. Ibid., p. 39.

29. Ibid., pp. 40-41.

Suggested Readings

Nye, F. Evan and Hoffman, L. W., eds. *The Employed Mother in America.* Chicago: Rand McNally Co., 1963. Research reports as well as reviews and summaries of research dealing with maternal employment and its effects on children.

Sjolund, Arne. *Day Care Institutions and Children's Development.* Trans. by W. Glyn Jones. Westmead, England: Saxon House, D. C. Heath, 1973. A comprehensive review of day care and nursery school research conducted in Europe and America.

Stanley, Julian C., ed. *Preschool Programs for the Disadvantaged.* Baltimore, Md.: The Johns Hopkins University Press, 1972. Proceedings from the first annual Hyman Blumberg Symposium on research in early childhood education. Good review of many studies and a description of Weikart's comparison of three curricula.

_____. *Compensatory Education for Children Ages Two to Eight.* Baltimore, Md.: The Johns Hopkins Press, 1973. Proceedings of the second annual Hyman Bluberg Symposium on research in early childhood education. Good description of major studies, including Bissell's comparative study.

Van Dalen, Deobold B. *Understanding Educational Research,* 3d ed. New York: McGraw-Hill Book Co. 1973. An excellent introduction to research in the social and behavioral sciences.

Chapter Fourteen

A Look Ahead

Philosophers and thinkers have repeatedly outlined the theoretical basis for a sound education with little effect. It remains for us to work out the theory in actual American classrooms. Neither theory nor glowing reports of good teaching will save us the effort of doing it ourselves.

Joseph Featherstone, Schools Where Children Learn
(New York: Liveright, 1971), p. 83.

The field of day care has not received the sustained professional attention other agencies, such as schools, have received. The efforts of a relatively small number of people in recent times, usually working with Head Start or other federal agencies, have managed to improve the quality of services offered to children in experimental or special projects. These people have also been successful in drawing the helpful attention of professionals from many disciplines and legislators from local, state, and national levels to the needs of young children. A need exists to survey the present situation and examine the trends for signs of the future. It would be tempting to write about pie-in-the-sky expectations, but the present state of the art dictates realistic projections about the near future. In spite of the rhetoric, social progress is more evolutionary than revolutionary, and small steps are more likely than leaps and bounds.

Trends

At present, day care settings exist in homes, nonprofit centers, and centers operating for profit. Some are government sponsored, a few are industry and hospital related, and a very few are integral parts of public schools. The number of family day care homes far exceeds the number of group care settings. If the number of group care settings increases, and there are signs that it will, the number of children being served in centers will approach and perhaps exceed the number of children receiving care in family day care homes. Some centers are likely to be attached to industries and hospitals that have the space and resources, but progress in these sectors will be slower than progress in the federal agencies and public school settings.

Federal employees, through their unions, are beginning to insist on day care facilities attached to or at least sponsored by the federal agencies that employ them. The concern some of the agencies have for implementing policies related to all kinds of social services is the lever such unions are using. What better way to enforce guidelines and policies than to set the example by providing employee benefits, such as day care? Government agencies that oversee the expenditure of millions of dollars for child services nationwide will be embarrassed not to offer high-quality services to their employees' families.

Public Schools as Delivery Systems

One of the least used facilities for day care today, however, shows signs of growing more rapidly than any other. We speak, of course, about the public schools. As a delivery system for day care services, the public schools have many advantages over other options. More than anytime in the history of the country, school buildings are standing empty because of the decline in the birthrate. Elementary schools, traditionally spread out through all the neighborhoods and in many instances now standing vacant, are nearly ideal for day care settings. The use of the conveniently located public schools would eliminate having to transport children long distances to receive day care. The available space they typically provide, both indoors and outdoors, is difficult to find in urban areas or too expensive to purchase and develop. Schools are usually equipped with food facilities, space for health care, administrative offices, and storage areas. Using these existing facilities for children in day care would prevent having to duplicate them elsewhere. Many schools also have gymnasiums, activity rooms, and music rooms that could be shared with the younger children. The existence within public school systems of administrative and professional resources encourages day care in public schools. Teachers, trained and certified, and increasingly out of work, represent a rich pool of resource persons and teachers for day care settings. Three prominent examples of day care in public school settings are the Kramer School in Little Rock, Arkansas; the Early Childhood Center in Galveston, Texas; and the Community After School Program in Norman, Oklahoma.

More Interest in Early Childhood and Parent Education

The use of public school buildings for Head Start programs has been the greatest impetus to housing programs for preschool-age children in school settings; and since the introduction of Head Start, public school officials and other professional educators began to see more clearly and speak more effectively about the importance of the preschool years. Focusing on children from disadvantaged homes in an effort to stem the seemingly inevitable school failures these children subsequently experienced, Head Start soon expanded its services in some locales to provide comprehensive all-day care to the children being served.

Health care and parent education were additional services offered by Head Start programs. Parent involvement in decisions about curricula and other matters was encouraged on the policy level and successfully carried out in many Head Start centers. Preschoolers are receiving more attention now than ever before. Indeed, parent education projects, such as Gordon's in Florida, involve training parents in ways of interacting with their infants before and sometimes in lieu of actual programs for the children. More high schools are offering courses in parenting, as well as being more accommodating than ever in regard to teen-age mothers. Attention is shifting to programs for younger children and their parents. The shift would be swifter, of course, if more money were available, but the likelihood of more money is dependent on the legislators at national, state, and local levels.

Legislative and Economic Actions

The increasing number of states that have established offices of child development is an indication of more activity on the state level regarding the kinds of services available for children. Community coordinated child care (4-C's) organizations have been and continue to be established on the local level. These agencies, usually made up of volunteers from the community, have as their charge the coordination of federal and state programs and resources to ensure effective and efficient provisions of services to children.

A comprehensive child development act is likely to be passed in the near future. The passage but subsequent presidential veto of such an act in 1971 was a serious setback for day care. Politicians, with the help of professionals in the field, again have mounted a campaign to pass a comprehensive bill that would provide the necessary economic resources for improved day care facilities everywhere in this country. The increased vocalization of women's groups and activities of child care professionals will likely result in the successful passage of a comprehensive child care act before long.

Whenever new bills affecting social services are passed, it generally follows that guidelines or standards are set to determine eligibility for funding. There will probably be an upgrading of licensing requirements for all kinds of day care settings and a raising of standards for the certification of teachers and assistants at the preschool level. Quality, like morality, cannot be legislated, but the money necessary for minimal quality control can be legislated to help ensure quality services for children.

The last ten years saw a great deal of money invested in intervention programs aimed at young children from culturally different backgrounds. There has been a leveling off of these funds, but compared to ten years ago, there is still a great deal of federal activity in the maintenance and careful expansion of Head Start programs and services, the latest of which is Home Start with its emphasis directly on the families of culturally different children. Great needs continue to exist for intensive intervention programs, but an even greater need exists for the millions of children from all socioeconomic levels who require day care facilities for their care and development. The 1970 White House conference on children and youth predicted 5.6 million children would need day care by 1980. A comprehensive child care act, with sufficient funding, would serve all of America's children.

The number of children requiring day care will continue to rise because there will be more of a willingness on the part of parents to place infants in group care settings. A decade ago, the prevailing attitude was against such a practice, but during the last ten years carefully controlled experiments have failed to indicate any deleterious effects on infants from group care as a supplement to family care.

The most heartening trend is the shift in the conception of day care from a place where only physical needs are met to the conception of day care as a setting in which all aspects of children's development can be potentiated. Adequate facilities, materials, training, and money for all these have been the obstacles to providing more than just physical care in day care settings in the past. The money has begun to come in, but with interests from many segments of society beginning to coordinate their political and social power, more monies will undoubtedly follow. In the not too distant future day care personnel will have only themselves to blame if services for children are not of high quality.

What Needs to Be Done?

The most outstanding need as far as this book is concerned is the verification and validation of procedures of curriculum development. There should be systematic efforts at curriculum development in all kinds of day care settings and a sharing of information about what works in what kinds of settings and with what kinds of people. Much of this book is speculative in regard to ways of working with people, both young and old, because there does not exist, at this point in time, very many reliable sources of information to guide such efforts.

Curriculum development has almost exclusively been an elementary and secondary school endeavor. Day care settings share some common ground with these facilities, but there are important differences as well. Whether or not procedures that work with elementary schools and their teachers will work with day care personnel remains to be seen. Every aspect of a curriculum system described in Chapters Three and Four needs to be examined, tried, and accepted as is or with modification before the benefits of such a system will be realized. The openness with which that approach is tried will be directly related to the likelihood of success.

There is no one way, let alone a right way, to proceed with organizations designed to provide a variety of services to a variety of individuals. There is an urgent need for the people in the business of trying to help children, including us, to admit they may be wrong about how to proceed. The fact that we should proceed in our efforts to improve the quality of experiences for young children is not debatable. How we go about the process is open to question. This book represents the suggestion that all of us need to be more mindful of the business we are in and the interests we are serving. And being mindful is not enough. We must be responsible and accountable to the parents, the children, and ourselves.

Appendix A

Two Statements of Purpose/Philosophy

Middle Earth's Statement
of Purpose/Philosophy*

Children need a happy, comfortable place to spend their time away from home. The children who attend a day care center look to the staff for the same affection, love, support, guidance, and discipline that they receive at home. The staff becomes substitute family members to the children during the day, but parents remain the most important people in a young child's life. Staff members strive to supplement the family and encourage family involvement in the program, so the child can feel a close bond between home and center. The physical, emotional, and intellectual needs of the children are considered the first priority of the program. The children's needs always come first and are considered before the needs or conveniences of the parents or the staff.

Each child is unique, and all children are respected for their differences. The same performance or behavior is not expected from any two children. All children are encouraged to develop their own personality; to hold their own thoughts, opinions, and ambitions; and to express these ideas comfortably and freely. The integrity of the individual child is always respected; this means expecting and accepting differences. If we want children to maintain their uniqueness and their differences, then we must provide an environment that will assist them to this end. Every child, regardless of sex, race, or religion will have the same advantages and opportunities as every other child. If children are to maintain pride in who and what they are and what they want to become, then they must never be faced with stereotyped sex, race, or religious roles or attitudes that will inhibit their choices.

Children have the right to develop to their maximum social, emotional, and intellectual abilities. It is the adult's responsibility to provide opportunities for this development to occur. Each child is allowed to progress at his or her own pace according to his or her own needs. All children have a right to grow with good self-image—a good feeling of personal worth. It is the responsibility of the staff and the parents to assist children to think well of themselves and to provide experiences that foster feelings of confidence, success, value, and pride. Children should never have to prove themselves to gain acceptance or attention from adults. All adults working

*Mimeographed (Norman, Oklahoma: Middle Earth Day Care Center, Inc., 1971).

with children have the responsibility to create an atmosphere of acceptance and cooperation among the children rather than a climate of competition.

All children need opportunitites to interact socially with their peers and are guided in respecting the rights and feelings of others. An atmosphere of gentleness, respect, and humanitarianism is a prerequisite for children to learn to care and be concerned for others and to settle differences in a peaceful way. Children are allowed to disagree with other children and adults, but they are not allowed to hurt one another or to be destructive. Likewise, all children need opportunities to be alone and are to be guided in becoming independent, self-sufficient individuals. To foster independence, children are given as much responsibility for their own lives as they can comfortably handle. The amount and kind of responsibility given to any particular child is determined by his or her ability to assume the responsibility. One of the major areas of responsibility that the children are encouraged to develop is an attitude of construction and cooperation where their environment is concerned. An appreciation for life, nature, and man's creative efforts is encouraged.

Independence is encouraged by giving the children freedom to make choices and decisions for their activitites during the day. Children have a propensity to make sense out of the world. They actively seek answers or some degree of resolution of the problems they perceive. When given an interesting, challenging environment, children will make wise choices for their learning activities and will learn those things they are interested in and capable of learning. This is not to say that children in need of assistance in a particular area of development shall not receive encouragement to participate in activities that will strengthen their deficiencies.

It is the responsibility of the staff to thoughtfully and consciously plan activities and experiences that meet the developmental needs of all the children. A program with many planned options available has more potential for children than a program that forces all children to do the same thing at the same time or a program that allows children to encounter activities and experiences randomly or fortuitously. Children are not forced to participate in activities, nor are they punished for not participating. It is recognized that in the best of situations with the most thoughtfully planned program, all children are not going to behave in an acceptable manner all of the time. However, physical punishment of children for misbehavior is unacceptable. Children are never physically, verbally, or mentally abused, and food is never withheld as punishment nor offered as a reward. Children need to be assisted in understanding why their behavior is not acceptable, and their actions should be redirected in a positive way. We are critical of a child's behavior, but we are never critical of the child. Children are loved and accepted at all times regardless of their behavior.

This program can be offered simultaneously with good physical care of children that includes a safe and sanitary physical plant, a nutritious food program, and careful supervision. With sufficient parental involvement and support, high-quality child care can be offered at a reasonable cost to families.

A Statement of Purpose/Philosophy
Regarding Multi-Ethnic Awareness*

As one of the ten demonstration day care centers across the nation, we at Headstart Day Care have been given the responsibility and unique opportunity of developing a multi-ethnic curriculum for preschool children. As we have approached this exciting task, so many questions have appeared; and we have spent many hours in conversation with parents, teachers, and staff

---

*Lucia Ann McSpadden, *Formative Evaluation: Parents and Staff Working Together to Build a Responsive Environment* (Salt Lake City, Utah: Headstart Day Care Center, n.d.).

as we search for what we feel our responsibilities to the children and to the parents are in dealing with being a multi-ethnic center in the realities of a multi-ethnic world. The following statement was prepared as a result of those conversations:

Every person is a special and unique human being who is of value just as he or she is. Part of a person's uniqueness is the ethnic group to which he or she belongs, and in our society this ethnic identity is a great determiner of who a person is, what a person believes and values, and what experiences a person faces in life.

One's race or ethnic identity is a fact of life that has no good or bad value attached to it. Therefore, at the day care center, this ethnic identity is treated as another important and interesting fact about a child along with his or her age, height, weight, sex, color of eyes, and color of skin. These are all facts which are discussed openly but not used to stereotype or label a child.

Our overriding goal at the center is to have children develop a positive and realistic self-image, to feel good about themselves as they are. This includes knowing and accepting their ethnic identity for the great thing it is. Children who feel good about themselves do not need to put other people down in an effort to make themselves feel more important. We hope such children will be better prepared to see the future as open and full of possibilities and be better able to meet a world that can be cruel. We hope that the children who go through the center will continue to be at ease with persons from all ethnic groups and will make judgments about persons on the basis of behavior rather than the ethnic group to which they belong.

Appendix B

Examples of Goal Statements for Young Children

Eight Goals for Young Children

1. Development of creativity and imagination.
2. Motor development in a physical and rhythmical sense.
3. Linguistic development.
4. Personal, autonomous development, independence, etc.
5. Development in a social context, that is, to learn to adapt to society.
6. Intellectual, cognitive development.
7. Learning good habits, keeping things in order, keeping to time, being polite.
8. Learning to behave spontaneously with confidence, removing shyness, inhibitions.

Early Childhood Goals of the Bank Street College for Education*

1. Positive self-image.
2. Becoming an active learner.
3. Cognitive development.
4. Affective development.
5. Ability to cope with the world.
6. Development of expressiveness in language.
7. Ability to function in social group interaction.
8. Respect for others.

---

*Ira J. Gordon, comp., "An Instructional Theory Approach to the Analysis of Selected Early Childhood Programs" in *Early Childhoold Education,* ed. Ira J. Gordon (Chicago: National Society for the Study of Education, 1972), pp. 206-7.

Goals Stated as Competencies
for Six Year Olds*

Social Abilities: Labels and Definitions

1. To get and maintain the attention of adults in socially acceptable ways.
   Definition: The ability to get the attention of an adult through the use of various strategies (e.g., moves toward and stands/sits near adult; touches adult; calls to adult; shows something to adult; tells something to adult.)

2. To use adults as resources.
   Definition: The ability to make use of an adult in order to obtain something by means of a verbal request or demand, or a physical demonstration of his need. His object may be to gain information, assistance, or food, and he may demonstrate this by declaring what he wants, making a request, making a demand, or by gesturing, acting out, or pointing.

3. To express both affection and hostility to adults.
   Definition: The ability to express affection and/or hostility through verbal and/or physical means (e.g., making friendly statements, such as "I like you," "You're nice," or hugging adult; making statements of dislike, such as "I hate you," "You're bad," hitting adult, or physically resisting adult).

4. To lead and follow peers.
   Definition: the ability to assume control in peer-related activities (e.g., to give suggestions, to orient and direct, to set oneself up as a model for imitation). The ability to follow the lead of others (e.g., to follow suggestions).

5. To express both affection and hostility to peers.
   Definition: The ability to express affection and/or hostility to peers through verbal or physical means.

6. To compete with peers.
   Definition: The ability to exhibit interpersonal competition.

7. To praise oneself and/or show pride in one's accomplishments.
   Definition: The ability to express pride in something he has created, owns, or possesses at the moment, or something he is in the process of doing or has done.

8. To involve oneself in adult role-playing behaviors or to otherwise express the desire to grow up.
   Definition: To act out a typical adult activity or verbally express a desire to grow up.

Nonsocial Abilities: Labels and Definitions

1. Linguistic competence (i.e., grammatical capacity, vocabulary, articulation, and extensive use of expressed language).
   Definition: Self-explanatory.

2. Intellectual competence.
   a. The ability to sense dissonance or note discrepancies.
   Definition: This is a critical faculty on the part of the child, an ability to indicate one's awareness of discrepancies, inconsistencies, and other forms of irregularity in the environment. It is almost always expressed verbally, but occasionally takes nonverbal forms as well. It is observable whenever a child comments upon some noticed irregularity. The effect that

---

*Burton L. White, "Evolving a Strategy," in *Experience and Environment*, ed. White and Watts. 1973, pp. 10-16. Reprinted by permission of Prentice-Hall, Englewood Cliffs, N.J.

generally accompanies it usually involves mild confusion, a look of discovery, or a display of righteousness, in pointing out and correcting the irregularity.

b. The ability to anticipate consequences.

Definition: This is the ability to anticipate a probable effect on, or sequence to, whatever is currently occupying the attention of the child. It is usually expressed verbally, but also takes nonverbal forms. It can take place in a social context or in relative isolation. It is not simply an awareness of a future event (e.g., "Tomorrow is Thursday"), but must somehow relate that event to a present condition. The relationship may be either causal (e.g., "If X, then Y") or sequential (e.g., "Now 1, next 2"). The second half of each relationship must be an anticipated future outcome. It cannot actually occur until after the child anticipates its occurrence.

c. The ability to deal with abstractions (i.e., numbers, letters, rules).

Definition: To use abstract concepts and symbols in ways that require building upon what is concretely present, and showing mental organization of what is perceived. The term *concept* means "a mental state or process that refers to more than one object or experience"; the term *symbol* means "an object, expression, or responsive activity that replaces and becomes a representative substitute for another."

d. The ability to take the perspective of another.

Definition: To show an understanding of how things look to another person whose position in space is different from the subject's, or to show an understanding of a person's emotional state or mental attitude when they are different from the subject's. (The opposite of egocentricity.)

e. The ability to make interesting associations.

Definition: When presented with visible scenes, objects, or verbal descriptions, a person with this ability shows a capacity to produce related kinds of objects or themes from either his own realm of past experience or some imagined experience. These productions are characterized by the ingenuity of the relationships or the elaborateness of the representation. Another form is the ability to build upon these events by assigning new and interesting labels or building coherent stories around the presented elements.

Executive Abilities: Labels and Definitions

1. The ability to plan and carry out multistep activities.

   Definition: This designation applies to largely self-directed activities, rather than activities in which the child is guided. At earlier ages, it would develop through gradual refinement of the use of means-ends relationships and the ability to plan and execute longer sequences.

2. Attentional ability—dual focus.

   Definition: The ability to attend to two things simultaneously or in rapid alternation (i.e., the ability to concentrate on a proximal task and remain aware of peripheral happenings; the ability to talk while doing).

Appendix C

Sample Objectives for Young Children*

Infant and Toddler

1. Follows people with eyes as they move about the room.
2. Follows people physically for short distances.
3. Responds positively to affection offered by another person.
4. Seems to try to elicit affectionate interchanges with adults.
5. Seems to try to elicit affectionate interchanges with other children.
6. Develops favorites among people he knows.
7. Shows pleasure at the sudden sight of a favorite person.
8. Shows displeasure at the departure of a favorite person or persons.
9. Expects attention on demand—looks at teacher when he cries.
10. Recovers fairly quickly (three to five minutes) from painful experience.
11. Accepts anxiety-provoking experiences when in home territory.
12. Accepts presence of strange adults or children in home territory.
13. Enjoys the company of others.
14. Tolerates solitude for short periods.
15. Recovers fairly quickly (three to five minutes) from frustrating experiences.
16. Can be distracted during crying episode.
17. Enjoys life—smiles, bounces, laughs, etc.
18. Accepts and seeks a broader range of experiences—does not automatically resist change.
19. Can delay gratification of impulses for five minutes or so.
20. Limits crying to situations that have clearly discernible causes.
21. Rolls over, front to back and back to front.
22. Sits without support when placed in sitting position.
23. Pivots about when placed on abdomen on floor.
24. Crawls for short distances, with or without an objective (obtaining an out-of-reach toy).
25. Locomotes by crawling—goes places for the joy of movement or to accomplish a specific objective.
26. Pulls self to standing position.

*Adapted from Center for Early Development and Education (Little Rock, Arkansas, n.d.).

237

27. Stands alone.
28. Cruises on feet while holding on to a physical prop or while hand is being held by an adult.
29. Abandons prone posture and walks.
30. Overcomes obstacle—can get around or over object in way of some apparent goal, or removes obstacle.
31. Can get up on sofa or standard soft chair and sit down, and can get down again.
32. Gets in and out of small chair without assistance and sits in proper position.
33. Climbs (crawls, or crawls and walks) up stairs; descends in same manner.
34. Walks up and down stairs if hand is held.
35. Walks up and down stairs using railing or with no support.
36. Can open a door that is slightly ajar or that swings (does not require a knob).
37. Can stoop to pick up objects or play in the stooping position.
38. Walks with push or pull toy, making the toy work properly.
39. Can ride and propel kiddie car, or other sit-and-ride toy.
40. Uses hands to help maintain position in swing.
41. Finger feeds self.
42. Holds own cup or glass for drinking and can set the glass down correctly (may spill some of the contents in process).
43. Eats table foods without rebelling or choking.
44. Manages adhesive foods (mashed potatoes, etc.) with a spoon.
45. Eats most of his meal with a spoon.
46. Does not try to eat inedible foods, or expels them upon request.
47. Eats a variety of foods.
48. Can pour from a small vessel into a larger one with accuracy (cup of water into a pan).
49. Accepts child-cleaning activities—diaper changing, hand or face washing.
50. Pulls off shoes (if unlaced) and socks (if uncovered) by himself.
51. Demonstrates awareness of function of different items of clothing (hat on head, coat on arms, etc.).
52. "Helps" in dressing—tenses arm or leg, does not resist or fight.
53. Takes off coat or jacket (may receive help with elastic cuffs or liners).
54. Can unzip (or zip if zipper is put together and started for child).
55. Can pull down underpants or simple boxer-type shorts or long pants.
56. Takes off hat.
57. Will sit on potty or toilet seat, if placed there, without pants or diaper.
58. Produces bowel movement on toilet or potty if placed when "signals" are being given or at usual time.
59. Occasionally lets adults know of desire to go to toilet, even if he does not produce when there.
60. Does not defecate in diapers or clothing while awake.
61. Takes a nap on fairly regular schedule (about same time each day and for about same length of time).
62. Takes only one nap per day, but takes at least one.
63. Identifies or finds own crib.
64. Settles down for rest or nap without patting or rocking (may be given toy with which to play.
65. Cheerfully signals adult (calls, shouts, babbles) upon awakening; doesn't wake and cry immediately).
66. Is undisturbed during sleep by ordinary household or school noises.
67. Achieves a balanced cycle of activity and rest.
68. Can sleep in crib with sides kept up only part way (could sleep on regular bed with minimum propping).

69. Can get out of crib by himself when side is let down.
70. Can climb into crib when side is let down.
71. Will pick up one or two toys with help and support and put them where requested or indicated.
72. Upon request will return toy or other object to its correct place without being shown where to put it.
73. Spontaneously returns one or more toys to a routinely used container or cupboard.
74. Regularly puts clothing in a specified location when reminded, without being shown where to put it.
75. Upon request, gets one or more articles of clothing from storage place and brings them to adult.
76. Responds correctly to request to bring adult a specific item of clothing (shoes, jacket, etc.).
77. Responds to request to "take your (shoes, coat) to your locker."
78. Demonstrates perception of correct function of toy (rolls or bounces ball, etc.).
79. Puts small object in and out of container in play (spools in bowl, plastic jar, etc.).
80. Persists at a self-chosen activity for as long as five minutes.
81. If given an array of small objects and a container, will, upon request, put all objects into container.
82. Can stack two small items (spools, blocks, etc.).
83. Can successfully place at least one piece of single-unit puzzle of no more than five pieces.
84. Can nest three loose-fitting round boxes (every other one in a set of nesting boxes).
85. Can stack three graded boxes in a tower.
86. Can replace a single-unit circle puzzle.
87. Can replace a single unit-square puzzle.
88. Can replace a single-unit triangle puzzle.
89. Can solve two-unit circle-square puzzle.
90. Can solve two-unit circle-triangle puzzle.
91. Can solve two-unit square-triangle puzzle.
92. Can listen to short book like *Pat the Bunny* or *Busy Timmy* if read to individuals or in pairs.
93. Can respond appropriately to request in *Pat the Bunny*.
94. Demonstrates by action correct comprehension of the word *on*.
95. Demonstrates by action correct comprehension of the word *in*.
96. Demonstrates by action correct comprehension of the word *up*.
97. Demonstrates by action correct comprehension of the word *down*.
98. Will act out comprehension of request to lie down.
99. Will act out comprehension of request to sit down.
100. Will act out comprehension of request to eat.
101. Will act out comprehension of request to drink.
102. Will act out comprehension of request to get down.
103. Will act out comprehension of request to stand up.
104. Will act out comprehension of request to show me.
105. Given a doll, doll's bed, spoon, cup, and a Kleenex, will spontaneously do at least two different things.
106. Given same items, will respond appropriately to at least to two requests ("Give the baby a drink," etc.).
107. Recognizes twenty-five to fifty labels of common objects in the environment (points to, goes toward, etc.).
108. Occasionally looks at a book by himself.
109. Can turn pages of book without tearing them.
110. Tries to touch screen upon seeing television.

111. Tries to get out of chair at end of meal.
112. Discovers correct function of toy (squeak, motion, etc.).
113. Pursues and retrieves a toy that rolls away.
114. Finds a hidden toy after one visible displacement.
115. Imitates pat-a-cake.
116. Responds to question "Want to play pat-a-cake?" when given without gestures.
117. Responds with gestures to the question "How big is . . . ?"
118. Imitates adult in touching (eye, chin, nose, etc.).
119. Imitates adult in making sounds (ba ba, ma ma, la la, da da).
120. Can generally signal needs and wants (using gestures, or gestures and words).
121. Can use some appropriate, easily interpreted gesture to indicate positive or negative reaction.
122. Can say six or more words (mommy, baby, no, go, up, down, all gone, cookie, juice, hi, milk, see, etc.).
123. Can follow instructions, including "Bring me," "Give me," "Come here," "Take it," and "Go to."
124. Knows names of all regular caretakers in own group (looks at, goes toward on request, etc.).
125. Knows names (looks at, etc.) of all other children in own group.
126. Recognizes own name (test by calling some other name).
127. Interprets clues indicating time for regularly scheduled change in activity.
128. Looks in direction indicated by pointed finger.
129. Points to pictorial representation of known common objects (shoe, ball, etc.) in choice situation.
130. Displays sympathy for children or adults.
131. Seldom appears frightened or apprehensive.
132. Is not unduly jealous when other children get attention.
133. Rarely has temper tantrums.
134. Can carry out certain types of play activities entirely by himself.
135. Enjoys games in which he participates and imaginative role playing.
136. Can shift activities if given a reasonable warning.
137. Accepts rules of social graces (when reminded, says "please," "thank you," "excuse me," etc.).
138. Is accepted (chosen) as a playmate by other children.
139. Generally complies with adults' requests without stormy protest.
140. Looks at speaker who is talking to him.
141. Demands or elicits recognition (applause, reward for job well done, etc.).
142. Recognizes himself in mirror and responds.
143. Shows enthusiasm for favorite foods and toys.
144. Can climb a three- or four-rung jungle gym without falling (appropriate size equipment).
145. Runs freely without stumbling or falling.
146. Strings large beads, getting ten or more past tip in five-minute period.
147. Can catch a ball.
148. Can hold a crayon or pencil for marking and produces marks on paper.
149. Builds with small table blocks, stacking as high as five or six.
150. Does lacing toys, correctly accomplishing the in-and-out effect.
151. Replaces nesting cups correctly.
152. Can unscrew a jar top.
153. Can screw a jar top on a jar.
154. Can replace a cover on a magic marker.
155. Knows labels for common perceptual phenomena (hot, cold, heavy, light, big, little, etc.).

156. Uses particular color or colors on request, demonstrating awareness of basic colors.
157. Uses toys meaningfully or correctly (sweeps with broom, places pegs in board, etc.).
158. Demonstrates knowledge of function of common object.
159. Can retain at least one instruction in memory long enough to carry it out.
160. Given the choice of three and two blocks, will say that three means "more."
161. Works with paints and colors in free-art situation.
162. Plays with clay creatively (makes bird's nest and eggs, etc.).
163. Sings songs with teacher or group.
164. Marches and plays rhythm instruments.
165. Dances or claps spontaneously to records and piano, TV, etc. upon direction.
166. Knows whether a person is a boy or a girl.
167. Knows day and night.
168. Knows his age.
169. Can show right hand and foot, left hand and foot.
170. Knows the name of his school.
171. Gives indications that he recognizes needs of others.
172. Can walk balance beam for six feet.
173. Can hop six hops on one foot (using both feet).
174. Can throw a ball with complete accuracy.
175. Solves simple form boards and places pieces correctly.
176. Can correctly respond to instructions involving locations when no gestural help is given.
177. Can respond to questions requesting labelling or identifying.

Three to Six Year Olds

Personal and Social Skills

1. Accepts, enjoys, "loves" teacher.
2. Develops preferences among the people in the daily environment.
3. Seems to "feel good" about himself.
4. Enjoys the daily activities.
5. Can wait as long as fifteen minutes for something for which he has expressed a desire.
6. Displays sympathy for children or adults.
7. Gives indications that he recognizes needs of others.
8. Is usually happy; seldom appears frightened or apprehensive.
9. Is not easily distracted by the activities of others around him.
10. Is not unduly jealous when other children get attention.
11. Rarely has temper tantrums (no more than one per week).
12. Can accept constructive criticism when he makes a mistake and can modify behavior accordingly.
13. Will persist at a task requiring ten minutes to complete.
14. Can correct his own mistakes when attempting a task.
15. Respects rights of other children (can take turns, does not hit, etc.).
16. Can carry out certain types of play activities entirely by himself.
17. Engages in parallel play (plays alongside another child at same type of activity).
18. Engages in cooperative play (takes roles, engages in give and take, etc.).

19. Shows pride in his own achievements—brings work to teacher for praise, etc.
20. Works carefully.
21. Can shift activities if given a reasonable warning.
22. Is responsive to praise from the teacher or other adult.
23. Accepts rules of social graces (when reminded says "please" and "thank you," etc.).
24. Demonstrates internalization of social graces (says and does accepted things on his own).
25. Has developed "generalized imitation" (seems to look to teacher as a model).
26. Is accepted (chosen) as a playmate by other children.
27. Emits anger.
28. Emits sadness.
29. Emits happiness.
30. Generally complies with adults' requests without stormy protest.
31. Demonstrates acceptance of differences (does not ridicule children with handicaps, etc.).
32. Does not scorn the accomplishments of others ("That's no good," etc.).
33. Can play simple group games (follow the leader, etc.).
34. Listens when spoken to.
35. Listens to a story being told.
36. Looks at a speaker who is talking to him.
37. Can watch a half-hour television program (appropriate for his level).
38. Can watch an hour television program (appropriate for his level).
39. Is curious about objects or events.
40. Enjoys new activities.
41. Is friendly (greets visitors, initiates contacts to visitors).
42. Can reward himself (does not require almost continuous praise to keep at a task).
43. Will work for future rewards.
44. Seems to seek more difficult tasks upon successful completion of easier ones.

Communication Skills

45. Recognizes name when roll is called.
46. Answers roll call with both names in a complete sentence ("My name is Joe Johnson.").
47. Gives name distinctly when asked by a stranger in the classroom.
48. Responds (looks, glances) when called by a teacher or other adult.
49. Uses word sentences ("Go out" meaning "I want to go out.").
50. Uses two- to three-word sentences.
51. Uses four- to five-word sentences.
52. Uses sentences containing subject and predicate.
53. Speech is clear, distinct, and audible (can be understood by a stranger).
54. Spontaneously relates experiences (tells something that happened on playground, etc.).
55. Talks to other children in play.
56. Can answer questions ("knows" that a question means an answer is expected).
57. Memorizes little rhymes and songs (up to four lines).
58. Can correctly respond to instructions involving locations when no gestural help is given.
59. Can respond to questions requesting labelling or identifying.
60. Can respond to questions based on symbolic representation.
61. Can respond to affirmative questions with a negative statement.
62. Can give rudimentary definitions of words.
63. Can form distinctly all the vowels.
64. Can make the sounds of all major consonants.
65. Can make the sounds of all major consonant blends (specify).
66. Can use comparatives ("He is bigger than I am.").

67. Can use the superlative form of adjectives and demonstrates that he knows what it means.
68. Uses future tense correctly.
69. Uses past tense correctly in regular verbs.
70. Uses complex sentences.
71. Demonstrates some grasp of language rules by "making up" past tenses ("I goed," etc.).
72. Correctly uses past tense in a dozen or so common irregular verbs (give examples).
73. Uses adjectives in sentences.
74. Uses adverbs in sentences.
75. Correctly uses past tense in a dozen or so common regular verbs (give examples).
76. Recognizes five letters of the alphabet (lower case, capitals).
77. Recognizes the numerals.
78. Copies letters of the alphabet.
79. Copies numerals.
80. Can print first name.
81. Can print first and last names.
82. Can print all letters of the alphabet in response to symbolic request.
83. Asks questions that generate information necessary for problem solving.
84. Can answer verbally questions involving "where" (gesturally would be a first level).
85. Asks "why" questions.

Motor Skills: Gross

86. Walks up and down stairs, one foot on each tread, without having hand held.
87. Can ride a tricycle, using pedals correctly and steering accurately.
88. Can climb a three- to four-rung jungle gym without falling.
89. Runs freely without stumbling or falling.
90. Can hop six hops on one foot (using both feet).
91. Can jump rope.
92. Can walk balance beam for six feet.
93. Can throw a ball with reasonable accuracy.
94. Can throw a ball with complete accuracy.
95. Can catch a ball.
96. Carries equipment from one part of room to another without spilling or dropping.
97. Can carry out simple gross motor acts upon verbal request ("Walk fast," etc.).
98. Can copy rhythm patterns with either hands or feet.
99. Can throw a bean bag so that it lands in a wastebasket from a distance of six feet.
100. Can play follow the leader through reasonable motor acts.

Motor Skills: Fine

101. Strings large beads, getting ten or more past tip in five-minute period.
102. Takes puzzle pieces out correctly (does not dump upside down).
103. Works five- to six-piece puzzles.
104. Works seven- to twelve-piece puzzles.
105. Solves simple form boards (circles, squares, triangles) and places pieces correctly.
106. Takes toys apart that involve manipulation (nuts and bolts, etc.).
107. Assembles toys (nuts and bolts).
108. Can hold a crayon or pencil for marking and produces marks on paper.
109. Draws an acceptable circle freehand, but with model to copy.
110. Draws an acceptable square freehand, but with model to copy.
111. Draws an acceptable straight line freehand, but with model to copy.
112. Can follow a straight edge (ruler, metal templet) with a pencil and copy a design.

113. Can copy a maze design when allowed a ½-inch track, staying within lines most of the way.
114. Can copy a maze design with only a ¼-inch track.
115. When given square to color, produces more area of color inside than outside design.
116. Can copy designs involving oblique lines, triangles, X's, etc.
117. Pastes small pieces of paper on larger pieces.
118. Pastes in such a way as to create a design.
119. Can put tone arm down on record with proper force and pressure.
120. Can put a record back into a record jacket.
121. Copies pegboard designs involving only one direction.
122. Copies pegboard designs involving two directions.
123. Copies pegboard designs involving three or four directions.
124. Copies pegboard designs depicted in drawings.
125. Builds with small table blocks, stacking as high as five or six.
126. Uses lacing toys, correctly accomplishing the in-and-out effect.
127. Successfully places graded cylinders in Montessori boards.
128. Replaces nesting cups correctly.
129. Stacks all discs on color cone correctly.
130. Can unscrew a jar top.
131. Can screw a jar top on a jar.
132. Can replace a cover on a magic marker.
133. Can cut with scissors.
134. Can cut out a simple design involving curves with reasonable accuracy.
135. Can cut out a simple design involving precise angles.
136. Can draw a recognizable man, woman, or child.
137. Can draw a recognizable animal.
138. Can draw a recognizable house or other building.
139. Can pour (rice, water, sand) from small container into larger one without spilling.
140. Can pour from large container into smaller one without spilling.
141. Can pour up to a mark with accuracy.
142. Demonstrates knowledge of function of common object.
143. Can verbally supply information about function of objects.
144. Knows functions of parts of the body.
145. Knows composition of common objects (hat, dress, etc.).
146. Can retain at least one instruction in memory long enough to carry it out.
147. Can retain two instructions in memory.
148. Can retain three instructions in memory.
149. Can retain four instructions in memory.
150. Remembers events done the day before.
151. Can answer "why" questions.
152. Can delineate similarities of different objects.
153. Can delineate both similarities and differences of objects.
154. Can classify on the basis of simple distinctions (big ones here, little ones there).
155. Can, with an assortment of objects, make functional groupings.
156. Perceives missing parts of objects from real objects.
157. Perceives missing parts in pictures.
158. Can conceptualize perceptual tasks.
159. Can specify impairment of function associated with missing parts.
160. Can make "not" statements about common objects.
161. Can make certain logical deductions relating to popular opposites.
162. Can perform simple if-then deductions.
163. Can perform simple if-then negative deductions.

164. Can use "or" in simple deductions.
165. Establishes logical perceptual-conceptual correlations.
166. Accepts perceptual-conceptual incongruities.
167. Counts correctly to ten.
168. Establishes one-to-one correspondence up to ten.
169. Knows positional terms—first, last, middle, next to last, etc.
170. Can correctly supply correct number of objects upon request (1, 2, 5, 9).
171. Can repeat numerals out of sequence.
172. Can repeat whole sentences containing six words.
173. Can repeat sequences of six unrelated words.
174. Shows beginning stages of conservation of volume, mass, weight.
175. Can ignore irrelevancies in problems.
176. Can describe pictures in sentences.
177. Can do simple addition of either one or two more than numbers smaller than ten.
178. Can show the order of progression of words in a book.
179. Can learn a list of four unrelated words in sequence.

Perceptual Skills

180. Can sort on the basis of one dimension (discs of different colors, etc.).
181. Can handle two-dimensional sorting and change basis for sorting (sorts by color and form).
182. Can handle three-dimensional sorting and use all characteristics as basis for different sortings.
183. Can successfully match complex geometric forms (requires comprehension of "likeness").
184. Can play lotto games.
185. Can upon request supply form or picture different from another form or picture.
186. Perceives size differences and knows appropriate verbal labels.
187. Can verbally describe forms haptically ("It's smooth, scratchy, round," etc.).
188. Can identify forms haptically (in hidden treasure box can feel forms and tell what they are).
189. Can copy a few simple tapped rhythms.
190. Unless discrimination required is too fine, can appropriately identify more and less.
191. "Hears" and distinguishes initial consonants (understanding of same and different).
192. "Hears" and distinguishes final consonants (cup and cut).
193. Knows labels for common perceptual phenomena (hot, cold, heavy, light, big, little, etc.)
194. Copies colors used by teacher.
195. Uses particular color or colors on request, demonstrating awareness of basic colors.

Expressiveness and Creativity

196. Works with paints and colors in free-art situation.
197. Manipulates clay nonrandomly (define).
198. Produces design with crayons or paints.
199. Sings songs with teacher or group.
200. Marches and plays rhythm instruments.
201. Engages in imaginative and creative play.
202. Tells fantasy stories.

Assumption of Responsibility

203. Enters classroom without dawdling, wandering about, running off, etc.
204. Hangs up coat or snowsuit in specified place.
205. Takes off coat or snowsuit by himself, including unbuttoning.
206. Can put on coat by himself.

207. Can unzip a jacket or coat.
208. Can button coat or shirt.
209. Can zip up jacket if zipper is started for him; can start zipper and zip.
210. Can loosen shoelace and insert foot in shoe (does not try to cram foot in).
211. Puts shoe on correctly (can identify left and right shoes).
212. Goes to toilet on request.
213. Takes care of self at toilet (arrangement of clothing, cleaning self, and flushing toilet).
214. Washes hands with assistance.
215. Washes hands without assistance.
216. Dries hands without assistance and gets them dry.
217. Turns faucet on and off without assistance.
218. Does not splash water on floor while washing.
219. After an accident, tries to brush off or remove food, dirt, etc. from clothing.
220. "Tries" to keep clothing clean.
221. Will put away toys upon request.
222. Puts away toys when finished with them without being requested.
223. Seems to try to "help take care of" classroom and playground.
224. Acts disturbed (concerned) if he breaks a piece of equipment.
225. Enjoys having work assignments given to him.
226. In general, conforms to school rules.
227. Remembers routines with minimum of reminder.
228. Eats a variety of foods.
229. Drinks from a straw, if one is supplied.
230. Eats good part of meal with spoon or fork, though may use fingers occasionally.
231. Follows local customs with regard to disposal of dishes.
232. Can be trusted not to bolt and run when group is moving from one locale to another.
233. Can be trusted on field trips.
234. Is not consistently foolhardy on equipment for large muscle activity.
235. Develops concern for school's materials (takes care when working with them, etc.).
236. Lies down to rest without prolonged protest.
237. Sleeps during nap time.
238. Will run errands for teacher or do other little chores within his capability.
239. Brushes teeth after eating.
240. Leaves school with parent or sibling without protest.
241. Permits parent to leave school without protest.
242. Blows when tissue is placed to nose.
243. Blows nose with tissue and disposes of used tissue.
244. Places napkins, used paper, etc., in wastebasket.
245. Ties shoes.
246. Knows whether a person is a boy or a girl.
247. Can give names of people in his family.
248. Knows day and night.
249. Knows his age.
250. Knows his birthday.
251. Can show right hand and foot, left hand and foot.
252. Knows his address.
253. Knows the name of his school.
254. Knows the name of all teachers in his group.
255. Knows the names of the days of the week.
256. Knows the name of the city in which he lives.

257. Knows the name of his state.
258. Can tell about some television program that he likes (name characters, describe an episode, etc.).

Appendix D

An Example of an Objective Bank*

Curriculum Bank
Format (1)

1.0 Self-Concept
2.0 Language Development
3.0 Concept Formation
4.0 Sensory Development
5.0 Motor Development
6.0 Living Skills

1.0 Self-Concept
    1.1 Body awareness
    1.2 Name and identify
        1.21 Silhouettes
        1.22 Photographs and pictures
        1.23 Mirror activities
    1.3 Family
    1.4 Role Playing
    1.5 Trust
    1.6 Positive guidance
2.0 Language Development
    2.1 Receptive language
        2.11 Attending behavior
            2.111 Acknowledges by action or expression when shown objects.
            2.112 Sustains attention for at least a five-minute period of time when listening to a record or sound film.
            2.113 Sustains attention for at least a fifteen-minute period of time when listening to a record, story, or sound film.
            2.114 Spontaneously responds by gesture or comment to changes in the environment such as new objects in the room.

*Henry Draper and Wanda Draper, *Horizons in Early Childhood: Education* (forthcoming).

2.12   Sound discrimination
    2.121   Responds to loud noises with facial expression or body movement
    2.122   Responds to own name by turning head in that direction
2.13   Directions
    2.131   Responds correctly to one familiar direction
    2.132   Responds correctly to two familiar directions at the same time
    2.133   Responds correctly to three familiar directions at the same time
    2.134   Responds correctly to a set of new directions given at the same time
    2.135   Responds to implied directions (i.e., it is juice time—he washes his hands, pulls up his chair to the table, and sits down)

2.2   Comprehension
  2.21   Object level
  2.22   Index level
  2.23   Symbol level
  2.24   Sign level
2.3   Expressive Communication
2.4   Labelling
2.5   One-word answers to questions
2.6   First-order identity statements
2.7   Second-order identity statements
  2.71   Modifiers
  2.72   Yes/no statements
2.8   Miscellaneous
  2.81   Polar statements
  2.82   Similarity statements
  2.83   Preposition and location statements
  2.84   Sub-class nouns
  2.85   Quality statements
  2.86   Action verbs
  2.87   Common sentences
  2.88   Personal pronouns
  2.89   If-then statements
    2.891   Logical thinking—and, all, only, some, and/or

3.0   Concept Formation
  3.1   Seriation relationships
    3.11   Seriation of length
    3.12   Seriation of two sets of objects
    3.13   Seriation of length and color
    3.14   Multiple seriation
    3.15   Seriation of shapes
      3.151   Triangles
      3.152   Rectangles
      3.153   Pentagons
      3.154   Hexagons
    3.16   Seriation of transitivity
      3.161   Big-little
      3.162   Large-small
      3.163   Tall-short
      3.164   High-low
      3.165   Long-short

INDEX

I hope what ever is wrong
with you that you straggling
up and turn Back to God

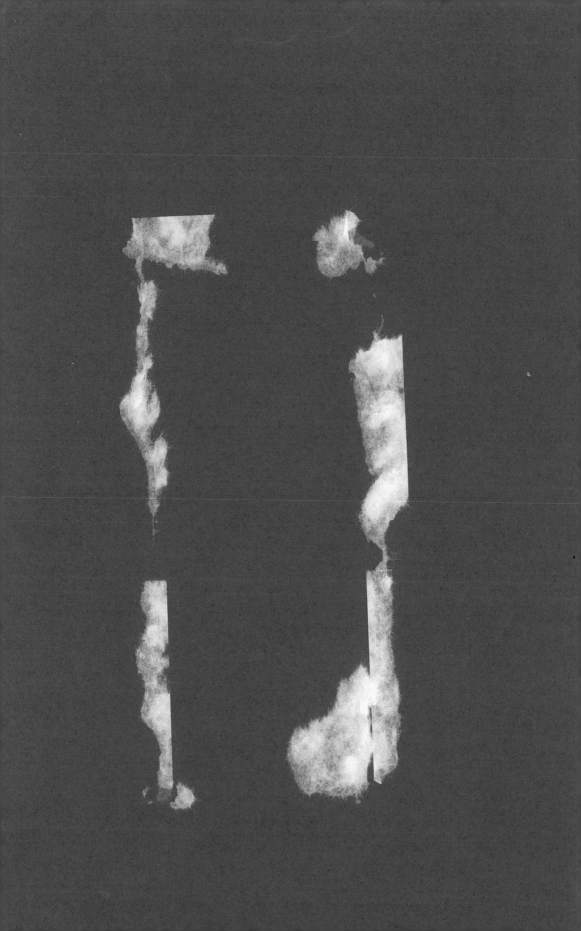